Contents

vi

THE UNIVERSITY OF WINCHESTER

The Dynamic Body in Space

Exploring and Developing Rudolf Laban's Ideas for the 21st Century

Edited by: Valerie Preston-Dunlop and

Lesley-Anne Sayers

Presentations from
The Laban International Conference
October 24-26 2008

DANCE BOOKS • ALTON

First published in 2010 by Dance Books Ltd., The Old Bakery, 4 Lenten Street, Alton, Hampshire, GU34 1HG

© 2010 Valerie Preston-Dunlop and Lesley-Anne Sayers

ISBN 978-1-85273-138-0

A CIP catalogue record for this book is available from the British Library

Printed and bound in Great Britain by Lightning Source

Foreword

We were delighted to host the Laban International Conference: the Dynamic Body in Space in October 2008, marking the 50 year point in contemporary developments of Rudolf Laban's work, since his death in 1958. The Conference offered us all a place from which to reflect on the enormous contribution his ideas have made, and, importantly, to acknowledge the significant contribution of contemporary exponents whose work evidences new and innovative ways of developing this work.

The response to the call for papers indicates a high level of interest in and use of Rudolf Laban's work within the performing arts across the world, and the three days of presentations, workshops and dialogue was witness to many creative, imaginative and experimental developments, testament to the relevance of Rudolf Laban's ideas today and of his substantial contribution to the history of ideas and practice in so many spheres.

The Conference offered a platform for practitioners and scholars to communicate their particular contribution to the growing body of practice as research and scholarship in the performing arts. Participants spoke warmly of the Conference as a wonderful opportunity to establish and rekindle professional links and to create new networks. All agreed that it is especially important to ensure that the relevance and vitality of Rudolf Laban's work is profiled to support its development as a continuing resource for future practitioners and scholars.

The speakers, presenters and events provided a wonderful mix of workshops, performances, lecture demonstrations, academic papers, covering a range of topics and offering a most stimulating three days.

I would like to thank the Laban Guild for their contribution through dissemination of publicity material, ensuring that our message was communicated to as many practitioners as possible to ensure that this Conference was truly international.

I would like also to extend special thanks to all who designed and organised the Conference, making it such a successful occasion. In particular, I extend my thanks to Lesley-Anne Sayers and Valerie Preston-Dunlop for their inspiration and unstinting support in realising a truly ambitious and invigorating project.

Anthony Bowne
Director, Laban
Joint Principal, Trinity Laban

Acknowledgements

Our special thanks to conference assistant, Isabelle D'Ambricourt whose energy and organisational skills greatly facilitated the Laban International Conference 2008. The conference also relied on Laban's exceptional technical and theatre staff, our wonderful catering team at Feast Your Eyes, and on the wide ranging expertise of academic and performing arts staff across the conservatoire. We would like to extend particular thanks to: Anthony Bowne and Mirella Bartrip for their unwavering support from the first moments the idea for a conference arose; to Jean Jarrell for her help and advice from the outset through to this publication, and to the Laban events and communications teams whose expertise, advice and organisational assistance greatly enabled the smooth running of the conference. We would like also to thank the Laban Guild, Sir Walter Bodmer, Brotherton Library, archivist Jane Fowler for the exhibition, our student volunteers, Alison Curtis-Jones and all those who gave their time to rehearse and perform the programme of performances, and everyone who attended the conference and helped make it such an unforgettable event.

The Editors

Editors' Note

Many of the papers in this collection are written up from verbal presentations where English is not the first language of the speaker. We have tried to keep editing to a minimum so as to preserve the individual voice of the presenter.

Introduction

In October 2008 Trinity Laban, the UK's first conservatoire of music and dance, hosted an international conference on the work of Rudolf Laban (1879-1958) dancer, choreographer and seminal theoretician of movement and dance. The conference posed the question: *How relevant are Rudolf Laban's ideas today and how are they being developed internationally?*

Presenters and delegates came from across the globe, representing 26 countries and a diverse range of fields. Over three intense days they addressed the conference question through papers, workshops, performances, films and lecture demonstrations. Rudolf Laban's ideas have influenced generations of practitioners and scholars and the conference revealed how these ideas are being used and developed today in a wide variety of fields. It became very clear that his ideas and methodologies continue to be a rich source of inspiration and innovation in the 21st century. The success of his ideas across such a variety of fields can however, when our focus is within separate disciplines, obscure the multi-faceted core of his work. Much of the excitement generated by the conference was seeing these *core* ideas in theory and practice, and discovering their inter and cross disciplinary connections.

There were well over seventy presentations, and this publication can only reflect a representative selection of that work, much of which was practice based. Former Ballett Frankfurt dancer, Ana Catalina Roman, led a practical session on the work of William Forsythe, who's innovations in choreography owe much to Rudolf Laban's ideas. Choreographer Johan Borghall performed his 'dance with the language of Laban', and a variety of other lively contemporary practice was much in evidence. Choreographers, dancers, therapists, movement profilers, and many others led workshops and lecture demonstrations. Gordon Curl from the Laban Guild treated us to an audio visual journey exploring virtualities across the arts which also defies reduction to the printed page. Practical sessions reflected a strong interest in the use of Rudolf Laban's ideas in the training of the actor and theatre director. Vanessa Ewan from Central School of Speech and Drama, and Juliet Chambers and Tracy Collier from E15 Acting School, demonstrated their use and developments of Rudolf Laban's effort actions and notions of physical truth. Rosemary Brandt from the Laban faculty (whose work is discussed in this volume by Claudine Swann) gave a workshop and lecture demonstration on her development of Laban based ideas for the training of the dancer in a contemporary conservatoire. These and many other intensely practical sessions cannot unfortunately feature in these pages. However, some of our contributors have felt able to write up their practical sessions for this publication. For example, drawing on her conference workshop, contemporary dancer and choreographer, Monique Kroepfli, explores how Rudolf Laban's methodologies and the terminology of choreological studies enrich her creative practice. Cadence Whittier and Julia Gleich discuss different uses of Rudolf Laban's ideas in the training of the ballet dancer, drawn from their lecture demonstrations. Paula Salosaari, who showed a film of her work on co-authored choreography with ballet dancers, considers ways in which Laban based choreological perspectives enhance creativity in working with ballet technique. (Claudine Swann's paper, referred to above and below, also looks at the ballet class). One of the core strands to the conference was a focus on the training of the artist, including musicians. Charles Gambetta, whose paper on the training of the conductor is included in this volume, was one of several speakers to address the use of Rudolf Laban's ideas in the training of musicians.

In many ways the conference made it clear that it is not until you *experience* Rudolf Laban's ideas in practice that their profundity and creative potential is fully revealed. Nevertheless, this collection hopes to go at least some way towards conveying the vitality and future potential of practice developed or transformed through the ideas of Rudolf Laban; it is dedicated to *all* our contributors whether or not their names appear in these pages.

The editors have striven to represent, as far as possible, the variety of work presented at the conference while bringing out the core themes that emerged and some of the surprises. This publication aims to disseminate conference findings and help to build bridges in terms of how, and where, and in what ways Rudolf Laban's work is being developed across the world today.

As might be expected, given one of Rudolf Laban's innovations was the development of a system of movement notation used throughout the world, a substantial part of the conference addressed practice and theory in the field of documenting the performing arts. Catherine Foley asks how one represents dance as a cultural practice within the context of an archive, for whom such representations are intended and to what extent they are partial. Joujke Kolff and Melanie Clarke discuss the challenges and rewards of notating Yvonne Rainer's Trio A. Katia Savrami introduces her system of DirectorNotation, a symbolic language for documenting the creative process of filmmaking. Jean Jarrell draws our attention in this digital age to the value of symbolising and analytic processes in the creation of a notated score and in reconstructing from a score; she emphases how this practice deepens understanding of a choreography. Valerie Preston-Dunlop explains her AHRC funded project to develop a mapping system for complex multi-media and process work. Used to document her research into William Forsythe's 'Loss of Small Detail', this interactive, multi-media resource was launched at the conference, opening up discussion about the value and importance of documenting creative *process* as well as product.

There were many interesting contributions in the fields of Laban Movement Analysis and profiling. James McBride explores Laban Movement Analysis in relation to current thinking and research. Reflecting on the seminal work of Warren Lamb since the 1940s, he looks at how ideas of movement profiling relate to 21st century perspectives on cultural specificities and to current thinking about the connections between the body, physical movement and cognition. Jane Carr's paper explores similar issues arguing that contemporary perspectives, while enabling critical distance from aspects of Rudolf Laban's cultural framework, should not obscure the importance and value of pursuing his ideas today. Dianne Dulicai discusses Marion North's pioneering work from the 1970s into the personality assessment of babies and young children through movement, and in the light of recent advances in the fields of genetics and neuroscience. She finds new reasons to look again at North's original research and its potential to inform and enable individual human development. Annabelle Rutherford looks at the value of using Laban Movement Analysis in grasping the physicality in the text of Senaca's *Phedra*; she reveals the extent to which the body and movement are referenced throughout as an essential part of the play's evocative literary means and its dramatic potential. In 'The Weathering Body: Composition And Decompostion In Environmental Dance And Site-Specific Live Art', Nigel Stewart explores the different ways in which Laban Movement Analysis can be integral to the creation of environmental dance. Loretta Livingstone explores the value of adding Laban Movement Analysis to her creative practice as a choreographer. She addressed the conference question with an inspiring directness and simplicity: 'Of what relevance is the work of Rudolf Laban today? I answer: It serves my art making in unanticipated and surprising ways.' She spoke, I think, for many of our contributors.

Held at Laban in London, the conference took place in its award winning building created in 2003 by Tate Modern architects Herzog and de Meuron. Purpose built for dance training and performance the building itself enhances a sense of relationship between the moving body and geometrical space. Connections between the building and Rudolf Laban's ideas are explored in Sarah Burkhalter's paper 'Living Architecture'. 'Living Architecture' is also the title of a paper by Anna Carlisle and Valerie Preston-Dunlop whose film, exploring the spiritual dimension of Rudolf Laban's ideas, was launched at the conference. Their paper explores relationships between 'space harmony', sacred geometry and sacred architecture.

Running up the centre of the building's forecourt was an exhibition relating to Rudolf Laban's avant-garde theatre work, researched and mounted by archivist Jane Fowler, evidencing his expressionist innovations and Dadaist leanings. This served to remind the conference of the centrality of his theatrical work. In The Bonnie Bird theatre a recreation of one of Rudolf Laban's dance theatre works, Die Grünen Clowns (1928), re-staged and directed by Alison Curtis-Jones, was performed by current Trinity Laban students, alongside the launch of my own documentary film which followed the processes involved in re-creating this work during 2008. There was looking back but also to the future. The conference brought together generations of Laban scholars to both reflect and imagine. Attendance by luminaries such as Ivor Guest and Ann Hutchinson Guest added to the excitement, while an inspiring number of undergraduate helpers volunteered to work hard over the three days in return for free access. Valerie Preston-Dunlop, in her key note speech posed an additional and centrally important conference question....'*what if?*' In doing so she encouraged students, scholars and practitioners to draw inspiration from the tradition of radical questioning and exploration associated with every aspect of Rudolf Laban's ideas and approach. All our contributors proved to be a living testimony to this approach. Many of them are working across the world, often in isolated situations and in the absence of well established networks of Laban practitioners. Amongst them, Anita Donaldson (Hong Kong), Linda Ashley (New Zealand), Isabelle Marquez (Brazil), Miriam Huberman (Mexico), Claudine Swann (Belgium), Monique Kroepfli (Switzerland) and Milca Leon (Israel): all inspired us with their personal vision, struggles and dedication.

Overall the conference enabled a greater appreciation of the extent to which Rudolf Laban's ideas continue to inspire creative practice across an extraordinary breadth of fields, around the world today. While the conference lamented the loss of a Laban basis to movement education in our schools, (along with the lack of music education in the average classroom), Maggie Killingbeck looks positively for a way forward for dance education. Gisela Peters-Rohse inspires us with her work with children in Germany, arguing for the all important potential of childrens' early dance education. Michael Huxley reflects on Rudolf Laban's ideas in relation to the history of 'body-mind' ideas, reinforcing and contextualising another of the conference's core themes that movement involves the *whole person,* – and that dance is a richer practice when that is recognized and addressed in training, creation, performance and spectatorship. Current practice in movement therapy is explored by Penelope Best in 'Creative tension: Psychotherapists shaping Rudolf Laban's ideas', and Dilys Price explores how Rudolf Laban's 'art of movement' ideas shape a creative and holistic approach to working with individuals with complex needs. Perhaps above all the conference imparted a tremendous sense of what *this* kind of experience of movement can offer, can heal, can reach and enable – not only in terms of enriching artistic practice – but in terms of developing human creative potential.

On behalf of the editorial panel at Trinity Laban, I hope this publication goes some way towards representing the range, vitality and potential of the work shown at the Laban International Conference 2008, and that it will help stimulate further development of Rudolf Laban's ideas in current and future practice.

Lesley-Anne Sayers
Conference Coordinator

Keynote address: What If?

Valerie Preston-Dunlop

The idea for a celebration in 2008, fifty years after the death of Rudolf Laban, came after a casual conversation with Jane Fowler, archivist at LABAN. Why not, we asked? We coined the catch phrase Laban Then and Now to identify the point of celebrating, the Now of his legacy, the incredible growth and development that has taken place, the diversity of it, in fifty years.

In the UK we celebrated in June in Manchester, where this institution began over sixty years ago, in a shabby room over a printing press, quite a contrast to this award-winning state-of-the-art building. In Manchester our young artists from Transitions Dance Company gave workshops in the schools, very much in 21st century mode, while performing Laban's 1928 Kammertanz dances in the evening at the Zion Arts Theatre to appreciative audiences. It was a real Then and Now event.

In July, through the generous support of William Elmhirst, we celebrated at Dartington Hall, a heaven-on-earth of a place, where Laban was given refuge on his flight from Germany seventy years ago. There we concentrated on dance for all, creative, spiritually-inspired communal dance for men and women, led by artists working definitely in 21st century mode. And there have been and will be further celebrations in Rio de Janiero, in New York, in Ascona, and in Germany.

Now to today, to this event. It was my colleague Lesley-Anne Sayers who suggested this conference. She was curious. How do Rudolf Laban's ideas function now, indeed do they? Are they recognisable, are they flourishing? Are they as strong as ever or are they diluted? Are his ideas valued today or struggling in a time of goals, outcomes and competition? Are they as they were or has his praxis sparked new material? Are there new interpretations, new criticisms? How has his legacy fared in the harsh but stimulating realities of the digital age? These are the issues that we will encounter and share over the coming three days as we give an eye to the future direction of scholarship and practice.

So who is here? In this conference people have come from across the globe, South America, Hong Kong, Ohio and New York, Cologne and Basle, Tel Aviv and Athens, Toronto and Lancaster, France, Japan, Italy, Spain, The Netherlands, Australia and more as well as from Wales, Scotland, Ireland and England. The age range is enormous from old hands like myself and Gisela Peters, Marion North and Ann Hutchinson Guest, who have spent a lifetime in Laban's work, to young artist/researchers just starting their careers and undergraduates eager to contribute as dancers instead of going away for their well-earned holiday week. My colleagues Rosemary Brandt and Alison Curtis-Jones have led the year-long preparatory work. The result: students vying for an opportunity to serve as a volunteers and find out at first hand if the Laban world will offer them what they hope it will.

We could be satisfied. We could say today Laban's work is in good shape, all is well, relax. But I for one am hungry for more, much more. I see this gathering as a staging post, a time and place to observe, to learn, to share, to assess and to plan for the future. I want to be able to identify opportunities for collaborative research, for exchange of expertise and methods, for ways of strengthening the core principles from which we have all emerged. We need to recognise that some of the central concepts and practices of Rudolf Laban have become diluted or muddied over time, or taken for granted and his work has largely been neglected and ignored by a host of people. Are we content with that situation?

One central issue for all of us must be his insistence on the integration of theory and practice in the lived experience of moving, and in its study. Who was it who said I am not a human doing, nor a human thinking, but a human being, involved in the phenomenal lived and integrating experience that moving is. Laban remarked that being an artist-researcher did not mean artist on Monday and researcher on Tuesday but a fusion, an integration in the event. Practice as research and practical scholarship are more accepted now but not universally and we need to press for it and strengthen methodologies. It is essential for the development of movement and dance as recognised disciplines, with an –ology of their own, to be taken account of in academia.

For this Laban introduced choreology. He did it at a time when he was prominent in dance theatre. It is the study of the hidden grammars behind movement and the movement arts, in particular the hidden grammar of spatial form in choreutics, the hidden grammar of dynamics and rhythm in eukinetics and the structural grammar of movement for rehearsal and in notating, kinetography.

Not everyone here today uses choreology as a term. But choreology operates in this institution in a way that fulfills the institution's mission. Here we are preparing undergraduates as dance theatre professionals, to enable them to forge careers in the dance and performing arts industries. For them we have developed Choreological Studies in which Laban's core ideas are juxtaposed with those of other dance and conceptual giants, Graham,

Cunningham, Paxton, Bausch, Forsythe, Merleau Ponty, Deleuze... Contextualising his ideas and praxis in this way makes the student aware what the core of his method is. It makes you as mentor ask does his work stand up to 21st century demands? What of his work must be held to against later introductions because it is valid, because no one has proposed a better analysis?

Where the study is not of dance but of human movement behaviour, we will hear other terms than choreology: Movement Pattern Analysis, Laban Movement Analysis, Sherborne Movement, Movement Preferences, Bartenieff Fundamentals, Ethnochoreology, Archeochoreology, Isometric modalities, Dance Movement Therapy and so on. Each of these is a post-1958 development and each offers the challenge of – how can we ensure its future? In what form? By what means? With what new discourse?

It is in the area of dance and movement literacy, including notating and reconstructing dance material that the challenge of the digital age has been most acute. The film is a lethal competitor to the notated score, quicker, cheaper, easier to use. But the analysis of movement that the notation system contains is second to none. Papers given here will show how people have made use of technology creatively to record not product but process, using film and interactive web file. Others are trying new methods and purposes for notating. Others are using the understanding of the grammar of the system in careers beyond score writing, as rehearsal directors where precision is essential.

Laban's own innovations in theatre are on the programme. Enjoy the exhibition of the posters of his Tanzbühne performances. It is the first time they have been shown since they were in use in the 1920s. We will have an opportunity to see a performance of his Kammertanz dances, solos and duos and Die Grünen Clowns. They give a glimpse of his burgeoning ideas on theatre making. What was his method? It was straightforward and simple. He worked on the WHAT IF principle to enable him to break the ossification of the theatre modes of his day. What if dancers speak as well as dance? What if nudity is used non-erotically? What if behavioural gestures are the vocabulary of the piece? What if music is taken away and the dance finds its own dynamics and rhythm, its own sound track? What if dances are abstract? What if they are political with social comment?

We will have a chance to see current work from performing artists who are asking their own WHAT IF, in a post-postmodern age. We can join a workshop on William Forsythe's choreography, he being a man who has operated a WHAT IF on ballet using Laban's choreutic theory as his catalyst.

Education was of great interest to Laban. This weekend we can see people's current work on the education of the actor, the education of the professional dancer, but also dance in the education of our children. In this country we have almost lost Laban's work where fifty years ago creative movement for boys and girls in our schools was wide spread. The cultural climate changed, technical prowess became valued over expression, the government prioritised examinations and diminished teacher training. But today there is a hunger amongst teachers to get back some of what has been lost, not through nostalgic longing for what can never be again but for Laban Studies for today, for today's children and today's culture.

Creative dance for all was a key value for Laban. His way was to create major group works for men and women with a celebratory and sometimes political message, Lichtwende, The Swinging Cathedral. But this is rare today. Why? Has the professional dancer working in the community shifted the whole centre of gravity of what community dance is? Are classes in techniques adapted for the amateur the way forward, or aerobics? Are hiphop and clubbing the current forms of community dancing? Or is the winner the craze for healthy exercise, treating your body as an object to be kept fit, fed properly, and cosmetically young? Or is there a place for the wider use of the kind of community dance we saw in the Laban celebrations at Dartington Hall? There 70 to 17 year-olds worked together expressively in sound, word and motion, a true integration of mind body and soul. I hope so. But it won't happen unless we make it happen.

So to work and to enjoy. I hope the weekend will go well beyond Then and Now and into Then, Now and plans for Tomorrow...

The metamorphosis of the Laban legacy in dance education for the culturally diverse classroom in a New Zealand context

Linda Ashley

Abstract
This paper examines ways in which the Western modern dance education *zeitgeist*, inherent in the Laban legacy, may metamorphose so as to retain its vibrancy and relevance in the present day within a New Zealand context. I contend that the Laban legacy requires complementary theory and practice appropriate for the 21st century multi-ethnic classroom, and consider how dance educators may inspire and support preservation of diverse dance heritages for future generations, without stifling the need for them to breathe and develop.

To annotate this paper I use examples from an ethnographic investigation, conducted between 2004 and 2006, from my recently submitted doctorate thesis.[1] Three sets of data were collected from teachers active in New Zealand dance education:

• An in-service teacher education course – researcher as participant observer (2004);

• Responses to a questionnaire from practising teachers in schools (2005);

• Focus groups involving teachers, tertiary dance educators and the dance genre experts – researcher as moderator (2005/6).

This fieldwork aimed to reveal an initial snapshot of *some* teachers' perceptions, preferences and practices as related to the Understanding Dance in Context Strand (UC) of *The arts in New Zealand curriculum* (New Zealand Ministry of Education, 2000) in comparison with the other three Strands.[2] Grounded theory was the method used to underpin the investigation as well as the interrogation and integration of theory.[3]

After presenting some general background, I will give a brief overview of the 20th century metamorphosis of the Laban legacy in dance education and identify shortcomings in current pedagogy. In the final section of the paper, three pedagogical strategies emergent from the legacy are presented. Semiotics, the study of signs and how people think *with* signs, mainly drawing on Peircean theory,[4] underpins these teaching strategies. I propose that the notion of readable signs, carrying diverse cultural meanings, has unexplored potential to promote relevance of the Laban legacy for the present day.

Background

I was introduced to Laban's 'Modern Educational Dance' in the 1970s at I. M. Marsh College of Physical Education in Liverpool. The basic student text was Valerie Preston's 1963, *A Handbook for Modern Educational Dance*. In my dance practice over the years as a dancer-academic, Laban theory has always provided a sustaining foundation from which to grow.

In the 1980s, as a frequent participant in African and Indian codified technique classes, I began to wonder about the purpose and effects of these classes as there was next to no explanation of the cultural significances of the dances and everyone seemed content to learn 'some moves'. In applying a reflexive lens on this, the questions that arose were 'How did we get to be this way?' and 'What are we going to do about it?'

On arriving in New Zealand, Aotearoa to use the Maori name, in 1997, I found Western dance education well-established. The lingering doubts about learning culturally diverse dances were reinforced as I took on the bicultural agenda of the country, as encountered in Maori *kaupapa* (heritage) in the form of *kapa haka* and the larger New Zealand Pacific diaspora.

The Laban legacy – one of many dance traditions

Amid the Romanticism and positivism of the dawn of the 20th century, a Western modern dance education *zeitgeist* emerged in Europe. Key characteristics of Laban's work rationalised the creative individual in physical experiment set within a universal cosmos of spiritual harmony. The then contemporary icons of the free individual pitted against a deterministic social system, and dance as a universal language, are not so easily transferable when dances nowadays are regarded anthropologically as culturally diverse 'evaluative ways of thinking' (Kaeppler, 2005, p. 210).

Later in the 20th century, the tried and tested creative dance education model continued to emerge as more of an artistic endeavour. Internationally there are many successful instances of dance education that are recognisable as being run on such a model.[5] The artistic account of dance education has historical continuities with the *zeitgeist* including: creativity; ownership of learning; elementary movement analysis; and 'emotional education in respect to life-issues' (McFee, 1994, p. 133). McFee's rationale for dance as art in education emphasises how emotions are educated, not feelings in the sense of liberal 'self-expression' as used by the early 20th century child-centred dance educators, but in the sense of the rationale of feelings that underpin cultural aesthetic shapings of dance. Mindful of tokenism and museum type pedagogy, McFee warns that, 'there will be no hard and fast answer to whether or not dance of another culture is understandable' (p. 133). However, he leaves the larger complexities of how to implement such pedagogy, as in much related literature, without further examination.

A necessary counter-move to Western dance-as-art in education is exemplified in Cowling's (2005) portrayal of how Tongan cultural values influence the manner in which individuals express, verbally or physically, emotional issues. Therefore, consideration that Western theatre dance would likely not only structure expression of feelings differently, but also carry different emotions as related to specific contexts than dances from other cultures, is crucial to developing pedagogy that is complementary to the Laban legacy.

Importantly, the recognition of Western dance education as one tradition among many is an essential starting point for this paper. Inclusion of dance genres on *their* terms is an emancipatory position for culturally diverse dances and dancers and offers clues to how to construct appropriate teaching strategies.

This sociological stance for dance education does not advocate abandoning the artistic analysis of dance but recognises that this is not all there is to the study of dance. In principle, this has been recognised in *The arts in the New Zealand curriculum* (2000), from within its underpinning notion of 'dance literacy'.[6] Although this curriculum continues to use the legacy of Laban's individual creativity and terminology to analyse dances as artefacts, it adopts a more culturally pluralist frame. However, as reflected in data from the ethnographic investigation, teachers working within dance literacy in New Zealand often retained a Western worldview:

> I think that the UC Strand is a basis for what you do and you've got to try and be creative and branch out in what you do. Not put blinkers on, as soon as you put blinkers on you ruin the creativity. (Primary school teachers' focus group).
>
> [The Curriculum Context Strand] has been forgotten because if you're doing practical dance work you can get those three [other strands] in without even thinking about it. (Secondary school teachers' focus group).

The confines of a short paper prevents presentation of a full range of data, so suffice to say that similar comments were numerous. Data also revealed that teachers rarely included contextual perspectives when working with creative dance-making or when learning involved viewing and responding to Western contemporary dance. I propose that the concern is not in the variety of cultural dances taught but a lack of rigorous interrogation into the relationship of tradition with innovation, and how to frame learning experiences that facilitate understanding of culturally diverse dance.

The review of recent literature also revealed few clues as to how to appropriately teach the understanding of diverse dance traditions on their own terms. I identify two gaps in current provision: first, provision of inclusive teaching strategies that develop meaningful appreciation of culturally diverse dances, complementary to the highly successful approaches of previous decades; second, identification of underpinning theory to support complementary pedagogy.

Complementary pedagogical strategies

In this final section, I examine how learners make and interpret meanings in relation to dance from a semiotic foundation. Semiotics is proposed as an appropriate theoretical foundation for the metamorphosis of current pedagogy because it explains how teaching can accomplish meaningful appreciation of culturally diverse dance within a tight school schedule.

Pedagogy that would emancipate culturally diverse dance traditions would, I argue, require the provision of meaningful, ethical and sustainable dance education theory and practice. From this platform, I present three pedagogical strategies that metamorphose from the Laban legacy and are part of a larger matrix from the thesis:

1. Meaningful physical learning
2. Culturally relevant creative innovation
3. Graphic movement notation as a discovery learning experience

1. Meaningful physical learning

As recognised by Laban himself, knowing how to perform a dance does not necessarily mean that the dance is understood. Furthermore, knowledge reproduction style pedagogy can disaffect some students.[7]

Data from the fieldwork showed that many of the teachers felt that they lacked adequate physical expertise to facilitate learning in specific dance genres and comments such as these three from the questionnaire responses were common:

'UC can be covered in classroom and wished to take advantage of my specialist space.'
'I am not a dancer, I have a drama background.'
'Videos are expensive and I don't always understand them myself.'

Physical learning offers learners enjoyment and health benefits, but it need not be confined to that *if* the teaching is infused with relevant contextual background, values and meanings. I identify an alternative view to behaviourist learning in dance that offers more in terms of contemplating the contextual semantics of dancing.

Using Peirce's *semeiosis* (1960), a triadic nonlinear thinking process, as a foundation provides a means to identify how humans think with signs. Here, I apply the three stages of *semeiosis* to learning to dance. In Peircean *firstness*, when learning a dance, an initial sentient response can motivate curiosity and even excitement, an experience which many readers may relate to. This is closely linked to *secondness*, when learners gradually deduce how to perform actions correctly through intentional physical action and spoken cues.

Interpretative understanding of the significances of a dance develops when, during *thirdness*, meanings are induced. However, Peirce locates *thirdness* and interpretation of meaning as always present and this clarifies how a viewer, performer or choreographer will use physical actions and verbal language simultaneously to interpret dance along with other contextually meaningful sign companions such as music, visual design, social rank and so forth. In this manner, *semeiosis* permits interpretation of meaning in dance when dancing *or* viewing if the teaching is designed that way.[8] An informed, insider view of blending contextual meaning *with* teaching dancing is eloquently described here by Tongan dance expert Niulala Helu:

> You explain the dance... when the dances were introduced into Tonga... during the peak of our empire, the Tongan Empire, we borrowed those dances and it marks a history – how Tonga at that time has been... it gives the student a feel of what we're doing...
>   This is a dance that was practised in 1100 AD – think of that time... They have that feeling of being dominated by a little kingdom and they come from somewhere else to bring their best food and they have to smile although they are colonised. Those kids will feel what it was like – that makes the emotions... (Focus group*).

I propose that indigenous dancers provide the necessary synthesis of dancing and authentic culturally-shaped emotional knowledge via inclusion of their specific worldview in dance education. Such inclusion, accompanied by appropriate financial reward, may even be recognised as, 'giving voice to the repressed, marginalised, or ignored' (Buckland, 2006, p. 16). Teachers may also facilitate students' own dance auto-narratives.[9] The learning is as much about the dancers' stories as the dancing.[10]

2. Culturally relevant creative innovation
Data from the ethnographic investigation revealed that the relative ease and enjoyable quality of creative dance was being chosen by the teacher research participants in preference to contextual study. For example, from the ques-

tionnaires 73% of teachers stated that they did not include the UC Strand in their teaching, as depicted in this statement:

> Because I believe that children learn and work in other Strands as they develop *original work* (Primary school teacher).

I argue that even though creative mixing of dance genres is seemingly harmless, potentially it is invasive and can perpetuate dominance by Western contemporary dance – inappropriately appropriating other codified dance vocabularies or compositional forms. This proposal was backed up by the members of the dance expert focus group, as in this comment describing innovation in Samoan *sasa* as only being achievable by experienced practitioners:

> once every stone has been turned over... there's nooks and crannies all over the place. You've just got to know how to get there (dance experts' focus group, Keneti Muaiava).

Muaiava's knowledge of the acceptable creative possibilities of *sasa* are not the same as a Western dance educator leading a creative dance fusion with *sasa*. His creative process is no less creative – just differently so. From this perspective, the creative learning experience is re-contextualised, shifting its previous Western profile to one that is informed by local parameters. Such a model incorporates creative, learner-centred learning, thus maintaining the motivation of the learner, but retains an ethical, culturally *relevant* sense of ownership.

3. Graphic movement notation as a discovery learning experience
Laban's movement analysis, already in use by teachers, aids learners in their application of analysis of body, space, time, dynamics and relationships to physical learning. In Peircean *secondness* such prerequisites of movement analysis can be learnt while dancing by targeting digestible chunks of dance vocabulary.

Once analysed, interpretation of meanings is possible in Peirce's *thirdness*. Graphic notation, a semiotic symbol recording the body in motion, can increase understanding of dances because it captures the culturally-shaped kinaesthetic. I propose that Labanotation is not theory-driven. Moreover, experience of the concept of graphic movement notation completes both the dance semiotic learning experience and the notion of dance literacy.

I am not proposing that all teachers and children should necessarily learn Labanotation or even Motif Writing, although these are valid options, but I offer a fresh idea for dance education – the use of discovery learning that is analytical and creative to create graphic notation. Indeed, recognition of

Laban's own creative discovery of his notation system, and later developments of it by others, highlight the apposite nature of this emergent pedagogy. Imagine, learning a short excerpt of *sasa*, choosing favourite gestures and drawing the body in motion as colourfully as possible on a large piece of paper. I believe that many learners would enjoy graphically recording their physical learning in the contextual study of dance.

In offering a more varied way to learn about dance, inclusion of graphic movement symbols also increases inclusiveness of current pedagogy with its dominant emphasis on dance creation. For instance, a broader range of students and teachers from musical, scientific, technological and mathematical education communities could be encouraged to embrace dance in mutually beneficial cultural exchanges between curriculum areas.

I suggest that developing analytical graphic accounts that engage imagination and depict meaning need not detract from the pleasure and value of the 'creative' learning experience, and would be acceptable to many dance educators in terms of inclusivity.

In conclusion, the metamorphosis of a socio-semiotic perspective on learning in dance education from the Laban legacy, as put forward in this paper, has potential to promote meaningful, ethical and sustainable dance education and enhance literacy in culturally diverse dances. Furthermore, from this emancipatory standpoint I identify the responsibility of dance educators to acknowledge and teach Western dance itself from a contextual perspective.

References

Buckland, T.J. (ed) (2006) *Dancing from past to present: nation, culture, identities*, University of Wisconsin Press.

Cowling, W.E. (2005) 'Restraint, constraint and feeling: exploring some Tongan expressions of emotions', in I Campbell & E Coxon, (eds). *Polynesian paradox: Essays in honour of Professor 'I.Futa Helu*, University of the South Pacific, Suva, Fiji, pp. 139 – 153.

Glaser, B.G. & Strauss, A. (1999) *The discovery of grounded theory*, 3rd edn, Chicago, Ill: Aldine.

Kaeppler, A. L. (2005) 'An introduction to aesthetics', in E. L. Dunn, A. von B. Wharton, & L. Felfoldi, eds, *Dance and society*, Budapest: European Folklore Institute, pp. 210 – 215.

McFee, G. (1994) *The concept of dance education*, London: Routledge.

New Zealand Ministry of Education (2000) *The arts in the New Zealand curriculum* (12711), Wellington: Learning Media.

New Zealand Ministry of Education (2002) *Dancing the long white cloud* (10426 & 10428), Wellington: Learning Media.

Peirce, C.S. (1960) *Collected papers of Charles Sanders Peirce.* C. Hartshorne, P. Weiss, & A. Burks, (eds), Cambridge, MA: Harvard University Press.

Preston, V. (1963) *A handbook for Modern Educational Dance,* London: MacDonald & Evans.

Salvara, M., I. Jess, M, Abbott, A. & Bognar, J (2006) 'A preliminary study to investigate the influence of different teaching styles on pupils' goal orientations in physical education, *European Physical Education Review,* Vol. 12, No.1, pp. 51-74.

Thwaites, T. (2003) ''Multiliteracies: A new paradigm for arts education', in T. Thwaites, (ed), *ACE Papers: Working Papers from the Auckland College of Education,* Auckland: Auckland College of Education, pp. 14 – 29.

1 Thesis submitted July 2008, The University of Auckland, NZ.

2 The dance component of this curriculum has four Strands: Practical Knowledge in Dance (exploring dance movement using Laban terms and learning practical skills); Developing Ideas in Dance (dance composition); Communicating and Interpreting in Dance (viewing and performing dance).

3 The method of grounded theory (Glaser & Strauss, 1999) was selected for this inquiry as suitable to develop local theory from field data. Grounded theory involves an ongoing deduction-induction as data and theory maintain close contact, stepping through the processes of detailed analysis and interpretation.

4 Charles Peirce's theories on human cognition are an appropriate means to examine learning and meaning in dance. These are less researched topics in comparison to other areas such as creativity, and choreography.

5 Two examples of dance-as-art models were formulated by dance educators in the UK and both retained components of Laban's legacy, such as movement analysis and creative aspects that were more pliable as tools to work with the recent theatrical developments of dance. At this point in time, the less helpful metaphysical dimensions were abandoned. Adshead-Lansdale's 1981 three-tier framework of creating, performing and appreciating dance for dance-as-art in education and Smith-Autard's 1994 'Midway Model' both formalised the possibility of combining student creative work with the study and appreciation of professional modern dance theatre.

6 Thwaites, who was part of the curriculum writing team, locates such literacy as being mainly derived from The New London Group's 1996 definition of 'multiliteracies' and recognises literacy in multiple fields such as science and media, thus placing the arts in an equitable position in education and society (Thwaites, 2003, p. 20).

7 Recent research into teaching styles in physical education, in which dance was included (Salvara et al., 2006), goes some considerable way to affirm teachers' longstanding anecdotal observations on the benefits of taking ownership via discovery, learner-centred teaching. Salvara et al. utilised four teaching strategies, based on Mosston's 1960s spectrum of teaching styles, with four different groups of 11 to 12-year-old boys and girls. Salvara's research found a noticeable increase in the motivation to learn in the guided-discovery group and reciprocally some decrease in interest to learn in the knowledge reproductive group.

8 An excerpt from the video resource *Dancing the long white cloud* (NZ Ministry of Education, 2002) shows a class of mainly Polynesian children (years 3 – 4), from an Auckland primary school making their own *sasa* gestures based on 'everyday' working actions. As Project Director for this video resource, tasks of planning with class teachers and selecting episodes for filming were two of my roles. The teaching utilised creative dance with Samoan *sasa,* as planned by their Samoan teacher,

Mele Nemaia. I contend that recognition of the thirdness of *semeiosis* in learning, explains why the learners in the video could clearly interpret the meaning of the sasa gestures *as* they danced. This video excerpt also illustrates culturally appropriate creative dance.

9 Another learning episode from *Dancing the long white cloud* (2002) illustrates how students' auto-narratives would be activated in dance education. The excerpt shows a New Zealand primary school class (years 4 – 6), learning in the Understanding Dance in Context Curriculum Strand from a unit based on a 'Celebration' theme. An Afghan boy, Farcel, who had not been long in the country, found a way of becoming a member of his new learning community. He demonstrated and explained a *Snake Dance*, a feature of *Nov-Ruz*, the Afghan New Year, as being celebrated concurrently in *his* community. Farcel's impromptu demonstration reached out to his new school community – the class joined in with his dancing and a meeting of cultures in the classroom was shared. Accounting for the learner within the preservation of dance traditions, is therefore possible in kinetic, socio-semiotic pedagogical practices that *allow* for difference.

10 A generic theory for these three teaching strategies is Peirce's principle that reflexive thought is an ever-present condition of what it is to be human and that all signs are self-reflexive (1960, vol. 5, p. 283). Reflexive thinking is key to understanding that learning about dance contextually facilitates individuals to be aware of their own identity. Therefore, I propose that, in an ephemeral sense, meaning in dance can be experienced as a sense of identity *itself*. This is explained in greater depth in the thesis.

Creative tension: dance movement psychotherapists shaping Laban's ideas

Penelope Best

Introduction

The stimulus for this paper arises from a practice-based workshop in which core concepts connected to Laban's rich legacy were introduced from the field of Dance Movement Psychotherapy (DMP). Laban's love for the art of movement and his keen sense of valuing tensions between the functional and aesthetic, between the individual and diversity connects well with a therapeutic stance (Preston-Dunlop, 2008). Dance Movement Psychotherapy combines psychotherapeutic, aesthetic and physical domains. Dance therapists make use of what they perceive as Laban's non-judgemental, descriptive, observational frame observing a client's movement qualities, spatial preferences and relationship patterns and then possibly refining diagnoses, treatment goals and interventions.

Within my own practice, as a DMP clinician, supervisor, educator and researcher, I prefer using movement observation to stimulate the therapist's curiosity about the co-creative spaces in between people and to encourage multiple meanings about interactions (Parker & Best, 2004). Moore & Yamamoto (1988) continually highlight the contextual dependence of observation. There is a tension within the DMP field between the need for rigorous diagnostics and contextualised narratives when using movement observation. For me, it is extremely important that the therapist's own movement, sensations and creative influences are taken into account. It is important that the shaping (both spatial and conceptual) between individuals, and amongst groups is also considered.

Within DMP movement observation there is a creative tension between a focus upon individuals, groups or upon the relational spaces between people. This paper suggests that this tension may be subtly influenced by official definitions within the UK and Europe in which the individual appears to be emphasised, rather than the relationship.

Within this paper two concepts which can enrich movement observation within DMP training, practice and supervision are introduced. Both of these, Interactional Shaping (Best, 2003) and Kestenberg tension-flow and shape-flow (Kestenberg, 1975) emphasise the centrality of relationship within therapeutic practice. These two concepts are animated through a description of the practice-based workshop and a conclusion is drawn that there is a need to maximise ways of capturing the observed co-creative spaces between people.

Dance Movement Psychotherapy and Laban legacy

Within the UK the field of Dance Movement Therapy was officially re-titled Dance Movement Psychotherapy (DMP) in 2008. Within this paper I will refer to the field as DMP, and to the practitioner as dance therapists, acknowledging that in most literature and in other parts of the world the field is referred to as dance therapy or dance movement therapy.

Dance Movement Psychotherapy practice is based upon a core belief in the interrelationship of body and mind and is defined by the UK professional association as 'the psychotherapeutic use of movement and dance through which a person can engage creatively in a process to further their emotional, cognitive, physical, and social integration' (ADMT, 2003).

While Laban's movement observation schema informed the development of Dance Movement Psychotherapy in different parts of the world, the soil which nourished DMP was quite different (Payne, 2007). Within the UK it was nourished by educational, community and special needs dance; in the USA through psychiatry, personal development, modern dance and action therapies; in Australia within social care, creative movement and cultural studies, and in mainland Europe within psycho-motor and bio-energetic work and primitive expressionist dance. Alongside these contextual influences dance therapists observed movement either intuitively or systematically, or both, and many searched for applicable schemas and frames. Laban Movement Analysis (LMA) became a significant platform for numerous diagnostic scales (see Davis, 1975 for full list including KMP (Kestenberg Movement Profile), MPI (Movement Psychodiagnostic Inventory), FAMP (Functional Assessment of Movement & Perception). Current developments within Europe demonstrate that as Dance Movement Psychotherapy establishes a unified professional body from diverse historic foundations the shared importance of Laban's legacy in movement observation remains a core feature of practice.

The European developments include the projected inaugural meeting in Spring 2010 of the EADMT, European Association for Dance Movement Therapy. This group has adopted the ADMT definition given above. One core word remains, for me, crucially missing from both definitions, that of 'relationship'. This omission does not resonate with DMP practice which requires understanding and experience of relationship building. I feel that the lack of emphasis upon 'relationship' within the public definitions may unconsciously champion LMA (Laban Movement Analysis) as a systematic tool or instrument of individual, rather than relational assessment. Laban's work has primarily been incorporated into DMP practice through observation of individual clients to create specific movement goals, establish baselines for the measurement of treatment impact, and to help the therapist better understand the resources and needs of the client (Cruz & Koch, 2004).

One development of Laban's ideas which I have found particularly useful, when training dance therapists to pay attention to relationship, is the Effort – Shape frame from the USA containing the concepts of tension-flow and shape-flow. According to American psychoanalyst Kestenberg who developed these two aspects, tension-flow underlies Laban's Efforts, while shape-flow underlies Lamb's Shape (Kestenberg, 1975). Kestenberg's longitudinal infant observations led her to establishing a developmental movement assessment, the KMP (Kestenberg Movement Profile), which she linked to psychoanalytic theory.

Linking movement observation parameters with psychoanalytic and developmental aspects has strongly influenced DMP practice (Karkou & Sanderson, 2000). This correlation has led many dance therapists to view movement observation data as information principally about a client's historic, inter-corporeal experience as foundations for contemporary relationship building (Bloom, 2006). On the other hand Karkou and Sanderson's (ibid) research into arts therapies praxis finds that there are alternative approaches within DMP which fit well with current social theories which support the possibility of fluctuating constructions when interpreting movement.

Interactional Shaping

My DMP training colleague, Gabrielle Parker, and I proposed the concept of Interactional Shaping (IS) as one means of conflating movement phenomena and psychosocial theories (Best, 2003). We wanted to find a concept which acknowledged the multitude of other terms looking at the psychological dynamics between individuals, while also ensuring a focus upon the shaping of bodies, and the shaping of ideas while in relationship. We found Interactional Shaping to be a creative construct for trainees, therapists and supervisors to help them appreciate how both verbal as well as non-verbal narratives shape relationships contemporaneously as well as historically. The idea of Interactional Shaping sits comfortably within current psychosocial theories which inform DMP embracing multiplicity, ambiguity, and complexity as well as linearity (Best, 2000, 2008; Allegranti, 2007).

Movement observation parameters can be used to support curiosity about how relationship building takes place. Kestenberg's Shape-Flow-Shaping system claims to assess an individual's personal foundation of relational development (Loman & Merman, 1999), while Interactional Shaping may add a view which combines the sense of inter-corporeality of body memories (Fuchs, 2008), the interpersonal, interactive space (Best, 2003) and the extraordinary mutual responses stimulated by mirror neurons within the observer (Berrol, 2006).

In my practice as a trainer and supervisor the concept of Interactional Shaping (IS) supports me to value shifting the attention of participants towards sensitively building relationships and noticing bodily feedback moment to moment. In addition, the constructs of tension-flow and shape-flow offer a wonderful experiential base for introducing dance therapists to LMA's Effort–Shape construct. According to dance therapists Loman and Merman (1999), tension flow arises from muscular tensions of binding and releasing related to inner motivations correlating within relationship to a sense of empathy. On the other hand, shape-flow arises from the bodily expansion and contraction of breathing related to one's experience of environmental safety and comfort, correlating with a relational sense of trust. Both empathy and trust are essential relationship building elements and require the therapist to pay special attention to the fluid, co-created aspects of the space in between. I have found that focusing upon IS and tension-flow/ shape-flow within introductions to LMA is a creative way of framing observation for dance therapists who in practice need always to locate relationship centrally.

Workshop: leading by following

My rationale for offering a workshop within the Laban conference rather than a written paper, stems from my passionate belief in the power of shared reflexive dialogue subsequent to action, in order to enhance sense making (Moon, 2004). Offering an experiential workshop acts as a soft centre around which I can construct a firmer frame of theoretical references. Experience has taught me that shifting from personal meaning–making outwards towards published theory helps participants make usable connections.

What follows is a brief description of workshop tasks as evidence of applied concepts. The session took place in a theatre-studio with dark, hanging drapes and erect lighting towers around the edge of the space. The session came immediately after a more formal presentation on DMP concerning research using diagnostic scales during which participants were assembled in raked seating. My first task was to shift participants' attention from being observers to being active agents. I began by asking them to sit comfortably on the floor noticing their bodily sensations and then to make themselves less comfortable, even uncomfortable, which I felt would wake up sensory experiences. I watched increases in tension and changes in shaping, twisting, perching and shrinking. I then asked for them to articulate their mini theories, their intuitive hypotheses, about what informed them to be able to accomplish these positions of comfort and discomfort. The responses varied from a focus upon physical tightness, to specific areas of pain, to associations of required posture at school, to memories of a family member's twisted body.

My main aim in this first task was to provide opportunities for participants to experience the extraordinary pull of personal narratives even before engaging with others. Next we walked around the room being aware of the spaces in between each other, squeezing and stretching them. Once they had found partners and organised who was A and who would be B, I asked how they chose to be A and B. Again stories emerged about their inner expectations of the other, their preconceived ideas of how one chooses, of status, of 'reading' the other's body, in effect bringing to this new relationship aspects of many other previous relational experiences. This took place before any indication of what task would follow; relational assumptions took precedent.

Each person was given a piece of blank A4 size paper and the group was asked, 'how does that feel?' which elicited responses such as 'wonder what we will have to do now?', 'anticipation!', 'oh no, I might have to draw!', 'it's smooth', 'it's blank and clean'. From here I asked them to make something together with their pieces of paper, without verbal planning. Many couples used non verbal 'call and respond' strategies, where one person would input and the other would react to what the first created. They used a lot of eye contact, and demonstrated a significant reliance upon positive response, as if getting it right somehow was the most important feature. This could have been influenced by my instruction to 'make something', perceived perhaps as a product which therefore, would be a right or a wrong end product.

Following reflection upon the production task I broadened it slightly by making the next task more ambiguous, 'find ways of placing your pieces of paper in relation without talking about it; put the pieces of paper in a "good enough" relationship with one another'. The concept of 'good enough' emanates originally from Winnicott's idea of the adaptable mother (1953) and developed by psychoanalyst Stern referring to the unpredictable, creative, relational space between the mother and infant in which they both continually create and repair mismatches in the service of maintaining relationship (Stern, 1985). In the workshop some couples kept the interactive space alive and dynamic, shifting, responding to each other's full nonverbal input via rhythms and shaping, while others made use of a more mimetic quality, checking each other's faces and particularly eye contact for acceptance. Both of these aspects were needed to get into 'good enough' relation.

Use of paper as a concrete prop in these preparatory tasks allowed us then to shift towards another iteration of dyadic interaction this time in movement alone. I asked them to move together silently acutely aware of the interactive space-in-between. In most cases, having had the prop to clarify the act of coming together the couples were able to re-create a sense of hesitancy in engagement, of checking out with each other non verbally, using breath, anticipation, call and response, stillness, fluctuation of flow and multi focus attention in space. These intuitive responses are core aspects of tension flow and shape flow and in the training of dance therapists need to be made conscious and accessible.

We then shifted the energy outwards towards the space away from the intimacy of the duet. I asked them to investigate the space immediately around them, and then quickly the whole studio and find three things which really interested them, which they found fascinating. Secondly, to find another person to whom they could impart this excitement. They excitedly guided their partners to their special spots and both shaping themselves into the new space, each vigorously explained why and what they had focused upon. Thirdly, this task was then repeated with the prompt that perhaps the follower might not be interested in going to observe. This brought in higher intensity of tension flow and fractured phrases, stopping and starting, pulling and cajoling. These three tasks facilitated abrupt shifts in tension flow and a need to adjust their shape flow continuously to engage another's attention and trust. A variety of relationships were engendered requiring intuitive attunement of tension and adjustment of shape to match the verbal engagement with partners.

We then changed the energy once more to focus back on the subtlety of the space-in-between, and the establishment through movement alone of beginning empathy and trust between partners. We considered the central relational dance of leading and following. The task I offered was a twist of a well-known trust game in which someone is unsighted and the other sighted person carefully shepherds them through the space. Generally one assumes that the leader will be the sighted expert or someone who has prior knowledge within a situation. Within this task, however, the essential element was that the one initiating movement had no sight, eyes were closed, yet at the same time that person remained the expert because they knew themselves better than anyone. The partner was asked to be the follower, while at the same time being a guide. Through light finger touch connections the person with eyes closed began leading, while the open eyed partner had to be extremely sensitive using tension flow shifts to find ways of being with and following the other, while at the same time providing sufficient safety through shape flow, with and around the other, to let them explore the space. This task resonates directly with the work of the dance therapist who has to empathise with, and attune to, the client by modifying tension flow, while at the very same time finding the means to guide through adjusting their shape flow towards providing a trustworthy, 'good enough', safe space.

Conclusions

The descriptions of workshop tasks within this paper highlight the extraordinary difficulty of adequately observing and acknowledging the ongoing shifts within relationships. Dance Movement Psychotherapy (DMP) leans heavily upon Laban's legacy of non-judgemental movement observation. The concepts of Interactional Shaping (IS) and tension-flow/shape-flow were introduced as a means of incorporating ongoing awareness of mutual influences when relating to another. The final leadership exercise described within it the core therapeutic skills of leading while following. The task holds the essence of relationship building from a Dance Movement Psychotherapy perspective; how to maintain relationship while at the same time observing oneself and another within the fluctuating bodily, psychological and social phenomena within interactions; how to stay respectfully present moment to moment.

There is tension within the DMP field between the focus upon the individual and the group; and between the need for the scientific rigour of diagnosis and the essential ambiguity within aesthetic processes and practice. There is tension between the uniqueness of relationship and the request for evidence-based practice asking for more generalised outcomes. These tensions are shared by other arts therapies and areas of arts based research. Different audiences require different languages, different rationales and interpretations. Dance therapists need to find ways of translating the extraordinarily sensitive spaces between people in relationship. Movement observation can serve both science and art; the field of DMP encompasses both. We need to keep the tension alive and well and focus upon the co-creative spaces in between.

> But in reality there exists no speech without bodily tension. Such tension is potential movement, revealing sometimes more of a person's inner urges than do his words.   Laban, (1992), p.90.

Acknowledgements

I would like to thank the participants in the conference workshop and also dance therapist Marie Kourkouta for her advice upon the paper from an external perspective.

References

ADMT, (2003) What is dance movement therapy? [Online] Available at: http://www.admt.org.uk/whatis.html [Accessed January 15, 2009]

Allegranti, B., (2007) A postmodern approach to dance movement therapy: a prequel from 1999. *e-motion: Association for Dance Movement Therapy Quarterly*, 14 (21), pp.4-12.

Best, P., (2000) Theoretical diversity and clinical collaboration. *The Arts in Psychotherapy*, 27 (3), pp.197-212.

Best, P., (2003) Interactional shaping within therapeutic encounters. *USA Body Psychotherapy Journal*, 2 (2), pp.26 – 44.

Best, P., (2008) Interactive reflections: moving between modes of expression. In H. Payne, ed. *Supervision in Dance and Movement Psychotherapy*. London: Jessica Kingsley.

Berrol, C., (2006) Neuroscience meets dance/movement therapy: Mirror neurons, the therapeutic process and empathy. *The Arts in Psychotherapy*, 33, pp.302-315.

Bloom, K., (2006) *The Embodied Self: Movement and psychoanalysis*. London: Karnac Books.

Cruz , R. & Koch, S., (2004) Issues of validity and reliability in the use of movement observation and scales. In R. Cruz & C. Berrol, eds. *Dance Movement Therapists in Action*. Springfield, Illinois: Charles Thomas.

Davies, M.,(1975) *Towards Understanding the Intrinsic in Body Movement*. New York: Arno Press.

Fuchs, T., Incorporeality. [Online] Available at: skript/fuchs.pdf" http://www.klinikum.uni-heidelberg.de/fileadmin/zpm/psychatrie/ppp2004/manuskript/fuchs.pdf [Accessed September 9, 2008]

Karkou, V. & Sanderson, P., (2006) *Arts Therapies: A research based map of the field*. London: Elselvier.

Kestenberg, J., (1975) *Children and Parents : Psychoanalytic studies in development*. New York: Jason Aronson.

Laban, R., (1992) *The Mastery of Movement*, 4th edition revised by L.Ullmann, Plymouth: Northcote House.

Loman, S. & Merman, H., (1999) The KMP as a tool for dance /movement therapy. *American Journal of Dance Therapy*, 18 (1), pp.29 – 52.

Moon, J., (2004) *A Handbook of Reflective and Experiential Learning: Theory and practice*. London: Routledge Falmer.

Parker, G. & Best, P., (2004) Reflecting processes and shifting positions in dance movement therapy. *Moving On: Dance Therapy Association of Australia*, 3 (3) pp.2-4.

Payne, H., (2007) Tracking the web of interconnectivity. *Body, Movement and Dance in Psychotherapy*, 1 (1), pp.7-16.

Preston-Dunlop, V., (2008) *Rudolf Laban: An extraordinary life*. Hampshire: Dance Books.

Moore, C. & Yamamoto, K., (1988) *Beyond Words: Movement observation and analysis*. Philadelphia: Gordon & Breach.

Stern, D., (1985) *The Interpersonal World of the Infant: A view from psychoanalysis and developmental psychology*. New York: Basic Books.

Winnicott, D., (1953) Transitional objects and transitional phenomena. *International Journal of Psychoanalysis*, 34, pp. 89-97

'Living Architecture':
skin and dynamics in the Laban Centre

Sarah Burkhalter

How does one build for dancers?
Such is the central question that guides my exposé today. I wish to address it by examining Laban's vision of 'living architecture' in and out of context – that is, first by situating it in turn of the 20th century aesthetics, and then by holding it up like a stencil or tracing paper to the building we are in right now. This is when this vision will resonate with Swiss architects Herzog & de Meuron's own phrasing of their practice – and how, in turn and according to them, architecture may come alive.

Particularly relevant to this investigation are skin and dynamics. I speak here of both the skin of the individuals composing the dance community, and of the sheathing of the Laban itself; I therefore refer to 'skin' in its embodied (organic), but also to its metaphorical (symbolic) meanings. Likewise, I understand 'dynamics' as the momentum at work in the articulations of the dancer – including that of mind-body – as well as the engineering of the Centre asking these bodies to move in a certain way.

I suggest that specific strategies and structures incorporated in the Centre dovetail with Laban's comments on architecture and the architectural quality of movement. But not all – it is indeed not my intention to read citations into the design, nor to overlook shortcomings that disturb the daily user. Yet I would like to point out the essential quality of surprise and continuous play with our senses which are orchestrated. Ultimately, I will follow the oxymoron 'living architecture', taking Laban's word for it literally and kinaesthetically, and see where it brings us.

> Movement is, so to speak, living architecture – living in the sense of changing emplacements as well as changing cohesion. This architecture is created by human movements and is made up of pathways tracing shapes in space. (...)[1]

Laban's statement, quoted here from his 1939 *Choreutics* (published posthumously in 1966), explicits thoughts that are apparent since the early 1900s. Valerie Preston-Dunlop has traced his interest in training as an architect while living in Paris with his first wife, Martha Fricke, in 1903: this drawing would indeed have been his entry project for the Prix de Rome class

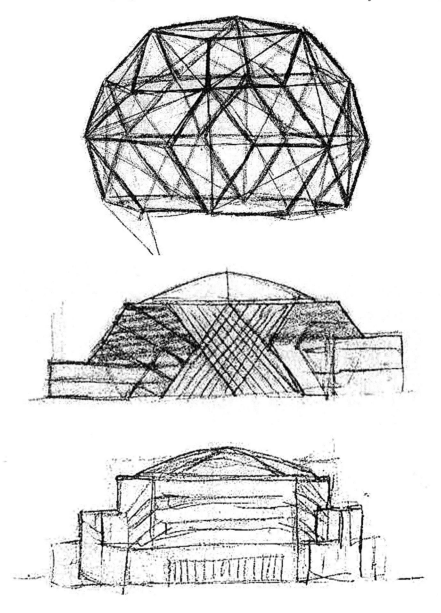

at the Ecole d'Architecture, for which he eventually failed admission, yet it apparently resurfaced and earned him a prize at a muscovite competition in the 1920s. Of interest here are the intuitions of dome-shaped volume – the pantheistic aspirations of Laban would require such a shape – and the crystal-like structure. Such a volume would, arguably, induce a heightened involvement of dancer and spectator thanks to the circular stage; moving

from the centre means performing from the middle-out. The crystalline network indicates already Laban's archaeology of movement, networked a few
years later in the kinesphere and dynamosphere.

By contrast, the Loïe Fuller Theatre built in 1900 for the Paris World Fair –
did Laban see it? – reflects the art nouveau line, the whiplashes of La Fuller's
appearances and disappearances, while Emile Jaques-Dalcroze and Adolphe
Appia's Festspielhaus in Hellerau plays on rhythmic counterpoint of geometric masses and levels. Here, the total experience of the theatre-goer is as

Katja Zehrfeld/Hellerau – Europäisches Zentrum der Künste

much in mind as is the ideal of the work of art. The 1912-1913 festivals launched it as stage of the future, at the same time as Laban was in Monte Verità. Proof that similar concerns were being debated in his close entourage during the months preceding World War I, a sketch by Suzanne Perrottet articulates spaces for the Labanschule, most probably with the Zurich site in

© Kunsthaus Zurich

mind (1914). To what extent might this design echo Laban's description in *Ein Leben für den Tanz* (1935)?[2]

> We also planned a beautiful building which would serve a dual purpose by having one half covered for use in bad weather and the other half open to the sky for fine days.

Moving now from graphics to words, many indications of the 'ideal show-place for dance'[3] emerge in this text. Neither a 'dark vault' nor 'dead and rigid tomb of the arts'[4] – rather, 'a dome, flattened at the top, with the audience sitting in circular tiers of seats (...) [which would be] only suitable for plastic dances [thus preserving] the subtlety of gesture.'[5] Still another vision is what he names the 'Kilometre-house'[6], a structure that

(...) would span a stretch of countryside and the whole area would be covered, as if by an artificial vault of heaven, without supporting pillars. (...) The dome would be held up by chains stretched as far as possible, in the same way that chain-bridges are suspended.

Writing in 1935, Laban is very hopeful about this idea – 'I do not think this project is impracticable.' One wonders what the 'many sketches and models of suitable places for dance performance' are!

Laban's remarks span three decades. Placing them in context, I have found mid-1800s art and architecture German-language thinkers insightful, those who contributed to what is now called *Einfühlungsästhetik*, or the aesthetics of empathy. My concern is less with the effective contact that Laban might have had with these topics through personal readings or public lectures; rather, I'm inscribing his thoughts within clusters of similar preoccupations across disciplines.

Robert Vischer (1847-1933)[7], in his doctoral dissertation entitled *Über das optische Formgefühl* (*On the optical sense of form*) published in 1873, describes our emotional projection into the work of art as *Einfühlung*; the literal 'feeling at one with' translates in English as 'empathy'. This projection, or 'structure of our imagination'[8], springs from our tactile sense: it is indeed crucial to our understanding of what surrounds us. If it weren't for it, according to Vischer, we would remain at 'stereoscopic vision' and miss out on 'the third dimension of space – depth'[9].

August Schmarsow (1853-1936), speaking twenty years later and specifically about architecture in *Das Wesen der architektonischen Schöpfung* (*The essence of architectural creation*, 1893 – inaugural address, chair of art history at Leipzig) would further elaborate on the sense of space[10]. And eventually offer a counterpoint to Vischer:

> The spatial construct is, so to speak, an emanation of the human being present, a projection from within the subject, irrespective of whether we physically place ourselves inside the space or mentally project ourselves into it, (...)[11]

Thus distancing himself from studies of form and its outside-in effects – as well as concerns with what he calls the 'art of dressing' façades (Gottfried Semper) – Schmarsow establishes an inside-out aesthetic. To support this, he casts bodily orientation into 'above and below, front and back, left and right' and emphasises that

> the most important direction for the actual spatial construct is the direction of free movement – that is, forward – and that of our vision, which, with the placement and positioning of the eyes, defines the dimension of depth.[12]

This insistence on the kinaesthetic grounds on which architecture appears to us is akin to Laban's explorations: here we find again the splintering of bodily orientations into three planes, and the sense of space being an 'extension', an 'expanse', a 'direction'.[13]

Finally, a striking feature of Schmarsow's thought is 'the kernel':

> As soon as we have learned to experience ourselves and ourselves alone as the center of this space, whose coordinates intersect in us, we have found the precious kernel, the initial capital investment so to speak, on which architectural creation is based (...) Our sense of space [*Raumgefühl*] and spatial imagination [*Raumphantasie*] press toward spatial creation [*Raumgestaltung*]; they seek their satisfaction in art. We call this art architecture; in plain words, it is the *creatress of space* [*Raumgestalterin*].[14]

Wouldn't we call this art dance, too? How tempting is it to see Laban's 'place' as an avatar of the 'kernel'?

These crucial decades at the turn of the 20th century indeed saw botanic and mineral models in the arts: the seed got along well with the Jugendstil, while the geologic stratifications provided Euclidian games in the name of which abstract and eventually cubist postures were taken. I would suggest that Laban, as a child of his time, adopted and developed these impulses. Overlooking his contact with the Deutscher Werkbund in Munich and Bruno Taut in particular, among other artistic and architectural circles, would extract him unduly from such discourses. 'The vital sense' owes as much to his own observations as to Bergsonian talks, and his landscapes and armatures, to Taut's crystalline constructions.

Crystal – chance has it that in Herzog & de Meuron *œuvre*, a crystal ring precedes the Laban Centre drafting in 1997. Perhaps anecdotal, this occurrence indicates nonetheless the architects' interest for mineral conglomerates. Bruno Taut is among the few references they cite, too, when explaining their approach. In a 1988 lecture, 'The Hidden Geometry of Nature', Herzog & de Meuron declare that 'the reality of architecture is not built architecture.'[15] Further, and in more detail, they expose their vision:

> Our interest in the invisible world is in finding a form for it in the visible world. That is, in breaking through the deceptive, visible and familiar guise to take it apart, to atomize it, before relating to it anew. The invisible world is not a mystic one, but it is also not a world of natural sciences, of invisible atomic crystalline structures.
>
> With this we mean the complexity of a system of relationships which exists in nature, in an un-researchable perfection, and whose analogy in the realm of art and society interests us. Our interest is thus in the

hidden geometry of nature, a spiritual principle and not primarily the outer appearance of nature.[16]

Yet this is what drives their highly material-minded practice. In their Pritzker Prize acceptance speech in 2001, Herzog & de Meuron specifiy that it is 'the materiality of architecture that paradoxically conveys thoughts and ideas – in other words, its immateriality.' From this approach – and to some extent, out of its conceptual tongue-twister – I would like to select two main focuses: materials and reversals.

Leading up to the Laban Centre project, the following examples indicate these thrusts: the Basel exhibition 'Architektur Denkform' questioned twenty years ago the reality of architecture with serigraphs on the windows, whereby built walls were measured with projected façades and words; the unbuilt Cultural Center in Blois, France (1991) explored digital media on the shell of the building and suggested a Janus-faced volume with two perform- ance areas; and finally the Eberswalde Library, in Germany, finished one year before the Laban competition – here, among the richly commented strate- gies, is the use of repetitive imagery that blurs form and function (a cube of posters for an archive of images), as well as surface and depth.

Their attitude is an unrelenting interrogative one – 'What is architecture?' begins the conceptual phase of each design. Their practice and career as a duo began in 1978 with a quasi ritualistic event: a carnival procession with Joseph Beuys in Basel, Switzerland. 'Carnivalesque' was overturned once more, as their *defilé* was composed of people in everyday clothes. This playful and yet acutely demanding position permeates their entire practice. They excavate, so to speak, uses of materials until these reach their 'specific grav- ity'.[17] This indicates at once rigor of thought and brief, a love for materials (departing from the postmodern taste for semiotics and typologies) and even- tually through this kneeding of substances, a love for the immaterial or virtual. When asking 'What is architecture?', they are in truth wondering 'What is reality?'

From London then came the demand to build for dancers. The competition initiated by Marion North included Scogin Elam & Bray, Eric Miralles, David Chipperfield, Tony Fretton, Peter Zumthor, and Frank Gehry in the early phases; the jury presided by Zaha Hadid chose Herzog & de Meuron. How, then, might the Centre today incorporate conceptions of space and corporeality developed by Laban in the first few decades of the 20th century?

In an undated essay written in French, Laban envisions space as dynamic: *L'Espace dynamique. Le sixième sens (Dynamic Space. The Sixth Sense)*. Drawing on turn-of-the-twentieth-century scientific discourse – 'electricity, magnet- ism, herztian waves'[18] – he describes space as essentially vibrating.[19] Even at night or blindfolded, he says:

we still feel our surroundings[20], we feel especially the presence of something moving, we feel the shapes we are approaching (thus the shapes moving towards us).[21]

Space is therefore 'living', as he indicates in *Living Space at Play*[22]: distinguishing matter and its element space, he names the former 'amorphous' and the latter, 'morphogen' (generator of form). Similarly, in *Choreutics*, space is never empty; rather, it offers an "overabundance of simultaneous movements"[23] and is always in flux, generating and participating in the 'universal flux'.[24]

Laban articulates corporeality through the same three dimensional planes mentioned by Schmarsow. 'Corporeal' is what engages the five anatomical zones of head, arms and legs.[25] Yet it is also the 'spatial sense' alluded to in an early fragment, again undated and in French, *Le sens spatial de l'homme motorique* (*The spatial sense of the motor man*): this sense originates from 'a centre from which six directions radiate'.[26] Laban describes inner and 'intercorporal' movement[27] as the fundamentals of the mover's intuition of space that emerges from his or her 'volition'.[28] Corporeality is then at once anatomical articulation and kinaesthetic sensing.

Are such ideas incorporated in the Laban brief for architects, which states 'movement', 'colour' and 'organic communication'? How, to begin with, is skin addressed in the Centre?

An exhaustive list this will not be, but rather some observations after experiencing the Laban, most recently during a two-week summer school in 2005. Metaphorically, skin is first the building's outer appearance: its membrane, oscillating between factory and storage space. Structurally, this is a shell of polycarbonate, a wall at once insulating from cold and yet porous to light; the sun-dried colours on the outside echo the starker colours on the inside, which act as orientation signals. This shell is independent from the greater structure. Attention to tactility comes up again in the resin coating on the black floors, lending a warmer touch to barefoot steps. It is likewise articulated in a wealth of materials – concrete, plasterboard, plastic, glass, wood, felt, moss, grass – and variations on these materials – transparent and translucent, glowing and absorbing. Skin is therefore thought as the divide – between indoors and outdoors, for instance – but also as the merging – of place and individual, of reality and illusion. At Laban, it is constructed as a chameleon signifier, thereby asking us to pay attention not only to what we perceive, but to how.

Turning to dynamics now – what dynamics at work in the Centre do I mean?

In *The Dynamics of Architectural Form* (1977), art historian Rudolf Arnheim describes dynamics as:

a property supplied by the mind spontaneously and universally to any form that is perceivable, i.e. organised in such a way that its structure can be grasped by the perceiving nervous system. (...)

Dynamics has generic qualities, such as straightness or flexibility, expansion or contraction, openness or closedness. These dynamic qualities are perceived not only as particular visual characteristics of a particular object, but as properties of a very general nature. (...)

To distinguish this view of expression from those of other theorists, let me assert that the objects and events we perceive are not simply endowed by us subjectively with human qualities, as the theory of 'empathy' has it. Rather, the dynamic qualities come along with the percepts of objects and events, and characterise them as possessing in themselves some particular way of being or behaving.[29]

Here is a set of dynamics that Jacques Herzog drew in the early stages of design. For the architect, a first dynamic is contextual – with the site, thus with St Paul's church designed by Thomas Archer (1712-1730) and with Deptford Creek.

In an interview about phenomenological research in their work[30], Herzog speaks of practising a 'tai-chi-like' method with the topographical context. This ushers in structural dynamics – the impact of the cityscape is indeed tracked into the danscape through landscape, as the ramp indicates, but also into the stairways and distribution of rooms centred on the theatre-atelier. Hollowing-out dynamics are also at work, as in the seemingly elastic studios or the inner courtyards.

One of the building's most significant shapes is the embrace. A built structure that has become highly symbolic, it is indicative of how contemporary architecture practice might be informed by dance. Indeed, it carries notions such as 'free' movement (through mastered engineering), 'abstract' move-

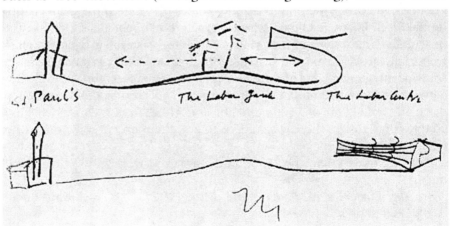

© Herzog and de Meuron

ment (through tensional and dynamic interplay) and finally, 'expressive' movement as it performs a sweeping gaze – or, in Laban's words, a 'piece of space'.

Current practice is indeed learning from the Laban Centre. Sarah Maxfield, Capital Project Director for Danspace in Brooklyn (New York), has highlighted the need to build surfaces that enable the dancer 'to spot', thereby reducing a sense of 'vertigo' or of being 'off-kilter'. Spaces must be adjustable, 'with options', and ought to create a 'sense of community' through sufficient enclosed spaces.[31] David Taylor, Leader at Arup for the Americas and working on the Danspace project, questions the allure of 'seeing the process, of how the dance gets put together' behind transparent walls. Throughout his 30-year experience as founder and consultant of Theater Projects he has tended closely to the 'tactile nature' of a building for

dancers, its ancillary spaces, and its footprint and scale[32]: 'the designer must learn to think like a dancer – it is less about telling and more about listening. It is about observing, rather than prescribing.'

At the Laban, I suggest Herzog & de Meuron stage perception rather than form. Through a nonchalant dismantling of our expectancies about the building and its purpose, they induce surprise, thereby demanding a renewed readjustment of our senses. This set of sensoria has been examined as epidermal and kinetic – that is, through skin and dynamics.

Rudolf Laban might certainly have enjoyed the open-air theatre land-scaped in Deptfordian meadows. He might have appreciated the seemingly 'light-weight structure' that curls along the creek. What would he have to say about the auditorium? And what about the sense of suspension – or loss of way – in the swirling staircases? Certainly he would have marvelled at the tipping points embedded in the design, such as – and this is a final dynamic I'd like to note, occurring by the way on the skin: the ultimate reversal at dusk.

Expanding on preceding projects, the architects indeed achieve the bow-ing down of the building to its dancers, who appear to constitute its primary material, its fundamental elements. The architecture's material is the ephemeral. Shadow-traces, initially defined by Laban as the colouring of movement, take on a particular connotation on the façades – the ephemeral. Mastering the oxymoron, Herzog & de Meuron stage here what Laban carved in the lemniscate: the workings of kinaesthetic perception.

Ultimately, how do you build for dancers? With them, and not only in mind.

1. Laban, Rudolf 1966 (1939), 'Choreutique', in Schwartz-Rémy, Elisabeth 2003. *Espace dynamique*, Nouvelles de danse, Brussels, p. 77. I devoted my Master's dissertation in Art History (2006, University of Geneva, Switzerland) to the interplay of dance and architecture at the Laban Centre (*Architecture danse. À travers le Laban Centre de Londres/Herzog & de Meuron, 1997-2002*).
2. Laban, Rudolf 1975 (1935), *A Life for Dance*, translated by Ullman, Lisa, MacDonald & Evans, London, p. 86.
3. *Ibid.*, p. 88.
4. *Ibid.*, p. 89.
5. *Ibid.*, p. 162.
6. *Ibid.*, p. 164.
7. Vischer, Robert 1873, 'Über das optische Formgefühl', in ed. Mallgrave & Ikonomou 1994, *Empathy, Form, and Space – Problems in German Aesthetics, 1873-1894*, Getty, Los Angeles, pp. 89-123.
8. *Ibid.*, p. 92.
9. *Ibid.*, p. 95.
10. 'The history of architecture is the history of the sense of space.' Schmarsow, August 1893, 'The Essence of Architectural Creation', in *ibid.*, p. 296.
11. *Ibid.*, p. 289.
12. *Ibid.*, p. 289.
13. *Ibid.*, p. 291.
14. *Ibid.*, p. 287.
15. Herzog & de Meuron, Jacques & Pierre 1988, 'The Hidden Geometry of Nature', in Wang, Wilfried 1992, *Herzog & de Meuron*, Artemis, Zürich, p. 144.
16. *Ibid.*, p. 145.
17. Herzog & de Meuron, Jacques & Pierre 1981, 'Das spezifische Gewicht der Architekturen' ('The Specific Gravity of Architectures') in Mack, Gerhard 1997, *Herzog & de Meuron 1978-1988/The Complete Works I*, Birkhäuser, Basel, pp. 204-206.

18. Laban, Rudolf (undated), 'L'espace dynamique. Le sixième sens', in Schwartz-Rémy, Elisabeth 2003, *Espace dynamique*, Nouvelles de Danse, Brussels, p. 22.

19. *Ibid*, p. 22.

20. 'l'entourage environnant', *ibid*., p. 22.

21. 'nous sentons des formes *dont nous nous approchons* (alors formes en mouvement vers nous).' *ibid*., p. 22.

22. Laban, Rudolf (undated), 'Le jeu de l'espace vivant', in *ibid*., pp. 62-63.

23. Laban, Rudolf 1966 (1939), *op. cit*., p. 75.

24. *Ibid*., p. 76.

25. *Ibid*., p. 91.

26. *Ibid*., p. 43.

27. 'Les réflexions d'un tel être s'effectuent et s'expriment dynamiquement. La pensée est pour lui un mouvement intérieur, intercorporel, l'esprit est pour lui une essence mouvante, peut-être le mouvement lui-même.' *ibid*., p. 44.

28. 'Volition' translates as 'will'. 'En examinant de plus près l'idée de l'espace qui se dégage de sa volonté, il découvre, avant tout, deux tendances. L'une est de rayonner, droit en dehors, et l'autre de contourner son centre dans un mouvement circulaire.' *ibid*., p. 45.

29. Arnheim, Rudolf 1977, *The Dynamics of Architectural Form*, University of California Press, Berkeley, p. 253.

30. Herzog, Jacques 2000, 'Herzog & de Meuron and Phenomenological Research – Jacques Herzog in conversation with Rita Capezzuto', in *Domus*, no. 823 (February 2000), pp. 3-5.

31. Phone conversation with Sarah Maxfield, October 17th, 2008.

32. 'The tactile nature is always hard to translate. That vocabulary of how materials touch each other [is complex]. The architect sees a clear room, and sits and fits the dancer in; the dancer comes in and sits down and starts stretching. That all the different parts of the dancer's body come into touch with the building demands different levels of scrutiny. Ancillary spaces – buffer zones – are as, if not more important than the platform or the studio. And space ought to seem in their control through adequate footprint and scale.' Phone conversation with David Taylor, October 17th, 2008.

Living architecture lecture demonstration: from the esoteric to the choreographic

Anna Carlisle and Valerie Preston-Dunlop

Brief introduction to the spiritual philosophy that underlies Laban's Space Harmony Practice. Anna Carlisle

Choreutics[1] was published several years after Laban's death. It is generally agreed that it is a difficult book to read. I would also contend that it is impossible to translate the content into a dance form without the expertise of a knowledgeable teacher. Further difficulties for the reader accumulate with the chain of references to the ancient wisdom of circles, to Plato and Pythagoras, to mathematics and geometry, to Leonardo de Vinci and the Golden Ratio,[2] to analogies with musical harmony. Laban writes of the relationship of human movement to the dynamics of the cosmos:

> Our body is the mirror through which we become aware of the ever-circling motions of the universe with their polygonal rhythms. (Laban 1966, p.26.)

As a young dancer studying at the Laban Art of Movement Studio in 1965, my studies raised two bewildering questions: what has Platonic geometry got to do with dancing? And, what is choreutic practice for? Thirty-five years later, the pathways of the research undertaken with Valerie Preston-Dunlop, go someway to answering these questions.

Laban specifically cites Plato's cosmology as a major source of inspiration for the development of space harmony, specifically Plato's *Timaeus*.[3] Seen as an esoteric text, and sometimes described as Plato's Theology, it offers an exposition of philosophical geometry, with references to bodily movements in resonance with cosmic movements. It includes the geometry of forms that constitute the scaffoldings for choreutic scales and rings. Here also the reader can discover the key to Laban's directive to embody the spiritual in space harmony.

For Plato, Pythagorus and the Esoteric Movements associated with this philosophy, geometry is sacred. With the knowledge that Laban joined an esoteric society in Paris in his early twenties, the Rosicrucians,[4] we are led to the conclusion that embedded in the geometry of his space harmony are the principles of sacred geometry and sacred architecture. Laban identified these principles in the organic geometries of the body and the living architecture of human movement. (Laban,1966 p.105). It would then appear that choreutic practice was designed as an *impressive* and *affective* practice, a means of opening a channel for the dancer to experience connections with the flux of the geometry of the cosmos. It is important to understand that engaging with space harmony via a spiritual perspective is by no means the only way. Laban's project was and remains multilayered. Practical training engenders a sophisticated awareness of spatial articulation and orientation and the embodiment of 3-dimensionality. It is also evident that the dynamic geometries can act as a resource for radical treatment in the architecture of choreography, as described by William Forsythe's commentators Heidi Gilpin and Patricia Baudoin.[5]

Background to the demonstration.   Valerie Preston-Dunlop
This demonstration took place after the screening the evening before of the DVD *Living Architecture: Rudolf Laban's geometry of dance*. The majority of the spectators would have heard and seen the account in it of the cultural background to Laban's development of choreutics (or space harmony) and would have heard Christopher McIntosh (author on Rosicrucianism and esoteric history) on the Rosicrucian belief of 'as above so below', the belief that experiencing space harmonies corporeally links the mover with the comparable harmonies that organise the cosmos. They would have seen Professor Keith Critchlow demonstrating and explaining Plato's sacred geometry and the golden ratio (or mean) through which Laban found what he termed the choreutic grammar of human movement. The DVD also shows the way the human body contains golden ratios in its proportions and how everyday objects and natural organic forms contain fundamental harmonic relations of arc surrounding axis (eg. the verticality and surround of a glass of water, a ring on a finger), and also the cultural issues of the communities in which Laban developed his space harmony, Munich and Monte Verita in 1910. These connections were presumed to be familiar and were not laboured in the demonstration.

The DVD shows dancers dancing the scales while the demonstration shows what their performance contains, through presenting to the audience the choices made in how the dancers embody the forms and the basic harmonic content of each form.

Two kinds of embodiment were demonstrated, the two being understood as poles on a continuum. At one pole is total integration of the dancers' body-mind and spirit in movement where limbs, torso, focus and intention all embody one single event in space, for example rising, or curving, organised around the dancer's body centre. At the other pole is choreographic invention where the dancers choose their own way of embodying the event in a dynamic polykinetic way and the choreographer spaces them to enable the spectator to see several versions of the harmony in space. Both kinds are used currently because they both have a purpose. The strength of the first kind is that the experience of the harmonic qualities of the event is intense for the dancer. It has a meditative quality. The strength of the second kind is that it offers the dancer creative freedom and should provide a spectator with a way into the content of the harmony so that they experience its qualities.

The second continuum in space harmony is the form continuum, between form governed by harmonic rules of sacred geometry, passing through free form, to deliberate disintegration of the geometry of the form, such as that investigated by William Forsythe. In this demonstration we kept within the bounds of rule-governed harmonic form with occasional free form.

The DVD *Living Architecture* contains reference to the Rosicrucian concepts that Laban embraced, especially the continuous cycle of life to death, death to rebirth, and the notion of the karmic shift that can occur and enable the soul to be released from this perpetual cycle. The demonstration shows how the rings and scales are all cyclic in their form, returning to their starting point on completion, so reflecting the Rosicrucian concept. The dancers end by demonstrating the form that contains in essence the karmic shift, as one half of a Seven-Ring (the zigzag from the Axis Scale) collides with its second half (the encircling Equator Scale).

The printed handout with the event gave the spectators the numbering of the twelve locations of an icosahedron given by Laban to the Primary Scale [6] and these were referred to in the demonstration as the way in which the harmonic connection of one scale with another can be followed.

Space harmony can be used, and was by Laban in his theatre work, with no reference to its sacred content but entirely as a useful choreographic tool and training method for his dancers[7]. However that sacredness exists and was his response to the quest of the period that artists must find a way of embodying the underlying spiritual dimension of human experience in their art. Wassily Kandinsky's *Concerning the Spiritual in Art*, 1911, is arguably the most well-known statement on this issue while Rudolf Steiner[8] and Jaques Dalcroze[9] were more specific. Both called for a new spiritually embodied movement art for the 20th century in 1912, the year Rudolf Laban began the development of his response, his art of movement. Spiritually imbued space harmony praxis was to form a major part of this endeavour.

Demonstration
Valerie Preston-Dunlop (speaker), Amanda Banks, Fumiaki Tanaka, Dawn Turner, Johan Stjernholm, Janine Harrington (dancers).

The demonstration is based on the two continua:
1. Of form: harmonic to chaotic
2. Of embodiment: integrated to fragmented

Dimensional scale danced in unison as the audience entered the Bonnie Bird Theatre.

> The directions of this basic scale link the dancer with the cosmos, the earth, the horizon, the past and the future. Their integrated embodiment is designed to maximise the impact of harmony on the mover.

The three planes study. 'The three planes study is choreographic, using the planes as a basic map, getting you into the "icosahedral scaffolding" is Laban's term, playing with the corners of the plane, feeling the demands that each plane makes on your body, feeling the discipline that the proportions of the planes demands. The golden section (or mean or ratio) that links us with other living matter is embodied in each plane.'

Peripheral A scale. 'We dance it with the right side leading with a peripheral pathway emphasising the long side of the plane you arrive at, with the harmonic experience of lability of weight and the harmonic opposite of the scale's second half.'
    Spiritual content of the form: the continuous cycle of life, death and rebirth.

Rotational A scale. 'We dance it with the left side leading as a canon, turning to face 4 different directions. A more complex harmonic emerges, the harmonic now visible to the onlooker as well as the performer.'

Axis scale. 'Referring to the numbers on the icosahedral diagram, the axis scale locations rise in twos, on the odd numbers
$$1 - 3 - 5 - 7 - 9 - 11 - 1'$$

'It is danced as a contact duo where the harmonic opposite is felt as a pull, and seen as a counterbalance.'

    Spiritual content of the form: Continuous cycle with the scale having a harmonic opposite second half.

Axis scale as dynamic duo 'We dance it with choreographic embodiment with jumps and turns but the harmonic form is the basis.'

Equator scale. 'The scale locations rise in twos on the even numbers
$$2 - 4 - 6 - 8 - 10 - 12 - 2'$$

3-rings. 'Starting with integration of the body performance of the equator we shift to choreographic choice of each dancer and the 3-ring (triangular) content of Equators emerges.'

Spiritual content of the form: Continuous cycle with harmonic opposite second half.

Cross stage line 'At first we dance with simplicity and integration of the esoteric, then with complexity and freedom of the choreographic embodiment. The two continua functioning in opposite directions, simple line and fragmented embodiment.'

Arc and Axis. 'From here on we lead up to the density of the 7-ring form.' 'The dancers use their own movement to demonstrate the content of this most basic of harmonic forms, in Arc-surrounding-Axis duos.'

Zigzag to arabesque. 'We develop the axis as a zigzag, ending with penetrating the space, This was associated by Laban to a balletic *arabesque* that penetrates the space but here into places not in the ballet lexicon.'

Curve to attitude. 'We dance curved paths into arced body designs surrounding space, associated by Laban to a balletic *attitude* but in places not in the ballet lexicon.'

7-rings. 'We place the axes and arcs into Axis and Equator scales; in 7-rings the scales collide as a three-part zigzag shifts into a four-part curve
$$12 - 1 - 3 - 5, 6 - 8 - 10 - 12,$$
$$2 - 3 - 5 - 7, 8 - 10 - 12 - 2 \quad \text{etc in a family of six rings.}$$

We dance each ring alone and then as a duo with each dancer's form being the harmonic opposite of their partner.'

The karmic shift takes place as the Axis shifts into the Equator and again as the Equator returns to the zigzag. For Laban this is a profound danced form of sacred geometry.

Dimensional scale. We invited the spectators to join us on stage and all dance this simple scale in continuous silent unison, as a means of including the experiential and meditative side to space harmony praxis.

1. Laban, R. (ed. Ullmann, L).1966. *Choreutics*. London: MacDonald & Evans.

2. Op. cit. p. vii and p.108.

3. Cornford, F.C. 1997. Plato's Cosmology: the *Timaeus* of Plato (c.350 BC). Indianapolis: Hackett Publishing Co.

4. Preston-Dunlop. V. 1998. *Rudolf Laban: an Extraordinary life*. London: Dance Books, p.10.

5. Baudoin.P. & Gilpin, H. 1989. *Proliferation and Perfect Disorder: William Forsythe and the Architecture of Disappearance*. William Forsythe Reggio Emilia Festival Danza. Vol. 2. p. 73 et seq.

6. See the numbering on Laban's drawing on the cover of the DVD Living Architecture (Laban Archive, NRCD) and Christmas card to Sylvia Bodmer, 1952, (Laban Collection, LABAN).

7. Preston-Dunlop, V. 1979. *Choreutics: the study of logical spatial forms in dance*. In Preston-Dunlop. V. ed. *Dancing and Dance Theory*. London: Laban Centre.

8. Steiner, R. 1926. *A Lecture on Eurythmy*. London: Anthroposophical Publishing Co.

9. Jaques-Dalcroze, E. 1921. 'How to Revive Dancing 1912.' In *Rhythm, Music and Education*. Woking: The Dalcroze Society.

The problem of significance:
revisiting aspects of Laban's discussions of the significance of movement and dance from a twenty-first century perspective

Jane Carr

From a contemporary perspective informed by poststructuralist theory, it is all too easy to critique the statements about the significance of movement made by Laban that have been passed on to us. Laban may have been inspired by dance and concepts emanating from different cultures, but he can be understood as doing so from the viewpoint of a European male, the son of an officer, born into a world in which the dominance of the west was often all too readily presumed. Yet, an understanding of how his work may be situated within a particular cultural framework should not be used to negate the continuing relevance of Laban's approach to dance – at least to those who approach theatre dance from a western orientated perspective. In revisiting some aspects of Laban's accounts of the significance of human movement, I will draw on my recent research among a small number of dance artists based in London to demonstrate why I think it is important to continue to pursue Laban's concerns about movement and dance.

Consider the following statements:

Movement in itself is the language in which our highest and most fundamental inspirations are expressed (Laban and Lawrence, 1974/1947, p.73).

Dance does not speak through the intellect to the heart as does the spoken word; it speaks directly to out hearts, and afterwards perhaps also to the brain, to the intellect (Laban, trans L. Ullman, 1975/1935, p.178).

In the teaching of children and the initiation of adolescents, primitive man endeavoured to convey moral and ethical standards through the development of effort thinking in dance. The introduction to humane effort was in these ancient times the basis of all civilisation.

But for a very long time man has been unable to find the connection between his movement-thinking and his word-thinking (Laban 1950, p. 18-19).

Taken out of context, and often relying on their translation, Laban's published statements do raise some theoretical problems. In relation to the first, it can be argued that while sign language and some codified mime may function in a similar way to verbal linguistic systems it has been recognised, even by Laban's most devoted followers, that approaching dance as a language is problematic if considered in the literal sense (Preston-Dunlop, 1998 p.7; Preston-Dunlop and Sanchez Colberg, 2002). However the notion conveyed in the second quotation, that dance speaks directly to the heart, may also be thought to reveal a resort to 'infection theory' expressionism in which in the 19th century writer, Leo Tolstoy's words:

> ...one man consciously by means of certain external signs, hands on to others feelings he has lived through [That] ... is a means of union among men, joining them together in the same feelings, ...(Tolstoy, 1975 /1898, p.123).

In the arts more generally, this infection theory of expressionism was first undermined by the formalist aesthetics that came to dominate modernist approaches to art in the mid 20th century. Then Beardsley's new criticism of the 1950s dealt with the problem of the intentional fallacy (Wimsatt and Beardsley, 1954), challenging the belief in the pre-eminence of the creator's intention in order to focus on the work itself; whilst the structuralists then challenged the very idea of meaning being generated by individuals. Finally the poststructuralist emphasis on the instability of meaning might be seen as the final assault on an understanding of one artist's work speaking 'directly to the heart' of others.

Specifically, in terms of dance, the philosopher David Best, writing in the 1970s, pointed to the issue of the problem of the implicit dualism of expressionist theories that purport to infer inner feeling from outer action. He included Laban in his criticism of those who, finding it difficult to provide logical grounds for the relationship between feeling and action, resort to beliefs that 'ultimately the mental or spiritual meaning of all physical actions is given by reference to a deity, or to cosmic laws, by a spiritual apprehension of truths beyond normal understanding' (Best,1974).

Notwithstanding the validity of Best's argument, it is interesting that in what is published as Laban's own writing, if in translation, can also be found a sensitivity to how context affects the interpretation of action and discussion of how cultural differences are revealed in different effort patterns (Laban 1950). Laban was not blind to some of the issues of interpretation and difference that would be important to the theories that came after him.

Perhaps more problematic in Laban's writings – exemplified in the third quotation – is what may be considered to be a suggestion of a hierarchy of levels of inspiration that reveal an adherence to a metanarrative of human progress; this may give rise to concerns with regard to just on whose terms some inspirations are 'higher' than others, and, how Laban knew about the dance of primitive man unless he presumed the customs of some cultures to be nearer to those of early humans. Moreover, that for Laban, movement expresses our most 'fundamental inspirations' may be felt to imply that movement is a 'natural' form of expression in some respects beyond the reach of culture. Yet 20th century anthropologists demonstrated the extent to which what may be considered natural physical behaviour is often an important aspect of culture (Polhemus 1998/1993, p.179). This is something that Laban himself seems to recognise in his discussions of the 'effort manifestations of social units' (Laban, 1950, p.17).

While Laban's words about movement and meaning can be viewed as revealing the influence of expressionism, in developing his actual means of conveying the spatial, temporal and dynamic content of bodily actions, he ironically seems to be more aligned with the structuralists; there are hardly clearer examples of a system of binary opposites than in Laban's choreutics (e.g. left forward low: right back high) and effort analysis (e.g. bound:free, sudden:sustained). Laban was beginning to develop his theories in Switzerland just after the death of the Swiss linguist Saussure in 1913. Saussure's students, by publishing their teacher's lectures posthumously, prepared the way for the mid 20th century's structuralist turn. By revealing an underlying structural system of differences Laban was not only showing how dance could be thought of as having structure but contemplating structure in accordance with the most recent developments in the intellectual climate of his time.

Having recognised all this I want to leave aside questions of how Laban's writings may be read as revealing a tendency to a universalism that could be deconstructed as situated within the cultural presumptions of his time and place. Rather I want to focus on the continuing relevance, in terms of the theatre dance presented in western orientated performance spaces, of key elements of his approach to dance as deeply meaningful. A relevance that continues because Laban perhaps can be best understood as confronting some underlying issues for dance as a performing art that, at least in western societies, are still pertinent.

Crucially, while Laban had the capacity to contemplate dance in precise structural terms, he did not reduce dance to formal structures but rather recognised both the experiential value of dancing to the person, and in a theatrical context, recognised the importance of 'contact with the audience' (Laban 1950 p.19). For Laban, the formal structures he explored were implicated in a spiritual realm. While, following Best's argument, metaphysics may not be felt to provide a satisfactory solution to the problem of how the significance of movement is understood, the important issue for dance is that *felt* experience is not disregarded.

The legacy of religious and philosophical doctrines that distrust bodily sensation may have been further challenged since Laban's era but they still have a substantial impact on how western orientated people experience their embodiment and conceive of dance. In this context it is interesting to contemplate that in his early years of artistic development, Laban allied himself with those who today we would view as seeking alternative lifestyles. Whatever else went on at Monte Verita, in the aims of this community (Green, 1986) may be recognised some of the same challenges to rationalist assumptions about the relationship between mind and body, and the desire to find a different way to experience the interrelationship of self-other-world, still sought by those groups who today set themselves against the norms of 'mainstream society'. The rationalist legacy, while having many positive outcomes for western society has distanced bodily from mental experience to the point where it is common for people to articulate a sense of lost wholeness. Dancers practise bodymind centring© or body awareness techniques so that what has been split asunder can be reintegrated. But in how, nowadays, dancers reintegrate themselves as mindful bodies or embodied minds, they can be seen as articulating the complexities of the relationship of bodily organism to the culture in which they are enmeshed and hence continuing in that exploration of body-self-world in a manner that links them to those pioneering spirits of the early Modern dance.

In considering the relationship of body and mind, the sociologist Charles Varela (1995) has suggested that the phenomenological concept of the 'lived body' provides a sensitising strategy that is useful in resisting the problems of dualism. However, he is also careful to emphasise that this concept falls short of providing an ultimate philosophical solution to dualism. Similarly Laban's exploration of 'effort' might be thought of as a tactical response to the rationalist legacy that prioritised reason, or analysis of the physically measurable aspects of movement, over feeling, or in this case, the perceived physicality of indulging in or fighting space, time and weight. While Laban may not have provided the kind of grounds a philosopher would require to resolve the problem of dualism, his development of a means of analysis of the effort combinations we become conscious of, does offer a conceptual framework for the analysis of physicality, or in his words of 'thinking in movement'. That an analysis of effort relies on the assumption that the bodily attitudes of others can be perceived objectively may raise issues of cultural factors that affect perception. Notwithstanding, Laban uniquely offers a way of bringing the embodied structures of being in the world into play with other aspects of discourse.

In contrast, in an account of approaches to literature that reflect on the role of the reader, I came across this statement:

The experiences or responses that modern reader-orientated critics invoke are generally cognitive rather than affective (Culler, 1983, p. 39).

Culler's statement reminded me of how as a student in the 1980s I had felt that accounts of art that focus on the cognitive response (to either aesthetic features or semiotic content) were somehow lacking something that was important to why I wanted to be involved in dance. But how is this missing 'something' to be accounted for?

As part of my research I asked the following question of six other artists who live and work in London:

> From your experiences as both performer and audience how would you describe what is happening between performer and audience when a performance 'works'?

My choice of questions and artists makes my findings far from 'objective' but their answers I think suggest that my concerns are not that unusual.

> I think it's a dialogue or an exchange... of sensations, of memories, of energies, of resonances with something the artist has communicated... (Informal Communication, Gaby Agis, 2003).

> If the performance is good and the performers are good at communicating and they have been able to communicate (and) it might be just for a moment, just a split second where they just come together. They journey together. You have taken the audience with you (Informal Communication, Mehta, 2003, edited 2007).

> For me, performers imbue the movement with some kind of meaning that they bring something of themselves into the performance. And they are the kind of performers that I like to watch (Informal Communication, Artist A, 2002).

> You feel that emotionally they've kind of got you somewhere... (Informal Communication, Anderson, 2003).

> It was very shamanistic and there were points within that where the audience, the whole audience went silent. The state of the audience changed, presence changed and it changed through her. (Informal Communication, Artist D, describing Deborah Hay, 2004, edited 2007.

> You can feel them [the audience] as well. They give you energy or they are like holding energy... I don't know how you just know.

> If you can't feel the audience you are not reaching out – by throwing

yourself over there – even if they are cold (Informal Communication, Artist B, March 2003).

It was interesting to me that some sense of communion between audience and performer was important to London-based dancers who between them drew on ballet, contemporary dance, Egyptian dance, jazz, hip hop and kathak. Like them if I perceive a performance as successful, I may feel I have connected in some way with the performers, but the grounds for believing this are fraught with philosophical problems. Yet while this sense of 'contact' is problematic in the light of 20th century understandings of the complexities and slipperiness of human communication, this does not mean that the sense of human interaction is not important to a number of dance performance traditions.

A sense of communicative interaction is something that has been discussed by Valerie Preston-Dunlop in her development and updating of Laban's theories within choreological studies that draws on a synthesis of semiotics and phenomenology.

> ...we have to remember that dance is not about understanding, primarily, but about engaging with the work phenomenally and searching for meaning, maybe (Preston-Dunlop 2002, p. 271).

The 'plane of intersection of phenomenology and semiotics'... 'illuminates the multi-engagement with a work from spontaneous, irrational, personal, corporeal absorption to intellectual searching for significance, concurrently, that audiences bring to an event' (Preston- Dunlop 2002, p. 270).

My own research suggested that the phenomenological experience of communicative interaction is dependent on, but not reducible to semiotics. This idea of the interplay between semiotics and phenomenology is informed by discussions of embodiment. For example, the cultural and psychological anthropologist Thomas Csordas has suggested that an understanding of embodiment may necessitate investigation of the relationships between a number of perceived dualities listed by him as being pre-objective:objectified, mind:body, representation:being in the world, semiotics:phenomenology, language:experience and textuality:embodiment:

> These pairs of terms define a critical moment in theorising about culture and self... our purpose is to identify the terrain on which opposed terms meet ...
> That terrain is marked by the characteristic reflectiveness and the process of objectification that define human consciousness, giving sub-

stance to representation and specificity to being-in-the-world (Csordas, 1994, p. 20).

It is interesting to reflect that in their dance practices artists may have been negotiating what Csordas identifies as the terrain on which opposed terms meet' (Csordas, 1994, p. 20) long before this became a recognisable theoretical proposition. Discussions with artists who make work they perform in themselves, revealed the skill with which they negotiate between their phenomenological experience of being in the moment of the dance and their understanding of how they may be perceived by others in relation to culturally understood systems of signification.

For performers this ability is an important part of their artistic development but it is also perhaps an extension of the skills necessary for social interaction in the conventional sense as explored by the sociologist Erving Goffman (1969/1956). Moreover in a society, such as that in London, that is thought of as marked by difference and in which people constantly have to respond to those whose life experiences and cultural backgrounds cannot be presumed to be similar, this skill becomes of increasing importance both in everyday life and in performance.

If it is accepted that:

> While physical culture may be viewed as a crystallization – an embodiment – of the most deeply rooted and fundamental level of what it means to be a member of a particular society, dance might be seen as a second stage of this process (Polhemus, 1998/1993, p. 179).

Then, dance may not only be understood to articulate culturally derived bodily ways of being, but in the current context of increasing globalisation, in which performers and audience members are informed by different cultural traditions, a dance performance might at times be viewed as the site of the negotiation of significance in the context of difference.

This was emphasised to me through discussions with those artists who might be thought of as second generation immigrants or black British. Their comments suggested that that sense of the problem of the rationalist legacy informing so much of the development of contemporary western theatre dance is encountered differently if other people have tended to assume that, by virtue of your ethnicity, you are somehow less the product of western dualism. For them, as for other artists who might be thought of as offering ways of being that do not fit into easily defined norms in terms of ethnicity, gender or sexuality, the success of their performance may to some extent be dependent on the audience being willing to enter into a reciprocal embodied interaction in which what it means to be male/female black/white young/old (and so on) is open to negotiation.

How cultural difference is contemplated has certainly changed since Laban first formulated his theories; and even during his life time Laban's own thinking about the relationships between the west and its others did not stand still.[1] In Britain today, informed by experiences of diversity, dance theorists may be more wary of accepting as universal what may be argued to be culturally learned patterns of behaviour. Contemplating dance within culturally defined semiotic systems certainly guides the understanding of dance in relation to appropriate codes and provides against approaching one kind of dance with the codes and values of another.[2] However, it is important to keep in mind that the experience of dance is enriched by an engagement that, in Laban's terms, requires thinking in movement, responding to the physicality of action. Those uncomfortable with resorting to universals or metaphysics to ground this kind of thinking, might rather contemplate the reciprocity of human interaction that informs how, in the moment, we make sense of action and allows for recognition that this too, at least to some extent, is culturally shaped. That this reciprocity of interaction is made more complex by the experience of diversity is a current challenge for dance, at least as it is understood in western orientated theatres. In contemplating those dance performances which rework different traditions and create hybrid dance identities in a global context, Laban's explorations of dance may provide the means to develop a sensitivity to how different ways of being in the world are manifested, and perhaps even negotiated, in performance. Hence they may be invaluable to the dance artists, and audiences of tomorrow.

References

Adshead-Lansdale, J. (1999) *Dancing texts: Intertextuality in Interpretation.* London: Dance Books.

Bartlett, K. (2007) 'What is intercultural dialogue?' *Animated*, Spring 2007, p. 14.

Best, D. (1974) *Expression in movement and the arts*, London: Lepus Books.

Bourdieu, P. (1984) *Distinction* (trans. R. Nice). London: Routledge. (First published 1979).

Burt, R. (2004) *Contemporary dance and the performance of multicultural identities.* Internet page at URL: http:www.akramkhancompany.net/html/akram_akram.htm (accessed April 2007).

Bridgewood, A., C. Fenn, K. Dust, L. Hutton, A. Skelton & M. Skinner (2003). *Focus on Cultural Diversity; The Arts in England.* London: Arts Council of England.

Crowther, P. (1993) *Art and embodiment.* Oxford: Clarendon Press.

Csordas, T., ed. (1994) *Embodiment and experience*. Cambridge: Cambridge University Press.

Culler, J. (1983) *On deconstruction: theory and criticism after structuralism*. Boston and London: Routledge and Kegan Paul.

Dragazis, Potter, Gray and Richmond. (n.d) Internet page at URL: www. uniondance.co.uk. (accessed 08.09.2008).

Duncan, I. (1983) I see America dancing. In R. Copeland and M. Cohen (Eds.) *What is dance? Readings in theory and criticism*. Oxford University Press: Oxford. (First published in 1927).

Featherstone, M., M. Hepworth & B. Turner, eds. (1991) *The body: Social process and cultural context*, London: Sage.

Geertz, C. (1976) Art as a cultural system. *Modern Language Notes*, 91, 1473-99.

Green, M. (1986) *The mountain of truth: The counterculture begins 1900-1920*. Hanover NH: University Press of New England.

Hylton, R. (n.d.) *Urban Classicism*. Internet page at URL: \t "_blank" www.urbanclassicism.com (accessed 05.05.2005).

Kant, M. (2004) German dance and modernity: Don't mention the Nazis. In A. Carter (Ed.), *Rethinking Dance History: A reader*. London: Routledge.

Khan, A. (n.d) *Loose in Flight*. Internet page at URL: www.akramkhan company.net

Laban R. (1950) *The mastery of movement on the stage*. London: MacDonald & Evans.

Laban R. (1975) *A life for dance* (trans. L. Ullmann). London: MacDonald & Evans. (First published in German in 1935)

Laban, R. (1959, May) The Educational and theraputic value of dance, Meaning, Dance as symbol , The aesthetic approach to the art of dancing, In *A collection of writings as a tribute*. LAMG Magazine.

Laban R. *(1966) Choreutics* (Ed. L. Ullmann) . *London:* MacDonald & Evans.

Laban, R. and Lawrence, F.C. (1974) *Effort*. London: MacDonald & Evans. (First published 1947).

Merleau-Ponty, M. (1972) Eye and mind, In H. Osborne (Ed.) *Aesthetics* pp. 55-85. Oxford: Oxford University Press (first published 1961).

Montero, B. (2006), Proprioception as an aesthetic sense. *The Journal of Aesthetics and Art Criticism, 64* (2), 231-242.

Polhemus, T. (1998). Dance, gender and culture. In A. Carter (Ed.), *The Routledge dance studies reader (*pp. 171-179). New York: Routledge.

Preston-Dunlop, V. (1998) *Rudolf Laban: An extraordinary life*. London: Dance Books.

Shusterman, R. (1997) The end of aesthetic experience. *The Journal of Aesthetics and Art Criticism*, 55. 1. 29-41.

Thomas, H. (2003) *The body, dance and cultural theory.* New York: Palgrave
    Macmillan.

Weiss, G. (1999) *Body images: Embodiment as Intercorporeality.* New York:
    Routledge.

1. An unfinished article on the value of dance published after Laban's death can be read as questioning the presumption of western society's place at a pinnacle of human development.
2. Certainly from the standpoint of Artist B it can be important to use more broadly understood
semiotic systems to direct the audience's attention.

The legacy of Laban: the uses of movement behaviour assessment in therapy, human development and education

Dianne Dulicai & Marion North

Introduction: Marion North

I had a unique opportunity to work with Rudolf Laban for over nine years before he died. During that time he was keen to convey as much of his ideas about movement and personality as possible, based on the technique of movement observation. As a young student I was sent into factories to observe workers' movements and I learnt to differentiate between practical movement with personal overtones, and personal movement which revealed an attitude to life and a way of behaviour. We developed together a system of teaching young people which provoked them to reveal their active and latent capacities, and we gave reports designed to enable a young person to find the most appropriate route for their life's work. This was called the Youth Advice Bureau (YAB). The original observations of these young people (mostly in their teen years) are in the Laban Archive.

I had always been interested in psychology, child development and personality assessment, and Laban's insights into human behaviour were very intriguing to me at that time. Briefly, there are three stages, which have to be considered if one is using movement in the conscious way that Laban did. The first is the skill of *observation* and learning the tool of notation, particularly effort notation. It is obviously necessary to have studied and experienced a range of movement possibilities in order to recognise them in others. This skill is learned best through the art of dance. The second skill is to take the observations and see the patterns and the relationships in the *preferred movement phrases and patterns* each human being has. The full range of movement is available to human beings, but none of us has an equal proportion, or necessarily the whole range. It is therefore necessary to know what is the size and content of one's vocabulary of movement, and then equally important, how it is *used*. The third aspect is to *translate the movement profile into everyday words* and language, so that it is possible to convey the information to non-movement trained people.

My long apprenticeship with Laban took many forms – the creation of dance for community groups, movement choirs, analysis and understanding, observing factory workers in the Manchester area, working with assessing young people's potential for particular jobs, teaching students at the Art of Movement Studio, teaching young people in schools and working alongside Laban in therapeutic situations. I also completed a research project which included the observation of six/seven/eight year-olds in a school in London where there were many problems for the children and staff. It was during this pilot scheme that the question arose of how early movement patterns and coping behaviour developed between birth and the age of these children.

The work which I developed in this field, originally thirty years ago, has now been followed up by Professor Dianne Dulicai in the United States, and I am grateful that she is here today to give you her findings and her thoughts about this work.

Dianne Dulicai

Laban's legacy to dance/movement therapists and other mental health professionals over the last fifty years has been outstanding. From his prescient work and from proteges such as Dr North and to those who applied and expanded it widely, we received contributions to our knowledge in mental health, child development and education. Today we present unpublished research beginning in 1971 extending to 2001 as an example of his contribution.

Many of you are familiar with Dr North's book, *Personality Assessment through Movement*, published in 1972. She wrote in the preface, 'This book is an attempt to describe and validate a technique of movement observation which, I believe, has a contribution to make to the assessment of personality.' She evaluated twenty-six children in elementary school with her adaptation of Laban's hypotheses of correlations between movement quality and its meaning. The data was then compared with results of four standardised educational and psychological tests. Correlations were high and dance/movement therapists and other mental health professionals use the assessment widely.

Equally important is her unpublished research project with thirty-one babies from three days to two years. Two important research questions were investigated:

1. Can you measure an infant's movement qualities while the nervous system is not yet fully developed?
2. Given a stable physical and emotional health through development, will those early patterns remain consistent despite development and elaboration of movement patterns?

We should be mindful that this research developed in the early 1970s did not have the advantage of neuroscience findings that became available in the late 1990s. We now know a great deal about our genetic endowment and the consequential effect on our personalities thanks to genetic and neuroscientists. A new look at Dr North's results can now be seen in light of the new information. Our new book will present the baby project and update it by our evaluation of two of the subjects now grown. Also included in the new book are other research projects that since built and expanded our knowledge of movement and personality and its multiple implications to child development and therapy.

In 1971, the parents of thirty-one babies at St. Mary's Hospital in London agreed to have their newborn children participate in a research project. Eight of the 31 sets of parents continued to allow their children to be observed at home at 3, 9, 12, 15, 21 and 24 months. Babies were scored by Laban's categories of body level movement, and use of space, time, weight, and flow, combinations and phrasing. To draw inference of the meaning of the movement, observers used Laban's hypothesised correlations. Two of the original subjects were visited in 2001, now grown. North and Dulicai collected movement data available, interviews and use of a psychological personality assessment.

New information emerged from the eight babies studied up to two years. First, it is possible to observe movement quality of infants as defined by Laban and others at three days old. Prior to evaluating this data, many researchers thought it impossible to collect this data. The three observers had seven opportunities of 45 minute observation over two years for test-retest reliability r=0.70. Internal consistency measured by split-half reliability at r=0.92. Practice with subjects outside their original group was not done. The second outcome was the level of consistency of individual patterns within a general pattern. For example, all infants scored present for body shapes of wide, narrow or alternates but the preferences were individual. Equally interesting is how all infants scored on three motion factor combinations with predominance of weight/flow/time that contains eight possible sub-combinations. The individual characteristics of a child appears when one assessed which of the eight the child preferred. In other words, there are movement qualities that all infants had, but within that the individual character begins to emerge. It would be extremely enlightening to repeat this study and include movement evaluation of the parents to examine whether one could identify combination of characteristics from parents.

For this presentation, we shall report a small example of the extensive data of two subjects compared with the data and predictions collected thirty years ago. Changing our focus to these subjects as adults we will focus only on areas of emotional and cognitive intelligence. A full exploration of all the data appears in our upcoming book. One of the subjects that I refer to as Jeremy lives in the UK and agreed to allow us to redo the movement assessment and take (BeMis) Behavior Management Information System Report (Collins & Adair, 2000) as well as a personal interview. The other subject, I refer to as Anthony agreed to take the psychological assessment but was working out of the country and could not participate in a movement assessment.

As a short review here are the components that appeared in the original assessment:

Body shape
Where the motion initiated from extension of torso
Inward/outward flow
Phrasing
Motion factors: space, weight, time, flow
Combinations of two motion factors
Combinations of three motion factors

For example, the item above, combinations of two motion factors contains the possibility of weight with flow, space with time, weight with time, space with flow, weight with space and flow with time. Each of these have four possibilities. Starting with combinations of weight with flow, the most frequently used combination in infants, Jeremy used neutral 31% of the observed time and 18% strong/bound associated with 'cramped concentration'. Whereas Anthony scored 3% neutral, 51% strong/bound, 10% light/bound associated with 'tentative' and 22% strong/free associated with vigorous exuberance. The two boys scored within the general score of favoring weight with flow as did all other babies but the variations between them are found in which of the combinations they used. These movement patterns remained consistent through two years.

Since the observer must consider the entire portrait of movement patterns to draw an inference, one must look at patterns in all of the above categories to suggest personality characteristics. A simple example to demonstrate this concept is after observing the eight babies who participated until two years old, the researchers could legitimately suggest personality traits emerging with each child. Human intellectual and social/emotional potential derives from genetic endowment, interaction with immediate environment and complex exposure to experiences. When there are truly rich and complex possibilities great potential may be open to us all. Professionals in early childhood education fully understand the importance of rich experiences for all children including, rather especially those children with disabilities. Before we return to Jeremy and Anthony, let me share some of the findings for the other six children. We will take the characteristic of inward/outward flow that is associated with relating well with others. To be able to score this characteristic as preferential, it should be consistently seen over time. Below are the scores of all eight babies on inward/outward flow and relational ability.

Subject	Inward/Outward Flow	Relational Ability
#1	Inward Only	Poor
#2	Inward/Outward Flow	Good
#3	Inward/Outward Flow	Good
#4	Inward Only	Poor
#5	Inward/Outward Flow	Good
#7	Inward/Outward Flow	Good
#8	Inward/Outward Flow	Good

All items were examined and displayed in the upcoming book which supports other research reporting on consistency of movement and personality characteristics over time in normal circumstances (Schwartz, Wright, Shin, Kagan and Rauch 2003 & Chess, Thomas, Birch and Hertzig, 1960).

For the rest of the paper the focus will be on the two subjects that we observed as adults allowing us to continue to observe whether personality characteristics remained consistent with early predictions. First, we will display some of the most salient movement characteristics observed, the research team's inferences that are still present as adults.

Jeremy
1. Inward/outward flow — same—lack of inner zest
2. Resists being held—same—adverse to support
3. Pauses between phrases—same—few leaps of ideas and enthusiasm
4. Falling away at end of phrases—same—poor follow through of ideas
5. Rich shadow movements—less evident—innate intellectual ability
6. Lack of body center—same—self involved more than externally involved

Anthony
1. Predominate impactive phrases—poised and ready for action—same
2. High level of passion drives—intense—same
3. Early use of inward/outward flow balance—easy interaction with others—same
4. Rich and complex phrases—very bright—same
5. Initiates from center of body—commitment to action—same
6. Early use of presenting face to face—desire for recognition—same

Now we will look at cognitive style and emotional intelligence comparing scores between the same subjects. The original research team had predicted that both boys would show above average intelligence but differ on interaction skills. Since that time we now have a reliable instrument combining a more complex understanding of intelligence and traits important to emo-tional intelligence (Goleman, 2006). Interesting to note that Dr North tempered her predictions of intelligence with interaction skills during her discussion of babies in the early study. Average scores range from 40-60 using (BeMis) Behavioral Management Information System (Collins, Adair, 2000).

Cognitive Style

Affected	Intellect	Pragmatic	Scientific
Jeremy - 68	Jeremy - 65	Jeremy - 32	Jeremy - 42
Anthony - 48	Anthony - 64	Anthony - 64	Anthony - 58

Affected is scored if feelings, emotions and action are emphasised over reasoning and evaluation suggesting informality and playfulness.

Intellectualistic is scored when both affect and rationality are emphasised, suggesting versatility, unconventionality, and individuality.

Pragmatic is scored when neither affect nor rationality are emphasised, suggesting a conventional approach to life, with feelings of contentment and optimism.

Scientific is scored when rationality and analysis are emphasised over feel-ings and emotion, suggesting logicality, industriousness, and cognitive clarity.

BEMis Emotional Intelligence

Emotional IQ	Jeremy	Anthony
Awareness	45	60
Motivation	42	61
Optimism	42	62
Impulse Control	40	48
Persistence	45	63
Interpersonal	43	62
Empathy	43	64
Social Skill	43	64
Average score	42.88	60

Of the above eight traits, the use of space is critical in five of them. Aware-ness, persistence, interpersonal empathy and social skills all require use of either direct or flexible use of space. A similar finding occurred in a research project examining the movement characteristics of children with cognitive deficits due to lead exposure (Dulicai, 1995)

For the rest of the presentation I used film clips from two sites in which I use North's assessment system for consultation and/or clinical intervention.

The first clip filmed in an early childhood education centre showed two children with very similar characteristics as the two subjects above. Their teacher reported both of above average in intelligence though they differ in cognitive style. Differences in emotional intelligence determines how these two children use their cognitive skills as evidenced by one child's higher social, interpersonal and empathetic skills. With this feedback, the creative headteacher can devise interesting movement games increasing one child's interpersonal abilities while teaching the other to modulate his impulse control.

The last film clip presented at the conference demonstrated how the movement assessment of a child with special needs assisted the dance/movement therapist design his goals and objectives for treatment. Important to note is how the assessment coordinated emotional, social and cognitive goals and the process of presenting them to school staff.

I am very grateful to the Laban Centre for fostering this conference and am sure that as we move forward in developing ever more efficient and insightful forms of movement assessment, we will continue to appreciate the legacy of Rudolf Laban.

References

Chess, S., Thomas, A., Birch, H.G. and Hertzig, M. (1960). Implications of a longitudinal study of child development for child psychiatry in *American Journal of Psychiatry*, No.117, pp. 4334-441

Collins, D.R. (2000). Behavioral management information systems. Williamsburg: Measurement and Planned Development, Inc.

Dulicai, D. (1995). Movement indicators of attention and their role as identifiers of lead exposure. Doctoral dissertation, Union Institute, Cincinnati

Goleman, D. (2006). *Social intelligence*. New York: Bantam Dell.

North, M. (1972). *Personality assessment through movement*. London: MacDonald & Evans.

Schwartz, C.E.,Wright, C.I., Shin, L.M., Kagan, J. and Rauch, S.L. (2003). Inhibited and uninhibited infants 'Grown Up': Adult amygdala response to novelty in *Science* 20, Vol.300. No.5627, pp. 1952-1953.

Dance, Collections, Representation, and Archives[1]

Catherine E. Foley

This paper looks at the notion of collecting and representing dance within the context of the archive. It examines the role of archives within the Western world and, in particular, how dance might be collected, documented and represented within them. Drawing from my own ethnographic experience as a collector of step dance in Ireland, I critically examine research methods and techniques in relation to documenting and representing step dance as a cultural practice for archival purposes. I posit the questions: How does one represent dance as a cultural practice within the context of an archive? For whom is this representation intended? And, to what extent are all representations partial?

The Notion of Collections
According to James Clifford,

> Since 1990 inclusive collections of 'Mankind' have become institution-alised in academic disciplines like anthropology and in museums of art or ethnology. A restrictive 'art-culture-system' has come to control the authenticity, value and circulation of artefacts and data. Analysing this system [he proposes] that any collection implies a temporal vision generating rarity and worth, a metahistory. This history defines which groups or things will be redeemed from a disintegrating human past and which will be defined as the dynamic, or tragic, agents of a common destiny' (1988, pp.12-13).

The notion of collections implies a worth, which deserves to be collected, remembered and treasured. Collecting therefore is concerned with what specific groups and individuals choose to preserve or value from the material and cultural world (see Clifford, 1988). For example, many anthropologists, folklorists and others have concerned themselves with collecting ethnographic data, including artistic products, from marginalised as well as more mainstream societies to shed light on human culture. And although collect-ing, classifying, and valuing are not restricted to the West, elsewhere 'these activities need not be associated with accumulation (rather than redistribution) or with preservation (rather than natural or historical decay)' (Clifford, 1988, p. 232).

Clifford suggests that in the West 'collecting has long been a strategy for the deployment of a possessive self, culture, and authenticity' (op. cit. p.218). It may therefore be safe to say that collections in the West gather what is of value or worth to a community and that these collections assist in articulating and reinforcing the group's identity both to themselves and to outside others. These collections are made in the name of education, research, history, heritage or tourism, and they give structure and continuity to communities.

Collecting within the context of archives in the West has a relatively short history and dance collecting is even shorter, although attempts at documenting dance date back to the fourteenth century. In Ireland, collections of indigenous music emerged during the eighteenth century to define and to promote cultural and national boundaries. With the emergence of the discipline of Folklore in the nineteenth century, collections of music, song and folklore et cetera, continued to be collated and became associated with the antiquarianism and romanticism of this discipline. Folklore emerged as a discipline in Ireland in the nineteenth century and by 1930 the Irish Folklore Institute was established with Government Funding. In 1935 this Institute became known as the Irish Folklore Commission and was responsible for all Folklore collections and their preservation until 1971. It was then replaced by the Department of Folklore and incorporated into University College Dublin, where it is today.

In the 1940s folklore was collected under the following headings:

Settlement and Dwelling; Livelihood and Household Support; Communications and Trade; The Community; Human Life; Nature; Folk Medicine; Time; Principles and Rules of Popular Belief and Practice; Mythological Tradition; Historical Tradition; Religious Tradition; Popular 'Oral Literature'; and Sports and Pastimes (A Handbook of Irish Folklore, 1940). Concerning dance, stories and information relating to indigenous dance practices were recorded and documented but actual dances were not documented or recorded within the discipline of Folklore.

In 1902 A Guide to Irish Dancing was published in London by J. J.Sheehan, a member of the London Branch of the cultural nationalist movement, the Gaelic League. This was the first collection or guide to Irish popular dances to be compiled or to be published. Other collections followed including O'Keeffe and O'Brien (1902), Burchenal (1925), O'Rafferty (1934, 1950, 1953), and An Coimisiún le Rincí Gaelacha, the Irish step-dance organisation established in 1929 under the auspices of the Gaelic League (1939, 1943, and 1969). These publications were not comprehensive collections of dance in Ireland but they documented selected dances in a verbal manner. This form of docu-

mentation was useful for teachers of *Irish* dance as an *aide memoir* in impart-
ing dances to their pupils; however, for those outside of this tradition of
dance, it was incomprehensible. In 1983, however, the first intensive regional collection of dance was undertaken. This was instigated by Muckross
House (then known as Muckross House Folk Museum) in Killarney, Co.
Kerry, Ireland, and was part of a broader regional collection of Irish traditional music, song and dance. I was employed to undertake this collection for
archival purposes and I concentrated on step dance since no collection of
step dance had ever been undertaken.

Collecting Step Dance in North Kerry

The traditional step dances of North Kerry were considered by Muckross
House to be authentic cultural products. Other dance practices co-existing
in the area at the time did not carry the same significance. The traditional
step dances were considered old and indeed, native to the area. Since they
were perceived to be in decline at the time, performed by only a handful of
elderly step dancers, they were considered to be endangered cultural and
artistic products and therefore collecting the traditional step dances of this
region implied, as I stated above, a worth, a value, and a rescue of dances
from inevitable historical decay and loss.

Although, the dances could have been collected solely by video recording
the dancers, I was reluctant to utilise this method alone. Also, the dances
could have been Labanotated from viewings of the recordings, but again, this
method alone I regarded as insufficient to give an understanding of step
dance as cultural practice. In her wide-ranging study, *Of Longing*, Susan
Stewart illustrates how collections, most notably in museums, attempt to
create illusions of adequate representations of a world by first cutting objects
out of specific contexts and then making them 'stand for' abstract wholes.
She gives the example of a Bambara mask which when placed within the
context of a museum becomes an ethnographic metonym for Bambara culture (1984, p.162-165; see also Clifford, 1988). In collecting dance for
museums or indeed archives there is also the danger that a dance will become an object cut out of its specific culture; an ethnographic metonym for
the culture out of which it has emerged. So, what constitutes 'good' collecting practice in relation to dance for archival purposes? This paper suggests
that an ethnochoreological approach, utilising ethnochoreological research
methods and techniques, assists in both combating a de-contextualisation of
dance while promoting an understanding of dance in cultural context.
These complementary ethnographic methods and techniques provide different kinds of information and knowledge while not neglecting the actual
dances. For example, my own collecting of step dance in North Kerry for
Muckross House applied a number of ethnochoreological research methods

and techniques. These included fieldwork, participant observation, learning the dances from the elderly performers which allowed for a personal embodiment of the dances; documenting and structurally analysing the dances using both a mnemonic native system of dance documentation and Labanotation; video recording the dancers; doing recorded ethnographic interviews; and historicising and contextualising the dance practice in written format. Since this paper does not allow for an examination of all these research methods and techniques, and since the focus of this conference is on Rudolf Laban and the influence of his work on dance, I will address the use I made of Labanotation as a documentation and analytical tool in my research of step dance in North Kerry (Foley, 1988).

Labanotation as a Documentation and Analytical Research Tool in Step-Dance Research

As an aural, oral and imitative tradition, step dance was not written down in North Kerry; in other parts of Ireland however, some step-dance teachers, including my own teacher, taught dance pupils to write steps mnemonically as an *aide memoir*. My research in North Kerry used both this mnemonic system and Labanotation.

From the 1960s linguistics became a model to follow in the social sciences in that language was seen as being central to culture and was able to elicit patterns of culture, or deep structures unknown to the speakers. Experimentation with linguistics was diverse – cognitive anthropology (Tyler, 1969), structuralism (Levi-Strauss), and symbolic analysis (Geertz, 1973). Linguistic analogies were also made within the field of dance. For instance, Adrienne Kaeppler's ethnoscientific work with Tongan dance (1972) and the structural analytical work of the IFMC's (The International Folk Music Council) Study group in Ethnochoreology (1972) all used Labanotation for documentation and analytical purposes.

Similarly, I also used Labanotation to document the traditional step dances in North Kerry. However, I also wanted to provide an understanding of the actual dance system as was practised by these dancers, particularly as it was in decline as a living tradition at the time. Therefore influenced by the field of linguistics, I carried out a structural analysis of the dances to elicit not only the vocabulary and patterns of movement within this tradition, but also to illustrate how these movements were combined together meaningfully; in a phrase the grammar and deep structures of the tradition. To this end I constructed Labanotated inventories of step-dance movements in each of the step dance types – Reels, Jigs, and Hornpipes, at this particular moment in this dance tradition's historicity (see Foley, 1988). This notion of movement inventories I borrowed from the anthropologist, Adrienne Kaeppler and her work with Tongan dance (see Kaeppler, 1972); the structural analytical terminology I used and developed was largely based upon the work of the IFMC Study Group in Ethnochoreology (1972) [1] The terminology is as follows:

- Element (smallest structural movement)
- Cell (made up of two or three elements)
- Motif (made up of one or two cells and has meaning for the dancer)
- Minor Phrase
- Phrase
- Step
- Repeat
- Dance (Reel, Jig or Hornpipe)

Elements:
I constructed and Labanotated 7 categories of Elements:
a: positions of feet
b: stepping movements
c: leaping movements
d: hopping movements
e: jumping movements
f: kicking and striking movements
g: gestural movements (tips, touches et al)

a, b, c, etc. Performed to the opposite side

I constructed and Labanotated a system of 73 elements in total.

Cells:
I also constructed and Labanotated a system of 7 Categories of Cells:
a: Cells commencing with a 'tip' or 'brush' ((a1), (a2), etc.)
b: Cells commencing with a leap or a step onto the opposite foot ((b1), (b2), etc)
c: Cells commencing with a hop
d: Cells commencing with a jump
e: Cells commencing with a kicking movement
f: Cells commencing with a stamp, ball of foot, or heel support
g: Cells commencing with a touch, toe, hell or stamp movement

(a8), (c1) etc. When underlined the Cell is performed to the opposite side

102 Hornpipe Cells
99 Jig Cells

75 Treble Reel Cells

Motifs:
M1, M2 etc.
I constructed and Labanotated the following number of motifs :
20 Hornpipe Motifs
18 Jig Motifs
17 Treble Reel Motifs

Minor Phrases:
P1, P2 etc

Major Phrases:
PH1, PH2, etc.

In cross referencing the Labanotated step dances with this Labanotated system I was able to illustrate not only the codes, grammar, and syntax of this traditional step-dance system but also personal and interpersonal variations of specific step dances as practiced by the traditional step dancers of North Kerry (See example – transcription 1 from Foley, 1988, p. 335).

Similarly to my own work, dance researchers continue to be interested in using Labanotation for specific research reasons: for example, to document and record diverse dance practices and their vocabularies (Foley, 1988); to illustrate the historical change of movement vocabulary within specific movement cultures; to structurally analyse movement for an understanding of the deep structures of that particular movement system (see Kaeppler and Dunin, 2008); to illustrate improvisation or variations in movement patterns; or to make manifest gendered ways of moving (Joyce, 2006). Labanotation is therefore an important documentation and research tool. However, when representing dance with Labanotation we need to bear in mind that all representations are "partial" (see Clifford, 1988); and when representing dance within the context of the archive we need to apply other research methods and techniques also in order to provide a more comprehensive or 'holistic' representation and understanding of dance as cultural practice.

1. The IFMC (The International Folk Music Council) was established in post-war 1947 and became the ICTM (the International Council for Traditional Music) in 1982.

Transcription 1. © Foley, 1988, p. 335.

Jig Step
Step dancer: Síle Lyons Bowler

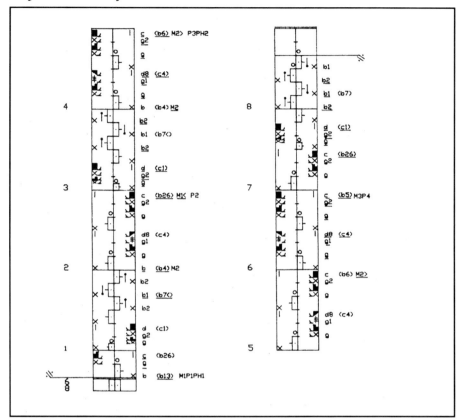

References

Clifford, J. (1988) *The Predicament of Culture: Twentieth-Century Ethnography, Literature, and Art.* London: Harvard University Press.

Foley, C. (1988) *Irish Traditional Step Dance in North Kerry: A Contextual and Structural Analysis.* Unpublished PhD Thesis. London: The Laban Centre for Movement and Dance.

Foley, C. (2008) "The Creative Process within Irish Traditional Step Dance" in Adrienne Kaeppler and Elsie Dunin (Eds.) *Dance Structures: Perspectives on the Analysis of Human Movement.* Budapest: Akademiai Kiado. Pp. 277-302.

Joyce, N. (2006) *Slipjigus masculinus* (Male Slip Jig): Extinct, endangered or dormant? Unpublished MA Thesis. Ireland: University of Limerick.

Stewart, S. (1984) *On Longing: Narratives of the Miniature, the Gigantic, the Souvenir, the Collection.* The Johns Hopkins University Press. US.

Laban training for conductors: creating a fresh approach to teaching conducting technique

Charles Gambetta

Introduction

In little more than 300 years, the conductor's art has evolved from its simple origins of time-beating and rudimentary directorial duties to become one of the most complex, demanding disciplines in the performing arts. It stands alone among musical endeavors devoted to performance because it is practiced in silence. Recognising this unique circumstance, conductor, teacher, author Hermann Scherchen (1966, p. 14) identifies gesture as 'the conductor's one and only medium during performance'. Even in rehearsal, when conductors often employ the voice to instruct or demonstrate desired execution, they still rely most heavily on the communication of musical expression through movement – conducting technique – to transmit their vision of the score to the ensemble.

While vocal and instrumental performers have at their disposal long established traditions and conventions upon which they can more or less concur, conductors and conductor educators have yet to reach substantial, meaningful agreements regarding the proper approach or methods for the acquisition and development of technique. Listing this deficiency among his primary motivations for writing *Lehrbuch des Dirigierens* in 1929, Scherchen (pp. 3-4) wrote: 'Indeed, there does not even exist a standard method of teaching the technique of conducting, a method providing teachers and pupils with materials for systematic exercises and dealing, in a gradual order, with the problems of conducting.' Sir Adrian Boult came to the same conclusion in 1959 (p. 9) when he observed: 'There has so far been no time for someone's "method" to be evolved and opposed to someone else's as we have seen with all other forms of interpretation, vocal and instrumental.' Nearly twenty-five years later, noted choral conductor educator Gail Poch (1982, pp. 21-2) maintained: 'There is [still] no source which offers a logical and meaningful learning sequence for the development of the techniques and skills of conducting.'

The need for a new approach

In the opening decade of the 21st century, prominent conductors and leading pedagogues continue to express similar concerns regarding these and other shortcomings that persist in traditional conductor training programmes. Yet little has changed since the publication of Hector Berlioz's groundbreaking 1855 essay, *L'Art du chef d'orchestre, le theorie du son art*. For over 150 years the common theme coursing through virtually all conducting texts and curricula of teachers who use them has been a concentration on the practice and mastery of highly prescribed, metrically based, two dimensional, repetitive patterns that trace the tip of the baton (or conductor's hand) through space as it marks beats and accounts for the intervening time between them.

If keeping time were the conductor's only task, these beat patterns alone might suffice. However, conductors either control or influence every aspect of musical performance including: tempo selection, starting, stopping, tempo changes, dynamics (changes in amplitude), rhythmic precision, ensemble balance and blend, entrances and releases, articulations, phrasing, shape, mood, character, style, even pitch and intonation. The conductor's performance should embody and transmit all of this information to her collaborators in the ensemble *without* making a sound, but most conductors fall short of these goals because the pedagogical system that produced them:

1) concentrates on the practice and perfect beat patterns rather than movements that reflect the expressive qualities of music;

2) fails to offer students the means to connect and engage the entire body in the act of conducting;

3) has yet to include the techniques and terminology needed to fully explain and describe conducting movements.

A new interdisciplinary approach that combines comprehensive musical education with complementary Laban training addresses these deficiencies and more.

Transforming conducting pedagogy through Laban training

Conducting technique is a highly specialised, extremely rich form of nonverbal communication through movement. Accepting this description, it logically follows that any 'school' or method of teaching conducting should include thorough grounding in the means by which the flow of musical expression in a given score is translated into movements that are immediately recognised and understood by musicians. The key to any successful training programme is, therefore, the identification and exploitation of the point in a conductor's cognitive process at which his movement thinking (Laban 1988, pp. 15-7, 47-9) and his powers of audiation (Gordon 1980, pp. 4-5) or 'music thinking' converge. In other words, a conductor's body and mind should be fused with his musical and artistic intentions through an awareness of the paired oppositional qualities that permeate both movement and music.

Laban uses the concept of bi-polar opposites to elaborate his Effort theory. He identifies eight Effort elements that arise from inner attitudes of indulging/accepting or condensing/resisting the four Motion Factors: Space, Weight, Time and Flow (Maletic 2005, pp. 9-11). Conductors who have honed their capacities to experience and observe Effort can make conscious use of these oppositional forces to create movements that accurately reflect their 'inner attitudes' towards corresponding pairs of musical qualities (i.e. loud/soft, fast/slow, etc.). These elements of musical expression coalesce with equivalent dynamic qualities of movement to produce the desired representation of the composer's notation in the score and the conductor's interior interpretation of the score. A list of these paired characteristics of music might include: loud/soft, sound/silence, fast/slow, long/short, high/low, thick/thin, firm/gentle, rhythmic/melodic, small/large, regimented/free, agitated/calm, connected/detached, consonant/dissonant, tension/release, complex/simple, expressive/plain, tender/brutal, etc. A short character piece may exhibit only a few paired qualities while a large extended work might include a much broader range of expression. Borrowing the concept of affinities from Laban and Lamb, the following table compiles and organises a group of six basic characteristics of music and their affinities with the eight Effort elements.

Table 1: The Effort/Conducting Affinities

Efforts	Elements of Musical Expression					
	TEMPO	DYNAMICS	ARTICULATIONS	CHARACTER	PRECISION	PHRASING
Light Weight	Increase	Decrease	Less Intensity	Light	Neutral	Neutral
Strong Weight	Decrease	Increase	More Intensity	Heavy	Neutral	Neutral
Flexible Space	Neutral	Neutral	Longer	Broad	Less	Pliant
Direct Space	Neutral	Neutral	Shorter	Focused	More	Strict
Sustained Time	Decrease	Neutral	Less Accented	Calm	Neutral	Stretched
Quick Time	Increase	Neutral	More Accented	Hurried	Neutral	Condensed
Free Flow	Neutral	Increase	Neutral	Carefree	Less	Fluent
Bound Flow	Neutral	Decrease	Neutral	Restrained	More	Controlled

The Efforts are listed in pairs in the first column, and six elements of musical expression extend across the top of the table. Tendencies for each Effort are listed across its corresponding row underneath each musical term so readers can choose to consider the affinities in relation to any given Effort or musical characteristic. For example, Light Weight tends to increase tempo and decrease dynamic intensity; but Strong Weight tends to decrease tempo and increase dynamic intensity. Cues, holds, releases and processes that occur over an extended period of time such as crescendos, diminuendos, accelerandos, ritardandos, etc., were purposefully left off the list. These types of events cannot be considered or properly represented in the context of a single Effort because, by definition, they normally appear together with one or more additional elements of musical expression. This simple list, although far from complete, helps conductors establish rudimentary connections between their powers of audiation and movement thinking. With practise and continued study these connections can ultimately lead to a genuine experience of the equivalence between movement and music.

Examining the Efforts and their relationships with the six categories across the top of the table, a curious yet logical pattern emerges. Each Motion Factor is active in four of the six categories and passive or neutral for the remaining two. An explanation of this passivity helps illustrate how the Efforts combine to emphasise specific qualities of musical expression. The tendency for any single Motion Factor to affect any of the six categories of musical expression is neutral if: 1) it exerts little or no obvious influence upon the considered musical quality, or 2) it is equally capable of communicating the effects at either end of the spectrum. For example, because Flow by itself suggests little or no sense of pulse, it is difficult to imagine the representation of tempo with Flow alone. Simply put, Free or Bound Flow may be applied to slow or fast tempos. Once Flow combines with Time or Weight (or both as in passion drive) the pulse emerges and tempo can be established. Space Effort is also neutral when considering tempo because one's attitude towards space alone does not affect tempo. Conversely, even though it may be difficult to conceive a tempo with Time Effort alone, it is equally obvious that accelerating or quick movements favour faster tempos while sustained, drawn out movements favour slower tempos. These affinities are justified because the tendency for each Time Effort is clear.

Effort/Space and Effort/Shape affinities
As Laban developed his Effort theory, he also noticed that 'the body and its limbs are able to execute certain dynamic nuances in movements towards certain areas in space better than towards others' (Laban and Lawrence 1974, pp. 30-2). He observed that lightness favours upward movement while strong movements correlate to downward directions. Movements across the body exhibit an affinity with the quality of directness or narrow focus, and roundabout, indirect movements favour flexible directions that open out-

ward. Quick or sudden movements relate to backwards directions while sustained movements tend to favour reaching forward. Further experimentation with these six Effort/Space affinities in groups of three and the continued refinement of his Effort theory eventually helped Laban develop the eight Basic Effort Actions and the Effort Cube. After validating the correspondence between Space and the horizontal dimension, Weight and the vertical and Time and the sagittal dimension, Lamb (1965, pp. 63-4) used these three Effort/Space affinities as the organising principle for his Effort/Shape affinities listed in the table below.

Table 2: The Effort/Shape Affinities

MOTION FACTOR	ACCEPTING EFFORT ELEMENT	SHAPE AFFINITY	RESISTING EFFORT ELEMENT	SHAPE AFFINITY
Space	Flexible	Spreading	Direct	Enclosing
Weight	Light	Rising	Strong	Sinking
Time	Sustained	Advancing	Quick	Retreating

These relationships provide conductors with the bond that joins the qualities of their movements (their Effort choices) to the shapes their limbs and bodies create as they carve pathways through space. Affinities frequently reinforce musical events like the downward stroke that may accompany a strong, direct, quick accent. Disaffinities (movements that contradict natural tendencies) often support some kind of musical tension, and they can appear simultaneously with additional affinities or disaffinities. An extended diminuendo, for example, might require a light, direct, sustained gesture with the left arm that sinks (a disaffinity), encloses (an affinity) and retreats (a second disaffinity).

Effectiveness confirmed through research
Years of Laban study had clearly produced positive results for me, but I needed to know if this new approach would help others as well. To find out I conducted a study of four student conductors at the University of North Carolina at Greensboro School of Music. Following a pretest conducting performance of the opening 154 measures of Beethoven's Coriolan Overture, Op. 62 (1808), the participants completed five hours of introductory Laban training. This mini-course included a brief exploration of Body, Effort, Space and Shape but focused on the material presented in this essay—Effort, the Effort/Space and Effort/Shape Affinities and their specific application to musical expression.

I designed and presented the Laban instruction, some of which was related to conducting, but I did not teach the course as a conducting class. No specific applications of the course materials to the study repertoire were prescribed, and the student conductors received no counsel from instructors outside the limits of the study. Participants were asked to use homework assignments and in-class participatory exercises as the means to incorporate newly acquired skills into their conducting. Upon completion of the course, the student conductors performed the same repertoire with the same community orchestra in a posttest. Both the pretest and posttest performances were documented with a video camcorder, and the resulting recordings were edited without any change in content and transferred to DVD. (Excerpts from these recordings are available for viewing using the links provided in the reference list.) Expert panels of two conductors and two Certified Movement Analysts provided analyses of the participating conductors' pretest and posttest performances, and a third channel of data was collected through post-study interviews with each participant.

The CMA panel was able to confirm significant changes in movement choices and an expanded range of movement possibilities that could be attributed to Laban training for all four participants. Focusing on the participants overall presentation, one of the CMA panelists noticed: 'In general the participants were more grounded (i.e. connected to their own bodies and aware of their potential power to communicate through movement) in the posttest than they were in the pretests.' Elaborating further, she continued:

> Each participant in the beginning of his/her posttest, standing in preparation to begin the music, had an awareness of his/her ability to communicate through the choices (s)he made in his/her inner attitude toward Space, Weight, Time and Flow Effort. This awareness of how those choices would affect the music produced by the orchestra was not as apparent... in the pretest (Gambetta 2005, pp. 269-70).

The other CMA observed: 'All conductors in the study seemed to be able to use shape change affinities to help crystallise Efforts better in the posttest that the pretest.' She explained:

> In the pretest many were working in a different plane of motion, which often seemed to counteract the chosen Effort: e.g. sinking with quickness or advancing with strength in the posttest versus retreating or advancing with quickness, and sinking with strength in the posttest (Gambetta 2005, p. 280).

The conductor panel was also able to concur that the changes they observed constituted a positive development for all participants. One found that 'overall, all four participants' general performance improved significantly in the posttest compared to the pretest. All four used a wider range of motion and involved different gestural solutions to inherent problems in the score.' He also reported that the participants 'were more relaxed in the posttest.' As a result, 'the ensemble was more relaxed and responded with overall better execution of the piece' (Gambetta 2005, p. 306). The second expert conductor noted: 'In general, the four conductors exhibited greater control of body language in their posttest performances as compared to the pretests. They seemed more poised and relaxed physically and more self-confident both physically and mentally.' Zeroing in on changes in the participants' gestures, he added:

> Their gestures were more focused and more purposeful with fewer extraneous motions in their arms or bodies. Contrasts of dynamics were more vividly delineated, as were certain, but not all, changes of character. Shaping of phrases also benefited from the greater physical focus, and, in some cases, eye contact with the players improved (Gambetta 2005, p. 332).

Lastly, the participants themselves expressed unanimous approval regarding the quality of the course content and instruction, and all agreed that they would eagerly recommend Laban training to their colleagues and peers. Participant 1 reported: 'I find that I am much more confident with my movement choices,' and he recognised that 'musicians react a lot more to a conductor's gestures than most of us realise' (Gambetta 2007, pp. 336-7). The course has helped participant 2 develop 'a better understanding of the connection between what I do and the sound I get and exactly how to describe that connection.' She plans to continue to use the skills she acquired during the course because LMA has, for her, 'become a very useful framework to analyse [her] movements, analyse what other people are doing and what works versus what doesn't' (Gambetta 2005, pp. 341-2).

Before taking the course participant 3 'didn't think of conducting in terms of gesture'. Through the Laban training she has developed 'much more appreciation for the art and the difficulty of conducting as well as the ability to convey a lot of things that, previously, I just could not figure out'. When asked how the course had improved the connection between her gestures and elements of musical expression she replied:

> At the most basic level, I now have choices to make. Before the class I felt like I was lost in the music with no tools or system to help me connect my gestures to the music. After the course I am able to look at a score and know that I can quickly find a solution to almost any problem or challenge I encounter (Gambetta 2005, p. 346).

After the study participant 4 realised: 'many of the things I already believed have been reinforced', and he added that the Laban training had provided him with 'some very useful terminology to describe movements [I am] already using'. He reported that since the course, he is 'definitely watching conductors more closely to try to see if their Effort choices match their musical intentions'. When asked whether or not he would encourage friends and colleagues to add Laban training to their studies he answered: 'I'm convinced that Laban training... should almost be a requirement for conductors' (Gambetta 2005, p. 351-3).

Conclusions

The expert panels' evaluations, the participants' observations, the pretest and posttest video recordings, and my personal experience combine to provide convincing evidence that Laban training offers conductors a comprehensive set of tools for conceiving and executing potent, persuasive movements that display genuine equivalence with the sounds of music. The Motion Factors, Effort elements and Effort/Shape affinities are the raw ingredients conductors combine to create 'recipes' for movements that perfectly reflect both the conductor's own personal movement style and the musical and technical demands present in the score.

Such a conductor's movements illumine the music and inspire the performers under his direction because he has firmly, irrevocably fused his musical intentions with his force of will and body by grounding himself at the point of convergence between his powers of music thinking and movement thinking. Lamb and Watson (1979, p. 81) describe Effort and Shape as 'the two processes from which movement is created'. From the evidence presented in this essay, it also seems abundantly clear that Effort and Shape together with audiation are the three processes from which music and, most specifically, effective, compelling conducting movements are created.

References

Boult, Adrian Cedric (1920-9?). *A handbook on the technique of conducting*, Oxford: Hall the Printer.

Gambetta, Charles (2005). *Conducting outside the box: Creating a fresh approach to conducting gesture through the principles of Laban Movement Analysis*. D.M.A. diss., University of North Carolina at Greensboro.

Gordon, Edwin E (1980). *Learning sequences in music: Skill, content and patterns*. Chicago: GIA Publications, Inc.

Laban, Rudolf (1980). *The mastery of movement*, 4th ed., revised by Lisa Ullman, London: MacDonald & Evans. Reprint, Northcote House, Plymouth (page numbers refer to reprint edition).

Laban, Rudolf and F. C. Lawrence (1974). *Effort: Economy of body movement*, 2nd ed., Boston: Plays, Inc.

Lamb, Warren (1965). *Posture and gesture*, London: Gerald Duckworth and Company.

Lamb, Warren and Elizabeth Watson (1979). *Body code: The meaning in movement*, London: Routledge and Kegan Paul.

Maletic, Vera (2005). *Dance dynamics: Effort and phrasing*, Grade A Notes, Columbus.

Poch, Gail B. (1982). 'Conducting movement analogues through effort shape,' *Choral Journal* 23, No. 3: 21-2.

Scherchen, Hermann (1966). *Handbook of conducting*, 10th ed., trans. M. D. Calvocoressi, London: Oxford University Press.

Video Resources
http://www.youtube.com/watch?v=bA8k_yF_EJs

Generating, analysing, and organising movement using the mathematical concepts of vectors

This written treatment of practice-based research is a companion to anno-
tated videos posted on www.youtube.com[1]

Julia K. Gleich

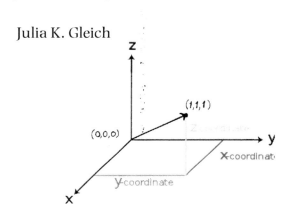

Dance can be seen as simple combinations of directed energy. This applies to
motion as well as apparent stillness. Directed energy could be a pathway or
line of direction with a length or magnitude, a vector. A vector is a mathematical concept, usually represented by a line with an arrow at one end. In
its simplest geometric sense, a vector has only direction and magnitude
(length).

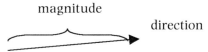

magnitude

direction

Vectors allow the possibility to strip dance down to its essential properties in
similar ways to Laban's development of Space Harmony and more. 'One of
the things that gives mathematics its power is the shedding of attributes that
turn out to be nonessential...' (Hoffmann 1966 p. 10). In developing this
research integrating mathematics, kinesiology, physics and dance, there are
implications for pedagogic practice as well as analysis and choreographic
invention.

Vectors exist in 2-d and 3-d geometric space as, in this case, Euclidean
vectors represented with Cartesian coordinates. For the purposes of this paper vectors will exist in 3-d space. It is worth mentioning that the concept of
a 4th spatial dimension exists in Euclidean mathematics (in theory there can
be infinite dimensions). In physics, there is spacetime. This is a continuum of
the three dimensions of space plus the single dimension of time. Certainly

1. Search for gleichdances and vectors.

this has relevance to dance and a 4-d vector dance space could be defined by adding a time element. Further discussion is beyond the scope of this paper.

Visualising vectors in 3-space

Each vector has an initial point or point of application and exists in three dimensions (3-space). For example, $(x,y,z) = (1,1,1)$ is a vector in 3-space with initial point at the origin $(0,0,0)$. The origin is the point where the x, y and z axes intersect.[1] In this study magnitude (length) of vectors ranged from 1-10. This is effectively a Likert item (or scale) so the numerical values are fairly arbitrary and based on judgment of a relative scale for the individual dancer. Vector equivalency is complicated. Free vectors are equal if they have the same length and direction. This model depends upon initial point or point of application and body position upon application. It will be unusual that any equal vectors (having the same direction and magnitude) will be equivalent (have the same effect).

The set of vectors in 3-space is infinite. Rudolf Laban's spatial models, which are widely known and analysed, are 3-space geometric shapes indicating specific points or directions in space, around individual kinespheres. In every case, there are a finite number of directional points. The vector model, however, has no defined points and no sense of orientation to a centre. But Laban is conceiving of space harmony, or harmonised movement. It would be safe to say that the vector model at this time in no way implies harmony and at early stages appears more often like chaos and disharmony – an atonal relative to harmony. But it has the advantage of embracing infinite vector space.

Motion vectors

Motion vectors, unlike position vectors[2], initiate movement or support stillness with directional energies of various magnitudes. They do not necessarily emanate from a joint, so the concept of the origin is less significant. Motion vectors (herein 'vectors') can lead to apparent stillness. Vectors can be associated with shifts or displacement, and are linked to force.

A short discussion of force

Force, in a mathematical model, is a vector with magnitude, direction and a point of application. 'It acts at a point and may be represented by a vector whose length is the magnitude of the force and whose direction is the direction of the force.' (Clapham and Nicholson 2005 p.177) The act of changing magnitude, direction or point of application leads to shifts in force. In dance, force is a generalised concept of energy input, pressure or tension, but is not necessarily named in relation to dance dynamics, though it may have some relationship with Laban's effort elements, Weight: strong-light and/or Flow:

bound-free. A search in *Dance Words* discovered a few mentions of force, including the force of gravity. In order to achieve clarity, however, the word force will be avoided. In this work magnitude will be treated as a quantifiable energy that causes changes in pressure that may lead to displacement.

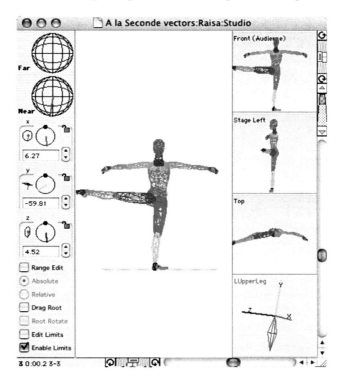

The single vector with responding vector

Armed with basic knowledge of vectors, it was time to begin research in the studio with three dancers over four sessions. The first area of research was the single vector activation. In most cases, activating a single vector of magnitude greater than or equal to 5 (≥ 5) lead to the dancer falling. Note that magnitude is effectively a Lickert item and that the dancers were applying the vector in stillness (not in a phrase). In the next investigation dancers created secondary or 'responding' vectors that would prevent, disrupt or recover the fall. This led to some interesting movement, but primarily created aggressive instability. Diminishing the magnitudes led to more subtle movement explorations. James-Paul Frost, a 2nd year student exploring vectors through this research, went on to employ vectors to generate original movement for his choreography. He created a dance in which all the dancers apply the same directions but each dancer applies a different magnitude. This created individuality within shared material. These vector explorations have similarities to spatial projection and to some methods from William Forsythe's *Improvisation Technologies*. Certainly any action of moving into space, projecting, leading with a body part, extrusion, etc. will have similarities. The Laban scales also possess vector principles.

A second single vector activity was 'up'. Up is a common dance idea. So when the dancers tried to fully activate the vector up – the one that goes through the middle of the head and pulls upward – they found they could not retain contact within their bodies, lost any sense of groundedness, and were desperate for a release of 'up'. In other words, up as a single vector was limiting and did not create 'up-ness'. This might be because the vector's initial point was in the head. Changing this point will achieve different results.

Vector addition

Vectors can be added. For example, the vectors in 2-space $(0,1)$ and $(1,0)$ will add to $(1,1)$. Also, $(3,-3) + (-3, 3) = (0,0)$, also known as the *null vector*. And finally, representing vectors in 3-space, $(1,3,-1) + (2,2,2) + (-3,-5,-1) = (0,0,0)$, also the *null vector*. The null vector is unique in that it has zero magnitude and no direction, or, as Hoffmann (1966) suggests, it has *all* directions. This is a relevant mathematical idea.

In analysing dancers moving in space the main process is vector addition. Identify the key or dominant vector and magnitude necessary for the movement. Explore secondary or sub-vectors and magnitudes as necessary.[3] There will be an infinite number of vectors both acting upon and acted on by the dancer. It is not possible in this brief treatment to identify each and every vector. Likewise, the vectors that act upon the dancer, such as friction and gravity are not addressed here. A dancer will act both consciously and subconsciously against gravity and the concern here lies primarily with the conscious vector processes. So certain vectors are assumed. There is a loose parallel here to the idea of voluntary and involuntary muscular actions in the body: voluntary muscle contractions are initiated in the brain, while the spinal cord initiates involuntary reflexes. Similarly, there are many actions that are not consciously performed but function in a supportive role. With vectors there are times to accept these additional vectors and times to prevent them or to adjust their direction and magnitudes.

The key vector(s) will initiate movement with sub-vectors offering extra directional activity or support. This applies both to motion and stillness. In general the vector model is about activating specific vectors, rather than making the vector visible. Especially with stillness, problems often arise because a dancer is trying to 'hold a pose'. Turning off all vectors, the dancer cancels out direction and magnitude in order to create what s/he imagines as stillness. This is both an error of technique and of philosophy. Even with the

minimum of muscular action (release or relaxation), there are always opposing tensions. And this introduces the first example of vector usage in
teaching ballet.

Zero-Sum vectors: A vector theory of movement without displacement.

One can imagine a set of high magnitude vectors that add to magnitude 0
(0,0,0), because in 3-space there are also vectors with negative direction. In
different fields of science there are conflicting attitudes towards the negative
magnitude. The term 'negative magnitude' will be avoided because it is clear
in the studio process how directions correspond to each other and apply to
vector addition. In this case, the null vector represents motion without displacement, stillness; it is always a sum of two or more vectors. The null
vector in this model is a philosophical concept since there is no single origin.
(Steve Paxton might have called the null vector, the 'small dance', with its
small adjustments to remain simply standing. Those 'adjustments' are vectors, probably of magnitude ≤ 2.)

Third year LABAN student, Pia Födinger, experimented with shifting
magnitudes that maintained a zero-sum. Vectors battled for dominance and
she struggled to keep to the zero-sum rule. The appearance of inner struggle
or free floating resulted from magnitudes of greater or lesser value, respectively. The Zero-Sum concept works differently with the typical ballet pose.

Vectors are straight

In dance literature there are many representations of lines with direction.
Many of these are curves or have two arrows, which will be labeled, *vectors
falsi* (pseudo-vectors already exist as a specific mathematical concept). My
model of vectors requires the rule from physics that force travels in a straight
line; it is, after all, a vector. If one considers the boney structure of the body,
there are, in fact, no curves possible. While this discussion is not fundamentally concerned with shape it should be mentioned that even along the spine,
a curve is apparent because the angled joints of each vertebrae are cush-
ioned with cartilage and the collection of joints adds up to what appears to be
a curve. Curve is visible because flesh fills out the form. Joints also create
axes; thus, the appearance of curve at the distal moving point. So there is a
slight problem accommodating these distal curves in the vector model. One
approach is to consider the calculus for measuring area under a curve. This is
done by creating infinitely narrow rectangles under and adjacent to the line
of the curve, breaking the curve into a series of very short straight lines.
Thus the straight line of the vector has a precedent, but what appears as
result is at this moment less important. Observations of shape or end result
are outweighed by rules of initiation. In studio there were some vector series
that led to a sense of an arc, but certainly not a swing.

Some examples of Vectors Falsi

In the drawing of a dancer in first arabesque, lines with arrows represent opposition in the arabesque. These lines are based on a drawing and discussion in *Ballet Beyond Tradition* by Anna Paskevska (p. 89). Paskevska makes great strides towards a Vector Model. She even refers to Paxton and talks about adjustments and pulls. The lines of opposition do seem to indicate a balance of energy, a Zero-Sum. But these are not vectors; at minimum the lines require a point of application. They are also curved. Finally, there is no magnitude and so all the lines share the same value without a hierarchy. At best this is a vague notion of curve and reach. Anyone who has read about ballet will have seen many *vectors falsi* in Lincoln Kirstein's *The Classical Ballet*, Valerie Grieg's *Inside Ballet Technique* and *Classical Ballet Technique* by Gretchen Ward Warren to mention only a few.

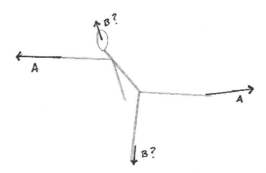

Zero-Sum first arabesque

In the studio the three dancers varied the vectors that dominate their first arabesque. The figures are line drawings to emphasise movement of the bodily structure, not the flesh. The vector pairs have corresponding lengths. It was first observed that different vectors affect style, from classic to romantic to Balanchine. Also, as in the 'up' investigation, the vectors associated with common corrections such as, reach with your arm, or reach with your foot (represented by vectors A), caused the arabesque line to disintegrate. The dancer became over-extended and lost the connection over the standing leg (vector B). The question marks for vectors B indicate a difficulty to activate these vectors in this instance. In general, there was concern about how literal work with the vectors compares with students' studio experiences with imagery. Some common ideas of energy were more akin to imagery, as opposed to functional efforts with concrete ideas of directed energy. Also, rather than building the arabesque from scratch, this process clarifies and strengthens the form. This is an effort to discover 'principles of movement that generate the classical form,'[4] specifically first arabesque, and not merely organise the shape, the flesh. Vectors only imply shape. Surprisingly, turning vector A around at the arm by 180° added power and support to the centre of the body.

In the image to the right there are vector pairs with equal lengths. Though this is an over-simplification the dancers found correspondence with these vectors pairs. C was the last set of vectors that seem unrelated, but a reactive connection existed between them. In general these vectors add to the null vector – no direction and every direction at once. (There is one more vector required possibly at the sternum pointing slightly downward and to the back of the dancer. This vector would make the zero-sum more obvious.) Consider also the sum of the magnitudes, by this definition they add to zero, but what a zero it is! It contains the magnitude of all the vectors (only a few are drawn here and are viewed in only two dimensions).

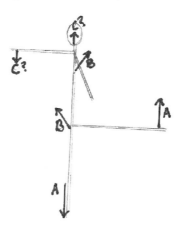

More examples of *vectors falsi* include Lulu Swiegard's Nine Lines of Action, illustrations for Bartenieff principles in *Making Connections* by Peggy

Hackney and technique drawings in *The Illustrated Dance Technique of José Limon* by Daniel Lewis. This is not an exhaustive list but shows how vectors exist in analyses of dance (not only ballet), but not in a precise mathematical abstraction. In no way are these representations incorrect, rather they are not vectors and should not be confused with the vector model. Interestingly, the Laban shapes of icosahedron, cube, etc. are all straight-edge shapes with angles. So the action of initiating a direction in the Laban models is very similar to the vector model. The artist Pavel Tchelitchew has made indications of vectors and origins in the body in many of his paintings, including cover designs for Ballet Russe and New York City Ballet. A list of his relevant paintings is attached as an appendix.

The application to choreographic invention
The studio research began with an exploration of single vectors and inverse vectors[5]. The next process used an ordinary ballet phrase with new vectors added. Used in a performance of Pelican (2008), the dancers had the appearance of diving birds, or slipping on ice in momentary departures from the phrase. This appears briefly in the video of the studio research and also in a video excerpt on youtube (gleichdances).

Pure vectorland
The final challenge was to generate movement only by verbal and tactile instructions that specify vectors; creating the mechanics for the movement prior to knowing what the movement will be. All three dancers took on this challenge with Michelle Buckley on pointe.

   The rules of the process follow:
   •   The subconscious vectors that deal directly with gravity are assumed.
   •   Vectors are only applied as straight lines.
   •   Vectors may emanate from any point within and outside the body.
   •   Space is a resultant of magnitude and direction only.
   •   The dancer must give in to the vector and vector outweighs shape.
   •   Vectors may affect body parts that are not adjacent to, or inside, the point of origin.
   •   There is no repeating of a movement. Each performance of the material is a re-creation of the vector map. The dancer must not 'learn' the result of the vector.
   •   Rotation about an axis is initiated with vectors (not curves).
   •   Several vectors can act at once or have a precise ordering.
   •   There may not be (visible) preparation to activate the vector. And a corollary, no vectors before the key vector. (This is similar to some aspects of Elizabeth Streb's method of Pop-Action.)

Definitions (and areas of further exploration):
- When a vector activates, a choice must be made regarding the vectors that were active in the prior moments. They can remain on or turn off altogether or in sequences.
- The 'dotted line vector' is a vector that turns on and off sequentially for a specified period. Possibly with increasing or decreasing magnitudes.
- Vectors can generate motion that goes through (blocking) or around (diverting) the body.
- Vectors may push or pull.

Variables in generating from vectors:
- Individual's 3-space spatial skills
- Strength – especially subconscious control
- Personality, the process is a kind of game
- Different dancers will require different magnitudes, directions or points of application to create inverse vectors in pairs.

In working with Michelle Buckley on pointe, who can be seen on the youtube video for this research, the process at the start was a bit difficult and frustrating. After two days, however, she grasped the concept of vectors and began to engage with the experimental nature of this work. Most of the rules above came out of this process. There were many discoveries such as; vectors can awaken places in the body 'undisturbed' by intentions of shape. The vector is not a direct journey and a single vector initiation may not result in the expected outcome. Dancers who have worked from shape may find themselves more open to this approach since it does not attack prior training, but rather focuses on specific rules for vector application. Buckley adds, 'As a classical dancer the most difficult aspect is to not think of the product of a series of positions. Not rehearsing is important in order to hold onto the element of surprise. In this case practise does not make perfect.' The vectors are a kind of game and remembering the next vector is the rehearsal. This also created an intensity of focus on task that enhanced performance.

Everyone in the studio accepted that the outcome of a vector would be unknown. When only one vector is applied results can be very clear and a dancer can discover their own habits. The back of the body is activated and concepts of body organisation become part of the process – contra-lateral, body half, etc. This was not expected. There was no focus on dynamics, though simply changes in magnitude affected time and duration. There were questions about defining words for faster or slower vector initiation. These were dealt with in magnitude, but that was not sufficient. The continuation of this work will include explorations of dynamics, notation and further development of the mathematical applications.

References

Clapham, C. and Nicholson J. (2005) *The Concise Oxford Dictionary of Mathematics*. Oxford.

Greenberg, M.J. (1972) *Euclidean and Non-Euclidean Geometries: Development and History*. 2nd ed. New York: W.H. Freeman and Co.

Laws, K. (1984) *The Physics of Dance*. New York: Schirmer Books.

Paskevska, A. (2005) *Ballet Beyond Tradition*. New York: Routledge.

Preston-Dunlop, V. (1995) *Dance Words*. Chur, Switzerland: Harwood Academic Publishers.

Weinreich, G. (1998) *Geometrical Vectors*. Chicago: University of Chicago Press.

Appendix 1:

Pavel Tchelitchew image list

- Design for Programme Cover (Ballet Russe)
- Projects and Considerations in Movement
- Costumes for the Man, Lifar
- Head IV, 1950, pink and white chalk on paper, 48.3 x 34.9 cm, Collection: Cleveland Museum of Art (1961.99)
- Spiral Head, 1952, Pastel on blue wove paper, 19 1/8 x 12 3/8 inches / 31.5 x 48.6 cm, Collection: Smart Museum, Chicago (1976.16)
- Garcon Nu, 1927, Graphite, watercolor on paper, 50.2 x 32.5 cm, Collection: The Samuel Courtauld Trust, Courtauld Institute of Art, London, UK

1. A vector can be bound, meaning it's initial point is the origin, or it can be free, where the initial point is not significant, but rather the magnitude and direction alone are valued. But vectors in this model are free *and* it matters where the initial point is. This raises some mathematical issues that won't be addressed here.

2. An Aside About Existing Digital Vector Applications
Digital graphics already represents bodies in terms of vectors that describe body location and body part place/position. What follows is a simplified description of the software, DanceForms. In DanceForms all positions of the dancer animation are represented by coordinate groups of numbers that indicate positions in 3-space at each joint's axis, the respective origin. That is, the origin is the center of articulation of a joint and vectors emanate from that origin for each joint. Let's call these 'position vectors'; they are all bound and there are many separate sets of bound vectors. For any moment of movement there are 28 DanceForms origins that have single vectors associated with each. Computer software extrapolates between the two position moments (or collections of vectors) in order to create a series of 'movement moments'. The appearance of movement, the animation, is achieved by flashing in order the series of 'movement moments' that represent the moments between the two positions. Similarly, the standard today for digital animation is called vector graphics.

(Read about OpenGL and vector graphics for more information.) A limitation of these animations is that they do not reveal weight or the appearance of force; they do not have gravity (a vector) acting upon them; and they do not have generalised muscular tensions (sub-vectors). A screenshot from DanceForms is below with position of the left upper leg is indicated.

3 Conventionally in technique classes we begin with a combination or phrase. Once the dancer begins the phrase I look for the vectors the dancer is activating. Are they the right ones? Could a different vector work better or be more efficient? Should I change the point of application, the magnitude or the direction? Do they have sufficient vector activation at all? Are there sub-vectors that will support the movement? Much of this is a trial and error process. Students don't always understand and may think that I am asking them to shift a body part or contract a muscle or hold in their stomachs. Sometimes I mention how muscles work, not by turning on a contraction once and locking it; electric signals must be sent over and over to the muscles that produce directed action. I touch a fine point of application; the touch is also giving magnitude information. For dancers who push into touch, find a point that the vector will push into (usually on the opposite side of the body). This is in the context of a technique class (not a somatic class) and all of its codified and modeled forms. This process will be reversed for the purposes of choreographic invention near the end of this document.

4. Rosemary Brandt quoted from her presentation at Laban International Conference October 2008.

5. For brevity, the discussion of inverse vectors is omitted. In short, inverse vectors are used when two dancers share weight. One vector inverts the other, creating equilibrium. This applies to contemporary and traditional partnering

Laban in Mexico – A choreological approach

Miriam Huberman

The story of my involvement with Laban's work begins when Bonnie Bird and Marion North came to the Dance Department of the National Autonomous University of Mexico (UNAM) in 1981 to give information about the then-called Laban Centre for Movement and Dance and its Summer School. At that time I was taking several dance classes, doing a B.A. in History with emphasis on art history at the UNAM since this was the closest I could get to a theoretical complement for the dance practice I was engaged in, and I was working as assistant to the head of the Dance Department, Colombia Moya. I was at the meeting with Bonnie Bird and Marion North to help with the translations and I was fascinated by what I heard. What they talked about was precisely what I had been looking for: a combination of theory and practice in dance which made it possible to describe, analyse and register objectively what went on when people danced or when they just moved.

The result of that visit was that I attended the 1981 Summer School at the Laban Centre. As soon as I came back from London I read and reread all of Laban's books I had bought and I began to experiment and search for ways of applying what I had learnt. This process changed how I danced, how I taught, and how I perceived dance.

My first opportunity to apply my newly-acquired skills came soon. In 1982, Ludwik Margules, one of Mexico's leading theatre directors, who was at that moment head of the University Centre for Theatre (CUT) at the UNAM, invited me to give a workshop to the students who were taking part in the new course for stage directors and set and costume designers. After a few conversations about Laban and his work, Margules chose Motif Writing, floor plans, body part signs and an introduction to Effort as the main elements of the workshop. The workshop was well received and it made me aware for the first time how useful Laban's work could be and of the wide range of areas into which it could be applied.

A year later, Margules was asked by the National School of Music, which also belongs to UNAM, to put together a team of teachers who would be able to give a summer course on acting for opera singers. The school was expecting a dance class to be included, but Margules suggested I go instead, arguing that what I did would have a deeper impact on their training. When the summer course ended, I was asked to continue teaching the opera singer students on a regular basis, which I did from 1983 to 1987.

Basically, the classes I taught there consisted of a systematic exploration of the relations that could be found between sound and space, sound and dynamics and phrasing, and movement and role interpretation. A typical end-of-term open class programme would be divided into two parts: the first half of the programme consisted of a series of short studies on breath and movement, changes of weight and falls, distortion/alignment, relationships, walking, running, jumping, lines and volumes, open space and closed space, changes of direction and level, and in the second half, the students would perform a selection of songs they had been working on to integrate choreological elements to their interpretation.

I began to study Labanotation through the Dance Notation Bureau correspondence courses. During this stage, whenever an opportunity arose, I would include Laban's work into what I might be doing: whether it was teaching movement to high school students, designing the performers' movement for plays or operas, or making my first attempts at notating the dances we staged in the Renaissance dance group where I performed. The influence of Laban's ideas was also present in the dance criticism articles I published in that period.

In 1985 I decided to interrupt my B.A. studies and go to New York with the intention of studying at the Laban/Bartenieff Institute of Movement Studies and the Dance Notation Bureau. However, almost as soon as I arrived, I came across information about the M.A. in Dance Studies that the Laban Centre offered and, as I realised I preferred this option, I returned to Mexico to finish my B.A.

Thanks to a British Council scholarship, I enrolled for the M.A. in Dance Studies in 1988. With Valerie Preston-Dunlop as my tutor, I wrote the final dissertation on a topic that intrigued me very much. I set out to trace the origins of Laban's ideas in an attempt to identify as closely as possible how, when and where Laban may have had access to his sources, and consequently, to determine to what degree the concept of choreosophy – the word Laban coined to refer to the wisdom that may be found in dance – permeates his work, arguing that it was such a predominant element in his thinking and in his life that it was what guided and motivated his work.

Upon my return to Mexico I taught workshops in different parts of the country using the term 'movement analysis' to describe what I did because the term 'choreology' provoked blank stares all too frequently. Using 'movement analysis' had two advantages: one was that students understood that the course or workshop would be movement-related instead of being another dance technique event, and the other advantage was that they were prepared not only to move but to go through a process of analysing what they were doing.

From 1993 to 1996 I was invited to work as dance consultant to the Department of Artistic Education of the National Institute of Fine Arts, responsible for elaborating the curricula for each of the art schools that would come together in the newly built National Centre of the Arts. I was able to explain the usefulness of Laban's work to the coordinators of the different sections of the National Schools of Classical and Contemporary Dance. As a result, the curriculum of the B.A. in Choreography of the National School of Contemporary Dance now has Movement Analysis in the first two semesters and Labanotation in the following two.[1] I also worked as advisor at the planning stage of the B.A. in Arts-Dance Option of the University of Sonora. There, the result was that students now have Movement Analysis on semesters III, IV and V.

In order to help teachers understand where I was coming from in terms of educational theory and how I was justifying the incorporation of choreology into the curriculum proposal for the above-mentioned institutions, in 1994 I published an article entitled 'Areas of Dance Knowledge'. Its purpose was to serve as a guide for deciding what subjects to include when designing a dance curriculum based on the idea that to be educated in dance means to cover all five areas that constitute dance since each one deals with a specific form of knowledge. Thus, the technical area provides the intrinsic practical knowledge of dance; the choreological area provides the intrinsic analytical knowledge; the choreographic area develops the creative aspect of dance and integrates all the acquired knowledge – theoretical and practical, intrinsic and extrinsic; the theoretical area provides the extrinsic theoretical knowledge; and the interdisciplinary area provides the extrinsic practical knowledge.[2]

Area	Type of knowledge
Technical	Intrinsic practical
Choreological	Intrinsic analytical
Choreographic	Creative aspect + integrates the intrinsic, extrinsic, practical and theoretical
Theoretical	Extrinsic theoretical
Interdisciplinary	Extrinsic practical

So, while it is expected that all areas will be present in a curriculum, what will vary from school to school is the amount of hours dedicated to each area because this should correspond to the school's aim; that is, more or less hours will be dedicated to each area according to whether the school wishes to produce performers, choreographers, teachers, etc.

Since 1990 I have worked with several dance and theater companies as a 'choreological counselor.'[3] When I have choreological counseling sessions I work directly with a choreographer or a stage director, on a specific choreography or play before opening night. The sessions are a movement conversation between a creator, an analyst and the performers; they consist of a series of questions that lead to movement exploration, with the purpose of clarifying whatever structural or interpretative issues arise in the movement. When working like this I have a practical problem in front of me that I must attend to and to do so I have to use the choreological tool that best solves the problem.

On the whole, the secret of these sessions lies in the fact that they are based on the application of an analytic method that is intrinsic to movement and dance, and is objective and thorough.[4] Choreology is what allows creators to clarify the relationship between intentions and what they actually do with the performers and their movement on stage. In the end, if I have done my job well, the creator will be satisfied because the result corresponds to his/her intentions and the audience will enjoy a work that has a clear and logical structure and, in Laban's words, is 'meaningful and understandable.'[5]

After attending the ICKL[6] 2007 conference in Mexico, I started a research project on the situation of Laban's work in Latin America, which was the subject of the paper presented at the 2008 Laban Conference. The project explores why Laban's ideas are still not integrated into the mainstream Latin American dance scene despite their relevance and the fact that Latin American people have been in touch with his ideas for several decades. So far, I have identified three possible lines of enquiry:

1. Because of the way dance is usually taught and perceived, people in Latin America generally have no need or interest in developing an intrinsic analytical understanding of movement and dance.

2. In Latin America, Laban's work is being studied and applied in a fragmentary fashion. This refers to the fact that few people take a 'choreological' approach to Laban's work; instead, they focus on Labanotation, Movement Analysis or Motif as independent aspects of a whole.

3. While Laban's work is slowly penetrating higher education institutions, there is no Laban-based training/certifying centre in any Latin American country, which makes it difficult to stay up-dated, maintain similar standards, and develop projects.

Just before the 2008 Laban Conference, Alejandro Schwartz, head of the Centre for the Arts in Veracruz, invited me to coordinate a diploma course on choreological studies. The programme will consist of a two-week intensive course and two intensive weekends for follow-up and the presentation of the students' application projects. Following Dr. Valerie Preston-Dunlop's advice to 'be inclusive,'[7] the programme brings together certified teachers in Labanotation, Movement Analysis and Language of Dance, and the contents have been organised according to the choreological 'star' (the body, action, space, dynamics and relationships) to achieve an integrated approach to the analytic and structural study of movement and dance. The programme will begin this coming July.

References

Huberman, M. La importancia del sistema Laban de notación de danza y del análisis del movimiento. Boletín Informativo del CID-Danza (1985); 5:6-8.

—La danza en México en 1986. México en el Arte (1986); 13:87-90.

—Lo mexicano en la danza contemporánea. México en el Arte (1987); 17:28-34.

—De maestro a maestro. Segundo Encuentro Normalista de Danza Contemporánea. Tiempo Libre (1992); 633:4-5.

—Pueden bailar los muertos? Pregonarte (1992); 9:26.

—Preguntas para coreógrafos. Bailamos? (1993); 1:24-25.

—Áreas del conocimiento dancístico. Educación Artística (1994); 5:72-75.

Huberman, M. Choreology and the Choreographic Process. Proceedings of the 25th Biennial Conference, International Council of Kinetography Laban/Labanotation. (2007) Jul 29-Aug 5; Mexico City.

Huberman, M. End-of-Term Open Class [programme]. Escuela Nacional de Música. 1984-1986.

Huberman, M. Rudolf, (1991) Laban and the Concept of Choreosophy [dissertation]. London: Laban Centre for Movement and Dance.

Laban, R. (1966) Choreutics. London: MacDonald & Evans.

Preston-Dunlop, V. (1995) Dance Words. London: Harwood.

1. The National School of Classical Dance has recently added a subject called Reading and Writing Dance which is based on Language of Dance.
2. In the original article each area was described more fully; it was divided into subareas, and a list of possible subjects was included.
3. In the paper I presented at the 25th Biennial Conference of the International Council of Kinetography Laban/Labanotation I gave a detailed description of this type of work.
4. Preston-Dunlop V. Dance Words. London: Harwood; 1995, p. 580.
5. Laban R. Choreutics. London: MacDonald and Evans; 1966, p. viii.
6. International Council of Kinetography Laban
7. Personal conversation with Dr Valerie Preston-Dunlop, Laban Conference 2008.

'Movement concerns the whole man'

Michael Huxley

In his final public paper of 1958, fifty years ago, Laban addressed the idea of unity. In his paper to the Joint Council for Education through Art at Whitsun of that year, a short time before he died, he talked of how 'movement concerns the whole man' (1958). This final public statement was given in the company of Lisa Ullmann and Marion North. It was published that same year in *Art, Science and Education* and in the *Laban Art of Movement Guild Magazine* and has been acknowledged by Valerie Preston-Dunlop and John Hodgson, as a 'major statement of holistic philosophy' (1990, p.87). Given the occasion of this conference, this statement seems an eminently suitable starting point for an exploration of the relevance of Laban's ideas today as part of an inter-disciplinary dialogue on his work and influence in the fifty years since his death. It goes without saying that this paper is just one very small part of Laban's considerable output – both published and unpublished. I will be using this as a starting point and make no claims that it is in any way *definitive* of what Laban had to say. Neither do I suggest that the totality of what he had to say does not merit close scrutiny, as many recent writers have pointed out.

Laban's 1958 paper was titled 'Movement concerns the whole man'. He develops this theme in various ways, typical of his writings. However, there are certain explicit statements that follow on from the title. It is not just the title that speaks of unity, but the very substance of the paper. It is expressed, here in 1958, in terms of unity, unitary, unified whole, integration, body-mind, brought together in movement as the whole man: he talks of 'unitary function of body and mind' (p.51), 'a unified whole an integrated being' and 'body-mind movement' (p.55), 'movement as the great integrator' (p.57) and 'unity at the basis of his natural tendencies and impulses' (p.57).

Although ideas of body-mind, unity, integration, and the whole person have considerable currency in 2008, they tend to do so largely from the point of view of what has become known as somatics. I would like to look a little more closely at the historical placing of Laban within the history of body-mind ideas in dance, dance training and dance education. My exploration is historiographical. Rather than putting forward an unproblematic linear narrative, I conduct a thick reading of his talk within its context in order to explore influence. My paper begins with the period celebrated by this conference, 1958-2008, and then looks further into 19th and 20th century ideas about unity, the whole man, and body-mind. In 1958 Laban had been in England twenty years and it was the twelfth year of the Laban Art of Movement Guild, and the Art of Movement Studio had been at Addlestone for just five years. As I read it, Laban was using the term 'body-mind' to talk of his movement practice, explicitly, in English, a quarter of a century before it was given common currency in dance by Bonnie Bainbridge-Cohen and others.

Terms like unity, integration and body-mind seem to have some currency in discussing dance in 2008. There are dance courses with somatics in the title, and the most recently founded British academic journal is titled *Dance and Somatic Practices*. Melanie Bales and Rebecca Nettl-Fiol's recent book *The body eclectic: evolving practices in dance training* gives a useful collection of writings on dance training practices. It is, albeit, based on their US experience, and addresses 'training' but much of what is said here is relevant to the British situation. Bales, in her introduction and essays, makes a convincing case in support of the 'assertion that contemporary dance training since the Judson era of American modern dance is distinct from earlier approaches in several ways' (2008, p.1). She considers recent approaches to dance training which foreground bricolage, eclecticism, and deconstruction. In doing so, she includes what she terms somatic approaches. When she writes of somatic approaches she includes Body-Mind Centering, Alexander Technique, yoga and Bartenieff Fundamentals. Bales, in locating these, says:

> When some part of a technique class incorporates yoga, or Bartenieff Fundamentals, or Body-Mind Centering, and so on, the resulting experience can reflect bricolage and deconstruction in that the somatic practice is added as an element of the whole training package (bricolage), but the process of examination and re-visitation during the practice may be deconstructive (2008, p.16).

Contributing authors extend the idea of the somatic. Wendell Beavers, for instance, also includes Ideokinesis, Release Technique, Feldenkrais and Improvisation (2008, p.128). He goes further than Bales contending that 'a revisionist dance history of techniques starts with Mabel [Elsworth] Todd and her book *The thinking body*, published in 1937' (2008, p.128). It should be added that Bales is a qualified LMA practitioner, Nettl-Fiol teaches Alexander Technique, somatics and kinesiology, and that Beavers studied with Bonnie Bainbridge-Cohen.

So dance training in the US and UK increasingly includes 'somatic' approaches. These approaches are characteristic of post-Judson dance in the States, and are thus located within the period 1962-2008. There is a broad diversity to what is included in these approaches but with Bales, and elsewhere, LMA and Bartenieff Fundamentals figure as somatic and it goes without saying that these are developments of some of Laban's ideas. There also seems to be an idea, encapsulated by Beavers, that an origin of somatic approaches can be located in Mabel Elsworth Todd's work. The matter is confused somewhat by the fact that the term 'somatic' gained currency after its use by Thomas Hanna in 1970 in *Bodies in revolt*. Many, but not I, have included the Alexander Technique within this somatic bricolage. The salient fact is that Rudolf Laban, F.M Alexander and Mabel Elsworth Todd were contemporaries with what seems to be a similar common interest in *unity* in their practices and writings. Their dates locate them within the same late 19th century, first half of the 20th century period:

Rudolf Laban (1879-1958)

F.M. Alexander (1869-1955)

Mabel Elsworth Todd (1874-1956)

This unity is variously expressed as body-mind, psychophysiological and psychophysical. However, the terms are not necessarily the same as what is currently meant by 'somatic'.

Bales and Nettl-Fiol, in looking at current eclectic approaches to dance, are talking about dance *training* in the US in 2008; specifically what goes on in American universities, which they bracket with professional training. Indeed, they go so far as to say that within the university context 'dancing to learn has shifted toward learning to dance' (2008, p.vii.). This seems to be drawing a contradistinction with the legacy of Margaret H'Doubler and her pioneering approach to dance as part of 'progressive education' (1925, p.3) and the broader legacy of John Dewey. Mark Franko identifies the 1930s as a key period for the formation of a dance canon centred on modernism. He (2007) has written most lucidly about how canonical approaches to dance performance have excluded certain works and artists from the serious consideration they deserve. Indeed, he carefully shows how the canon is based in the canonical techniques that formed the basis for professionalised discourses of university dance. He identifies Graham and Cunningham in particular, locating the former in the developments through the Bennington summer schools of the thirties (2007, p.173). However, if you look at dance from a transatlantic perspective, distinctions between dance education and dance training seem to me to exemplify some of the differences between European modern dance and American modern dance of the 1930s. My research suggests that the type of modernist discourses based on dancers' techniques is primarily an American affair and dance education occupied a different place. As Janice Ross has pointed out, H'Doubler was not interested in and distanced herself from the theatrical. The European (German) approach to dance at this time is modernist, but of a different sort. Laban linked lay dancing, pedagogy and the professional. My reading is that the German approach is more open than the American one, whilst still professional.

Whilst it shares some of the progressive aspirations of H'Doubler, it does not separate itself off from the professional world. In this sense, it has not been susceptible to the same canon formation that Franko critiques, precisely because it is not based on techniques to underpin it. Whereas, in the 1930s Graham and Humphrey most certainly offered techniques, Hanya Holm offered a more holistic approach to a dancer's training. A fuller discussion around these differences, highlighted in particular in the writings and oral history of Jane Dudley, is currently being worked through for publication in the near future.

Laban's view of movement and the whole man was far from an accepted view within the totality of transatlantic dance training, education and practice in the year that he spoke. So what was happening in 1958? In the USA Doris Humphrey had just completed her manuscript for *The Art of Making Dances*. Lulu Sweigard had been teaching Ideokinesis at Martha Hill's invitation for two years at Juilliard in New York City, supplementing the teaching of choreographers that included Anthony Tudor and José Limon. Anna Halprin was improvising and collaborating in San Francisco. It was four years before the first concert of dance at Judson Memorial Church in New York City. In England, Jane Winearls' book *Modern dance: the Jooss-Leeder method* had just been published. Ballet Rambert had a largely classical repertoire and premiered Norman Morrice's *Two Brothers*. The Arts Council had no dance department. There were no British university degree courses in dance. The Art of Movement Studio was still in Addlestone. The extant dance literature in England did not make an explicit case for unity, mind-body approaches or anything similar.

The four years from 1958-1962 in America show a significant shift in approach.[1] When Robert Dunn gave his workshops at Cunningham's studio, which gave rise to the first concert of dance at Judson Memorial Church in 1962, he deconstructed ideas about compositional form and structure that are to be found in *The Art of Making Dances*. A secondary effect of this approach was to open up possibilities of conceiving the dancing body as a thinking body and opening up a space for Anna Halprin's ideas to enter the New York dance scene via Simone Forti, Trisha Brown and Yvonne Rainer. The changes in thinking about choreography around Judson lead to a change in thinking about the nature of the dancing body, which includes Todd, Alexander and Laban. This, I would suggest, posits a different view of Todd's place, to a generally accepted one that links it to post-modern dance practices via Thomas Hanna and somatics.

Laban did not talk explicitly of body-mind, integration and unity to any extent in his main published books of 1947, 1948 and 1950. He did so in published talks of 1958 and 1939. Laban's use of 'body-mind' as a term is exceptional in the dance literature at this time, 1958. The term does appear a decade later in the UK in the second edition of Winearls' book (1968), in a chapter by Gerald Wragg based on the Alexander Technique. However, I have yet to find reference elsewhere, in English. It does occur in a talk of Laban's 'Dance in general' published posthumously in 1961. The original text is from a series of open lectures at Dartington Hall given twenty years earlier in 1939. Here Laban says:

> Why does man dance? Why are all these dance-like motions in nature? The solution can only be found by studying the history of dance as a poetic and spiritual emanation of man's body-mind (1939,1971, p.64).

In the same year that Laban gave his series of lectures at Dartington, only a year after his arrival there, he wrote to Leonard Elmhirst, in March 1939 about:

> Kurt Jooss told me that you would like to read something about modern community dance, that means about the new way of our body-mind training for laymen (March 10th 1939).

This approach, as Nicholas (2007) has shown, was part of a subtle and complicated movement at Dartington to refocus dance education there: to give it a greater community emphasis. Accompanying the letter were documents on a proposed centre and on Lisa Ullmann's WEA work in Plymouth, and a translation from the German of part of an address from 1936. What struck me when I first read this letter and some of the accompanying documentation in the Dartington Trust Archives was the use of the term 'body-mind training' as early as 1938. I have been looking at 'body-mind' or 'somatic' approaches to dance, education and training for over a decade, and this was the earliest use of the term that I had come across. The second thing that struck me was two of the documents that accompanied the letter. The first is the much discussed and contentious programme for the 1936 Movement Choir Performance *Vom Tauwind und der neuen Freude – Wir Tanzen*. The second is headed 'Extract from an address held by Mr Laban on a meeting for community-dance in 1936' and Laban's letter makes it clear that this is an English translation of his address to that meeting. It was published posthumously in 1974.[2]

The extract begins:

> The idea of psycho-physiological training, fitness, movement-culture etc., deals with the only and absolute reality which mankind possesses: with the human body and its functions (1936, 1974, p. 6).

He says:

Our motto is: go ahead towards oneness with nature, towards psycho-physiological synthesis. For this we need those time saving improvements of our civilisation, and therefore also your work and your fresh spirit in the factories and offices. For this we need firstly the unifying point of view which is given to us by the discovery of the power of movement (1936, 1974, p.9).

So here in the letter Laban talks of body-mind and in the extract of the psycho-physiological.

I'm now going to take all these documents together – the 1939 letter, the 1939 talk, the 1936 'extract', the 1936 *Wir Tanzen* booklet and the 1958 talk on which this paper is based and consider them in relation to the context that has already been suggested, especially in terms of publications of the period and the etymology of some of the terms to do with unity. I stress that for today's paper I am looking only at one context and would stress that there are, as others have commented, political implications to anything produced in Germany in 1936.[3] Further exploration of these implications is for another paper.

As I said earlier, Laban and his contemporaries in England and the US, Alexander and Todd, espoused unity in their practice and writings. They expressed it in terms of body-mind, psychophysical and psychophysiological. These three terms were well established in the literature by the 1930s. G.H. Lewes had used the term body-mind in 1877 in *Physical basis of mind* where he says:

We know ourselves as Body-Mind; we do not know ourselves as Body and Mind, if by that be meant two coexistent independent Existents (1877, p.350).

The term psychophysiological had been common currency in physiology since the 19th century. Psycho-physical entered the English language in Lloyd's 1847 translation of von Feuchtersleben's term *psychisch-physischen* from the German edition of *Principles of medical psychology*. Dee Reynolds, in her recent writing around kinaesthetic empathy (2007, p.65), identifies Laban's use of unity in 1958 with the earlier German context where Schikowski in 1924 had talked of dance in terms of *körperseelisch*, which Reynolds translates as psychophysical. Ramsay Burt, in his paper for this conference, has re-examined modernist Laban's ideas in *Die Welt des Tänzers* (1920) and suggests that his ideas on unity are evident as early as this. Todd introduces the idea of the psychophysical in her early writing of 1929 and stresses unity in 1937 in *The thinking body*. Alexander first uses psychophysical in 1910 in *Man's supreme inheritance* and is at pains to stress the indivisibility of the mental and the physical in his approach, thus psychophysical unity, which he defines in *Constructive conscious control of the individual* in 1923 and further explores in 1932 in *The use of the self*. It could be argued that Todd's ideas are continued, and brought directly into the American dance training context at Juilliard in the fifties by Lulu Sweigard, and that her term Ideokinesis is a movement-based development of psychophysical. It should also be said that whilst both Alexander and Todd treated the person in action, neither isolated *movement* as a determining factor, as Laban did. Thus Laban in 1939 talking about dance in general makes claims for body-mind unity that are in intention quite different to those of Todd and Alexander:

> Dance is often described as born out of a kind of frenzy, that means, that all dancing involves a change of mental state, a change from a comparative inner quietude and stillness to exultation and excitement. This excitement is connected with or results in that kind of extreme concentration which we call unity of body and mind and in which subconscious awareness of unified space and time is present (1939, 1971, p.65).

I am making no claim that Laban, Alexander and Todd were saying the same thing. They were not. However, they were all developing ideas within a discourse that is now used, partially, as a particular part of the bricolage of post-modern dance training/education.

So I would like to reinstate 'Movement concerns the whole person as a 'major statement of holistic philosophy' (1990, p.87) relevant for the 21st century. I began by saying that I would be using this as a starting point and make no claims that it is in any way *definitive* of what Laban had to say. My starting point has taken me to the present and back to the twenties and thirties. I believe that there is value in considering Laban's work within a broader context with which he might not usually, historically or otherwise, be associated. This context includes the particular approaches of Mabel Elsworth Todd in the States and F. M. Alexander in England and the States. I would contend that on closer examination there is not such a clear distinction between pre-Judson and post-Judson dance education practices. This suggests a basis for a reconsideration of Laban's place within modernism and/or modernity. It also suggests a re-examination of Laban's work, and indeed that of his contemporaries, in present day dance pedagogy, and here I embrace both dance education and training.

References

Alexander, F. M. (1910) *Man's supreme inheritance*, London: Methuen.

Alexander, F. M. (1923) *Constructive conscious control of the individual*, New York: E.P. Dutton.

Alexander, F. M. (1932) *The use of the self: its conscious direction in relation to diagnosis, functioning and the control of reaction*, London: Methuen.

Bales, M. & Nettl-Fiol, R. (Eds.) (2008) *The body eclectic: evolving practices in dance training*, Chicago: University of Illinois Press.

Beavers, W. (2008) Re-locating technique. In Bales, M. & Nettl-Fiol, R. (Eds.) *The body eclectic: evolving practices in dance training*. Chicago: University of Illinois Press. pp. 126-133.

Burt, R. (2006) *Judson Dance Theatre: performative traces*, London: Routledge.

Burt, R. (2008) Dance's immanent potential: Laban and early Twenty First Century European Theatre Dance. *Laban International Conference* 24th–26th October. Laban, London.

Feuchtersleben, E. Von (1847) *The principles of medical psychology*, Trans. H. Evans Lloyd, London: Sydenham Society.

Franko, M. (2007) Period plots, canonical stages, and post-metanarrative in American modern dance. In Gitelman, C. & Martin R. (Eds.) *The returns of Alwin Nikolais: bodies, boundaries and the dance canon*. Middletown, Conn: Wesleyan University Press.

Guilbert, L. (2000) *Danser avec le IIIe Reich. Les danseurs modernes sous le nazism*, Paris: Éditions Complexe.

Hanna, T. (1970) *Bodies in revolt: a primer in somatic thinking*, New York: Holt, Rhinehart and Winston.

H'Doubler, M. N. (1925) *The dance and its place in education*, New York: Harcourt, Brace and Company.

Hodgson, J. & Preston-Dunlop, V. (1990) *Rudolf Laban: an introduction to his work and influence*, Plymouth: Northcote House.

Humphrey, D. (1959) *The art of making dances*, New York: Grove.

Kant, M. & Karina, L. (2003) *Hitler's dancers: German modern dance and the Third Reich*, New York: Berghahn Books.

Kew, C. (1999) Weimar movement choir to Nazi Community dance: The rise and fall of Rudolf Laban's 'Festkultur'. *Dance Research*, 17, 73-96.

Laban, R. Von (1920) *Die Welt des Tanzers*, Stuttgart: Walter Seifert.

Laban, R. (1936, 1974) Extract from an address held by Mr. Laban on a meeting for community-dance in 1936. *Laban Art of Movement Guild Magazine*, 6-11.

Laban, R. (1939) letter. To Elmhirst, L. *Dartington Trust Archive* T/AD/3/A/4. Dartington.

Laban, R. (1939, 1971) Dance in general. In Ullmann, L. (Ed.) *Rudolf Laban speaks about movement and dance.* Addlestone: Laban Art of Movement Centre.

Laban, R. (1958) Movement concerns the whole man. *Art, Science and Education.* London: JCEA.

Lewes, G. H. (1877) *The physical basis of mind,* Boston: James R Osgood.

Manning, S. (2006) *Ecstasy and the demon: the dances of Mary Wigman,* Minneapolis: University of Minnesota.

Nicholas, L. (2007) *Dancing in utopia: Dartington Hall and its dancers,* Alton: Dance Books.

Preston-Dunlop, V. (1998) *Rudolf Laban, an extraordinary life,* London: Dance Books.

Reichsbund Für Gemeinschaftstanz (1936) *Wir Tanzen,* Berlin: Reichsbund Für Gemeinschaftstanz.

Reynolds, D. (2007) *Rhythmic subjects: uses of energy in the dances of Mary Wigman, Martha Graham and Merce Cunningham,* Alton: Dance Books.

Schikowshi, J. (1925) *Der Neue Tanz,* Berlin: Volksbühnen Verlag.

Sweigard, L. E. (1974) *Human movement potential: its Ideokinetic facilitation,* New York: Harper & Row.

Todd, M. E. (1929) *The balancing of forces in the human being: its application to postural patterns,* New York: Privately Published.

Todd, M. E. (1937, 1968) *The thinking body: a study of the balancing forces of dynamic man,* New York: Dance Horizons.

Winearls, J. (1958) *Modern Dance: The Jooss–Leeder method,* London: A&C Black.

1. See Ramsay Burt's *Judson Dance Theatre: performative traces* (2006) for a recent re-examination of this area.
2. It was published posthumously in the *Laban Art of Guild Magazine* in 1974. Neither the original nor the Laban Guild publication gives any indication of who translated it, but the title suggests that it was not Laban himself.
3. The broad terms for this debate are to be found in the writings of Kant and Karina (2003), Preston-Dunlop (1998), Guilbert (2000), Kew (1999) etc.. This debate is acknowledged in recent accounts by Manning (2006) and Nicholas (2007): I take a similar view, noting that there is much more to be examined in further research.

Understanding dance through the process of symbolisation
with reference to Shoal, Rafferty, (1992)

Jean Jarrell

It is well recognised that social communication involves the organisation of the flux of impressions that constantly bombard us into meaningful systems of signs and/or symbols. Each symbol system, be it linguistic, mechanical or aesthetic presents a way of codifying and making sense of reality.

Rudolf Laban identified two main objectives for his notation system, the first being the recreation of 'dance ideas fixed in script' – in other words a text for movement enabling its re-instantiation (Laban, 1956 p.14). The second, and according to Laban far more important, was the 'defining of the movement process through analysis' (as cited in Preston-Dunlop & Lahusen, 1990 p.32).

Much theoretical discussion has focused on whether a notated score can provide a 'text' for dance, enabling 'authentic' recreation. Less attention, however, has been given to the value of the symbolising and analytic processes involved when creating a score, reconstructing from score and using Laban's schemas for dance/movement analysis.

The encapsulation of dance in Labanotation draws attention to intricate features of the body moving in space and time. The act of transcription involves countless decisions by the notator in an effort to represent the three dimensional phenomenon of the body moving in space and time and with a view to expressing choreographic intention. At the deciphering stage a myriad of different pieces of information is gained from the symbolic representation on a score. No symbol can be ignored and the eye is consequently less selective than in the visual learning of dance movement.

A further superimposition of structural parameters based on Laban's other systems of movement analysis highlights additional information not necessarily embodied within the notation which, in turn, aids in the conceptualisation and realisation of a choreography by the reconstructor working from score. For the performer re-instantiating a work subsequent to its conception these different avenues of symbolic information serve to enhance the experience of its embodiment.

This presentation elucidates ways in which symbolisation can facilitate in-depth understanding of a choreography, in this case *Shoal* by Sonia Rafferty, (1992). The word shoal may for most of us evoke a series of images,.... thousands of individual fish moving as one mass,.... the flash of colour as the water reflects on different surfaces of their bodies,.... perhaps notions of unity and harmony. However, while the title makes reference to the movements of a shoal of fish, in no way are the movements of the dancers 'fish-like'. Rather the images produced evoke qualities associated with the movement of a shoal of fish in their ever-changing formations and beyond that images of water, light and harmony.

By superimposing selected elements of a movement analysis based on Laban's principles and by examining the Labanotation symbology that documents the dance piece, I aim to explore the ways in which the choreographer has communicated the images that formed the stimulus for her work, how the images of unity, harmony, waves, water light are embodied in the material organisation of *Shoal* as the dancers will demonstrate at the end of my discussion.

A primary focus of *Shoal* is the aspect of spatiality – the use of stage space, the spatial relationship between the dancers, the ensuing floor patterns and the particular spatial focus of the movement motifs. Detailed floor plans of *Shoal* have proved to be an efficient means of examining the use of general space for this particular choreography. When viewed in their totality, they highlight the specific spatial choices made by the choreographer, either consciously or unconsciously, during the creative process. The element of group forms, group formations and floor patterns appears to be structurally important serving to punctuate the overall development of the work.

The group of five dancers remain onstage throughout the twelve and a half minute choreography and are in motion virtually throughout the piece. The visual impact of five dancers moving as a unit is a strong pervading image, primarily established by the dancers' spatial relationships within selected geometric formations.

Spatial Formations

The prevailing spatial formations in *Shoal* are:
- Parallel lines
- The triangle
- Combinations of parallel lines and a triangle
- The square with one dancer in the centre
- The pentagon which at times becomes a circle

These are introduced in the first section of the dance and are increasingly reinforced as the dance develops with the five dancers moving within and through the formations.

The next series of slides, taken from the original production of *Shoal*, and their corresponding notation floor plans, provide examples of each of these formations.

Parallel lines

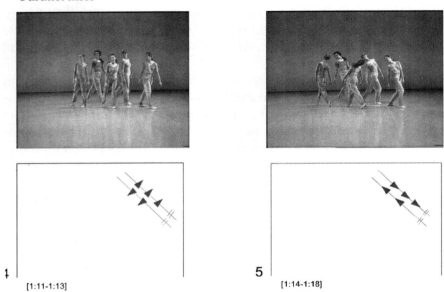

The blue wedges on the floor plans indicate the group of all 5 dancers and their body facings, while the brown lines highlight their formation in parallel lines.

Triangle

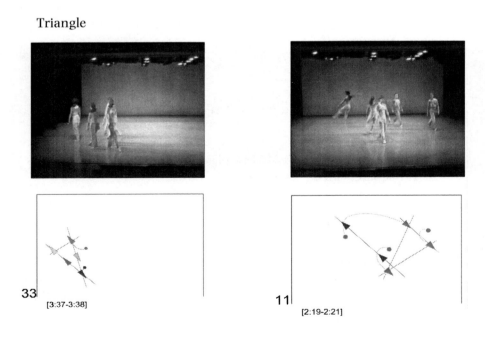

In floor plan 33, all 5 dancers form a triangle - here each dancer is depicted with a different colour. The corresponding dots represent where the dancers were placed before moving momentarily into the triangular formation; in floor plan 11 three dancers, shown in red, form a triangle while the other two dancers, in blue, are in a straight line.

Throughout the dance there are frequent examples of combinations of parallel lines and the triangle. Here, floor plan 1 represents the starting formation. A similar combination of parallel lines and triangle occurs a minute later, at the end of the first section, as seen in floor plan 6.

Combinations of parallel lines and triangle

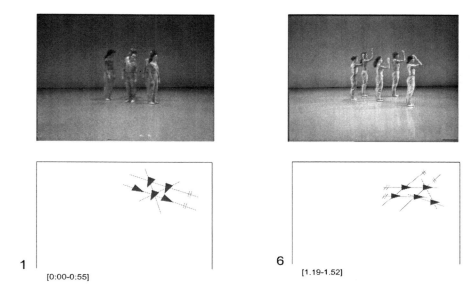

1
[0:00-0:55]

6
[1.19-1.52]

The square with its 4 equal sides is a shape that epitomises uniformity. In *Shoal*, 5 dancers are made to fit this formation through the placement of one dancer in the centre.

Square

Finally, we come to the pentagon which occasionally rounds out to become circular and is frequently associated with unison motifs.

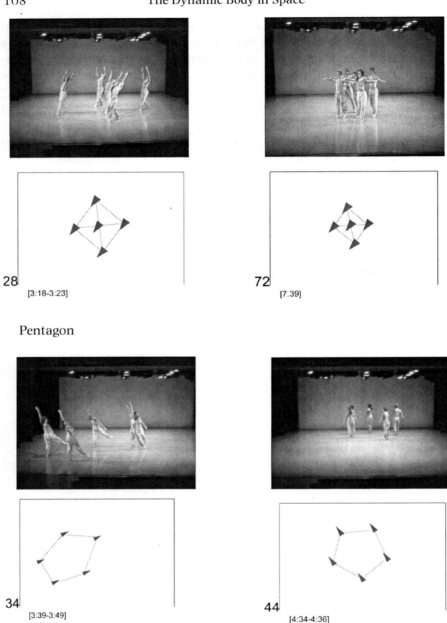

28
[3:18-3:23]

72
[7.39]

Pentagon

34
[3:39-3:49]

44
[4:34-4:36]

All these geometric formations suggest a spatially harmonious relationship between the dancers – the distance between them is either equal or in
proportion; the facing of the dancers is either parallel or in opposition; it is
the fleeting emergent shapes of their formations which unite them.

As can be seen from the above examples, the group formations are one of the key unifying elements of *Shoal*. For these to impinge on the consciousness of the spectator they must be drawn to our attention and a number of devices are used to achieve this including synchronisation of facing, timing and action.

Synchronised facing, timing, action

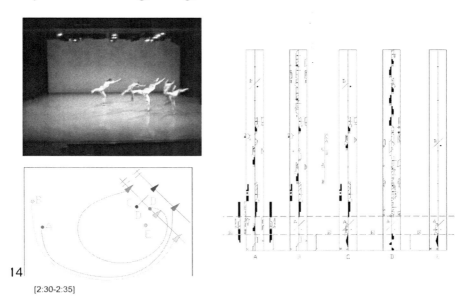

14

[2:30-2:35]

Floor plan 14 shows a moment of unison in both time and action with this extended flat back or arabesque position. What was previously a duet and trio, come together for one single position – this unison is visibly identified in the notation by the use of repeat signs, highlighted here between (Two dashed lines). Following this one brief moment the dancers break apart once again into a duo and trio.

Another device, which draws our attention to the formations, is synchronisation in action but where the facing may be complementary as in the two instances shown here. Synchronisation may also be one of timing and body facing or simply focus, although the body shape is different; this nevertheless establishes a sense of unity between the duet and trio and these momentary snapshots punctuate the continuous motion that characterises the choreography to give it coherence.

Synchronised action – complementary facing

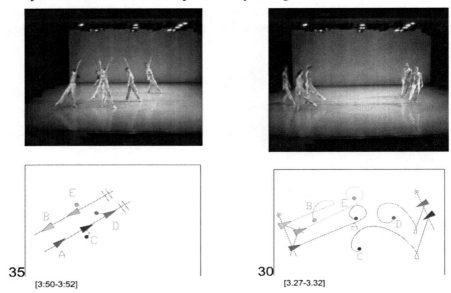

35   30

[3:50-3:52]   [3.27-3.32]

In spite of the potential rigidity of the unison movement and angular geometric patterns, one manner in which a certain flexibility is maintained, and which could be interpreted as a sense of 'freedom within the group', arises from the interplay of the division of five dancers into duet and trio and the changing formations. The dancers, however, are never confined to either duet or trio or to particular formations but constantly change reinforcing the impression of ever varying patterning within the group as the four slides below illustrate.

Interchange of dancers between trio and duet 1

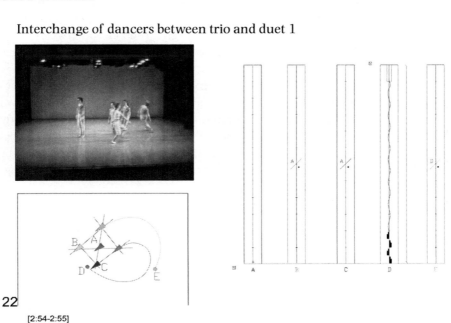

22

[2:54-2:55]

In floor plan 22 dancers D and E arrive in the square formation.

Interchange of dancers between trio and duet 2

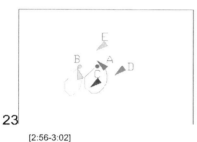

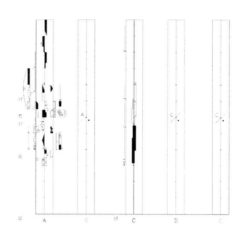

23

[2:56-3:02]

Subsequently, dancers A and B introduce one of several 'wave' motifs and then circle to return to their previous positions.

Interchange of dancers between trio and duet 3

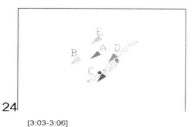

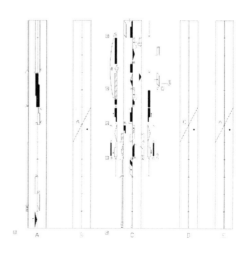

24

[3:03-3:06]

As they arrive, dancers C and D pick up the motif but perform it on the opposite diagonal, from downstage right to upstage left.

Interchange of dancers between trio and duet 4

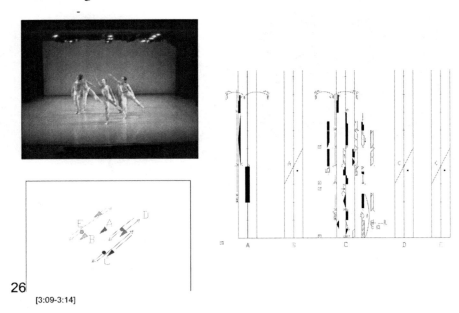

26

[3:09-3:14]

The motif is performed sometimes by 2 sometimes by 3 dancers until they all end in the square formation from which they started with one of those moments of unison which always precedes or resolves a split of the group into trio and duet.

A close relationship is established between the pentagon and the circle depending on where the dancers are facing. For instance having established the circular formation through the inward facing group of dancers, as can be seen in floor plan 68, this expands and contracts but the illusion of circularity is maintained. This is then broken by the apparent parallelism of the dancers, materialised through their facing and projection, so that the straight lines and angularity of the pentagon shape is once again emphasised

From circle into pentagon

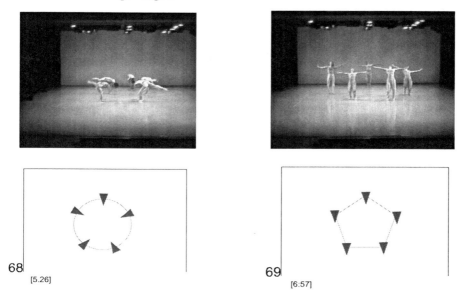

68 [5.26]

69 [6:57]

The notion of circularity is also embodied in other spatial features of the dance, such as the floor pathways travelled by the dancers as opposed to the circular formations. Whereas the group formation of the circle only occurs in one instance, this is both anticipated and echoed by instances of continuous circularity of the floor patterns which 'soften' the very angular nature of the group formations of triangle, square and pentagon.

Predominance of circular pathways

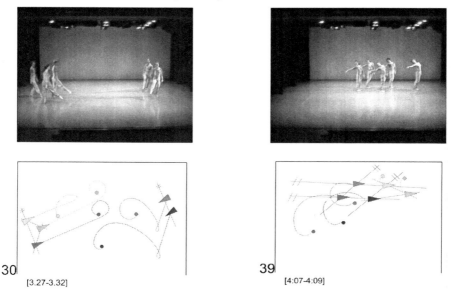

30 [3.27-3.32]

39 [4:07-4:09]

Here, however, as in many instances, the circularity of the pathways through space is followed by linear formations, body shapes and dimensional forward and back movement almost like a breath in the turbulent flow of movement.

Most significantly circularity can also be found in the manner of materialisation of much of the movement motifs. Curved progressions of the torso, arm and leg gestures are a recurring feature. They tend to be performed within a particular plane – table, door or wheel – which at times imbues a certain linear flatness to the movement. One such movement with numerous variations is what could be called the 'wave motif' which we see right at the start of the piece and which establishes the particular movement quality.

• As Louise Tanoto has shown us, the 'wave' motif is initially a slight movement as in A, only performed by the heads and torsos of the dancers – it is an even, gliding action with virtually no change in energy and almost no accent. The dancers are close together within the geometric formation previously identified and move as one body. The apparent tranquillity and dominantly sustained movement quality is at times juxtaposed with sudden impactive changes of direction
• In version B this increases with a very slight accent as it were 'at the crest of the wave'.
• A stronger accent appears in the two versions of C when the movement travels and both arms and legs are involved.
• The strongest accent and this time, clearly impactive, can be seen with motif D

All these motifs occur in the forward/backward wheel plane.

'Wave' motifs – wheel/sagittal plane

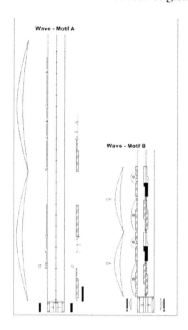

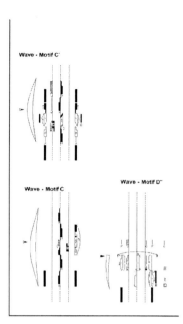

In motif E, the wave motif is transposed into the lateral plane. Interestingly, although in relation to the body the movement is sideways, because of the forward and backward direction of the pathways through space, along the stage diagonal, it gives the impression of a sagittal movement. This forward and backward motion along straight paths is a recurring characteristic throughout the choreography echoing, as it were, the introductory wave image.

'Wave' motifs – door/lateral plane

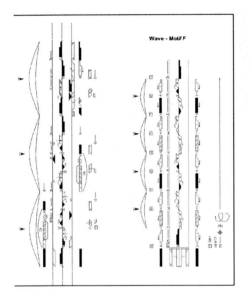

Wave - Motif F

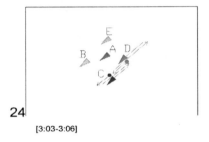

24

[3:03-3:06]

In this paper I have attempted to highlight just a few of the ways in which the superimposition of selected symbolic systems of analysis may help to clarify the inner structures of a dance. The focus has been primarily on spatial features because these are essential characteristics of this particular dance work. Through study of the notation we could identify all the movement motifs and their variations and examine the use of canon. We could document dynamic phrasing and understand more about the manner in which movement accents are passed from one group of dancers to the next and so on.

The question could be asked: Is this the only way to go about analysing a dance? Not necessarily. Does this dissection of an artistic product destroy its mystique as is frequently claimed? When asked whether she was happy for us to restage her work, the choreographer, Sonia Rafferty who was only minimally involved in the restaging process, said: 'Marc (Dodi, the reconstructor), has understood what it's about – he is saying all the right things – it's amazing to see everything that was in my head.... out there!' (Rafferty, October 2008).

So perhaps as Claxton quoting Richard Feynman said with reference to creativity: 'it does no harm to the mystery to understand a little about it' (Claxton in Bannerman, 2006, p.60).

And finally – Does this analysis make us 'like' a dance work more? Not necessarily – that has to do with taste affected by so many other factors

However, I would claim that the interface of the different analytic perspectives we have seen, does help us to understand and appreciate the inner workings of a dance – in this case the complex interweaving of spatial, rhythmic and dynamic features that, embodied by the dancers, and together with the costume, sound and lighting contribute to the production of an evocative dance work. But that is something I will leave you to decide for yourselves as the dance is viewed in its totality. [Presentation accompanied by a performance of *Shoal*].

References

Bannerman, C., Sofaer, J., Watt, J. (Eds.) (2006). Navigating the unknown: the creative process in contemporary performing arts. London: Middlesex University.

Laban, R. (1956). Principles of dance and movement notation. London: MacDonald & Evans

Preston-Dunlop, V. & Lahusen, S. (Eds.) (1990). Schrifttanz. London: Dance Books.

Conference Contributors:

- Choreographer: Sonia Rafferty, MSc, BA graduate, faculty Laban
- Music: Philip Chambon, Composer, faculty University of Kingston
- Costumes: Deb Thomas
- Lighting: Fay Patterson
- Conference presenter: Jean Jarrell, MA, faculty Laban
- Notator: Andrea Treu-Kaulbarsch, SDDN graduate, faculty Laban
- Choreological analysis: Ingrid Reisetbauer, Transitions, BA graduate, Laban
- Reconstruction from score: Marc Dodi, BA graduate, Laban
- Dancers:
  – Victoria Beck, BA graduate, QUT, Australia
  – Jessie Brett, BA graduate, LSCD
  – Pauline Huguet, BA graduate, Laban
  – Megan Saunders, Transitions, MA graduate, Laban
  – Louise Tanoto, Transitions, MA graduate, Laban

Laban: the way forward in dance education, research project report

Maggie Killingbeck

Aim of research project

This research project aimed to discover the extent to which extended knowledge, skills and understanding of Laban's work enhances the teaching of

dance in an educational setting. Recognising that those training to teach dance in education do so with a reduced amount of contact time, the researchers were aware that many dance teachers have limited knowledge and understanding of Laban's work. In addition, where training follows the principles identified by Smith-Autard's 'Midway Model', fewer training hours are required to address twice as much content ie the content of both the Professional and Educational models. In such circumstances it was felt that training could not address Laban's work in significant depth. This research therefore, attempted to discover the impact of greater knowledge, skills and understanding of Laban's work on the teaching of dance in education. It should be noted however that in the time available this represents a mere 'toe in the water'.

Methodology of the research project

The research project involved seven experienced specialist dance teachers [and one selected group of pupils per teacher], twenty hours of intensive Laban studies, pre and post project questionnaires [teachers and pupils], reflective diaries, filming [teachers and pupils], reading and sharing experiences. This report/presentation shares the outcomes of the research project.

Background of the research subjects

All of the dance teachers participating in the research project had a first degree in dance [their degrees had been awarded by a range of Higher Education institutions] and the majority had completed a PGCE in dance. In addition most of the group had been teaching dance for at least five years with, sufficient success to have received significant promotion. Moreover it was clear from the pre-course questionnaires that all of the dance teachers participating in the research project were wholly confident with action, space, dynamics and relationships, and, with their use of Laban's analysis of movement in the teaching of composition and appreciation. Two of the seven participants expressed reservations about the extent to which they made reference to  Laban's analysis in their teaching of performance. Three of the participants felt that their initial training had made extensive reference to Laban's analysis. Not one of the participants claimed in depth knowledge, skills and understanding of Choreutics or Eukinetics.

The Laban Studies content

Choreutic material was at the heart of the twenty hours of Laban Studies. Participants were required to orientate themselves two dimensionally in space in order to respond to demanding performance and choreographic tasks based on the planes. A similarly rigorous approach characterised performance and choreographic tasks related to the A Scale. Whilst spatial architecture: arcs and axes, harmonic opposites, spatial counterpoint, spatial progression, spatial tension, spatial pathway and body design were substantial features of the Laban studies sessions, attention to specified: uses of the body, movement qualities and relationships together with tasks demanding polyphonic action increased the complexity of performance and choreographic outcomes. The sessions also included reference to Commedia dell'arte and the work of William Forsythe.

Findings – pre-course reflections

The pre-course questionnaires indicated that all of the research subjects used Laban's principles to inform their teaching although they acknowl-

edged that they did not explicitly share this with their students. Typically Laban's analysis provided a framework for discussion in the context of appreciation. It is fair to note however that one research subject found the use of Laban's analysis in this context gave rise to 'vague' responses [generic terms such as 'jump', 'turn' perhaps as opposed to more differentiated responses]. In the context of composition, there was more consensus; most research subjects agreed that they encouraged students to 'use Laban's analysis as a guide when creating composition work, in order to create variety and interest within [their] work' The use of Laban's analysis in the teaching of performance however, again gave rise to a range of opinions. Some of the research subjects referred to Laban's analysis in the context of teaching performance, for example addressing dynamics in relation to expression/ interpretation and flow/phrasing in relation to musicality. However some of the research subjects made no reference to Laban's analysis of movement at all in their teaching of performance. At A Level Laban featured more strongly in the context of Labanotation.

Findings – performance

In their experience of using their 20 hours of Laban studies to inform their teaching of performance the research subjects reflected upon 'how quickly students picked up the material' and how much more spatially accurate their performances were following input on the planes. One of the research subjects, speaking personally, commented,

'learning the different [planar] orientations has given me insight [into] how to perform actions with accuracy .... I had a new awareness and constant evaluation of what I was doing and whether I was being accurate' [RS4].

Indeed as a group the research subjects reflected on the extent of the challenge associated with this degree of accuracy commenting on the need for extreme attention to detail. Such an approach they felt enabled both themselves and their students to analyse and refine their performances against a clear set of guidelines which consequently increased their capacity for self evaluation and in so doing enabled them to become more autonomous. In some instances research subjects used the planes as the basis for a perform-ance audit; the impact on their students' work was described as dramatic; performances were seen to have increased purpose, intention and integrity as a result of the students' greater knowledge, skills and understanding of these spatial concepts. Research subjects noted however that such a focused approach on spatial issues can have a detrimental impact on the dynamic quality of students' work initially.

The research subjects found that CHUMM [spatial projection, body design, spatial pathway, and spatial tension] also informed their teaching of per-formance insofar as it helped their students to understand the concept of performance through the provision of accessible 'further qualities'. These additional qualities/features of performance not only enabled students to excavate performance issues in more depth, it gave them also access to in-creasing discrimination/subtlety in performance through the possibility of attending to the placing of more/less definition/significance on these aspects of their performance.

Also considered of value by the research subjects for teaching perform-ance were the choreutic scales generally.

'I think that the A Scale [and consequently all of Laban's scales] would be great to develop technique – they are spatially challenging as well as addressing alignment, extension and placement.[RS1]

Findings – composition
In their experience of using the four days of Laban studies to in-form their teaching of composition the research subjects noted a number of outcomes. One re-search subject observed in her students' work richer/more com-plex content as a result of their exploration of the planes; 'there was without doubt more detail in form, shape and space in their cho-reography as a result of understanding the planes' [RS1]. Indeed not only was the visual im-age richer it was more innovative. The spatial limitations of the com-position task, the research subjects

noted, required significant invention in order for their students to answer the task and remain spatially accurate. Originality, the research subjects commented was something with which students typically struggled.

Choreutic tasks resulting in choreographic material exemplifying spatial counterpoint and harmonic opposites excited the research subjects and their students. This work introduced entirely new concepts; the research subjects were completely unfamiliar with Laban's choreutic scales.

And, whilst a number of the research subjects expressed confidence in their use of dynamics, the eukinetic tasks, because they encouraged use of a greater range of dynamics, resulted in less predictable, more exciting and challenging qualities in the students' own work. This was particularly so of the exploration of direct and indirect intention [space motion factor] which through use of a prop produced exceptionally inspiring dance material. Indeed the paired eukinetic tasks through providing a 'safe' framework within which to work improved students' non verbal communication,

> 'pupils' knowledge and demonstration of dynamics improved as well as their ability to engage with another dancer. I think it developed their non verbal communication through responding to others' dynamics and use of space' [RS3].

The polyphonic action task challenged the research subjects' ability to create dance material as well as their students. Indeed all of the research subjects considered it to be an excellent strategy to further develop their students' appreciation of the potential complexity involved in creating dance material. This was particularly so when the possibility of creating primary/subsidiary emphases became an option and research subjects realised that they had further decision making opportunities which increased the likelihood of their developing uniquely interesting material.

Findings – post-course reflections
One of the research subjects who started the research project confident in her use of Laban's analysis said,

> 'I strongly feel that whilst much of what we have learnt is already present in my teaching, it is the breaking down, labelling and identifying of specifics that has had the greatest impact. Firstly because my confidence in my knowledge and understanding has increased and secondly because students [particularly A Level] like and need information and learning to be legitimised. They want to know theories, academics, research etc and where it comes from' [RS1].

Laban's analysis, the research subjects reflected, in providing a uniquely universal yet incredibly discriminating theoretical framework, is a valuable tool offering the possibility of access to high standards whilst permitting a significant degree of autonomy. The research subjects considered that central to the value of Laban's analysis was the language, which, through its comprehensive application, facilitates accuracy, precision, depth, innovation and subtlety. This combined with the systematic approach to understanding human movement they felt, enables progression from the very simple to the extremely complex. Such a means of articulating movement they agreed was of value for the performer, choreographer and/or viewer of dance.

Future plans

Arising from this research project it is hoped to develop a series of Scales workshops, a Masters module and a Phoenix 2 for dance practitioners in education.

This project has confirmed the need, for those involved in teaching dance to have increased opportunities to study Laban's work in greater depth. Interestingly having presented this paper at the International Conference at LABAN it became clear that this 'hidden legacy' is in need of renewed attention more generally. This project along with many others shared at the conference revealed the significance of Laban's work in a range of contexts and confirmed the need for a return to and development of the work such that its value is not lost.

Reference

Smith-Autard, J. (2002) *The Art of Dance in Education* 2nd edition. A & C Black.

Preservation and reconstructing of Yvonne Rainer's Trio A

Joukje Kolff and Melanie Clarke

Trio A

Trio A was originally performed as *The Mind is a Muscle*, Part 1 in 1966 by Yvonne Rainer, David Gordon and Steve Paxton. The piece of around six minutes can and has been performed in a variety of places and contexts and by any number of dancers.

Yvonne Rainer, as the other members of the Judson Church in the 1960s, rebelled against some of the characteristics of the established Modern Dance and Ballet. With *Trio A* Rainer's objective was to eliminate such aspects as phrasing, development and climax, character, performance, virtuosity, the fully extended body and variation in dynamics. She also did not use a glamorous costume, décor and music. Instead she substituted every-day, 'found' movement, equality of parts (as opposed to development and climax), task-like activity, neutral performance, real body weight and time (Rainer, 1966).

Yvonne Rainer taught her seminal work *Trio A*, from 1966, during a week-long workshop organised by London International Summer School at Greenwich Dance Agency in 2003. During this workshop Kolff and Clarke recorded the piece in Labanotation. Clarke then reconstructed the work from score on students at Laban in 2006, 2007 and 2008.

The on-going life of Trio A

In the 2005 spring issue of the *Dance Theatre Journal* Rainer writes:

> For the first decade of *Trio A*'s existence I was teaching it to anyone who wanted to learn it – skilled, unskilled, trained, untrained, professional, amateur – and gave tacit permission to anyone who wanted to teach it to do so. I envisioned myself as a postmodern dance evangelist bringing movement to the masses, …. Well, I finally met a *Trio A* I didn't like. It was fourth or fifth generation, and I couldn't believe my eyes. It was all but unrecognisable (Rainer, 2005 p.6).

Besides Rainer herself, there are three people authorised to teach *Trio A*: Pat Catterson, Linda K. Johnson, and Shelley Senter. Another potential resource for learning the dance is a videotape from 2002 in which Rainer fine-tunes *Trio A* on Senter and Johnson. And there is also a film from 1978 by Sally Banes in which Rainer performs *Trio A*.

The 'certified' teachers will continue to pass on the work. Rainer wrote in email correspondence to Kolff (12/08/2004): 'As for after my demise, so far Pat Catterson is the best versed in the intricacies of the dance, but she's getting on in years also.' Rainer herself is now in her 70s. The 1978 film contains mistakes, so it cannot be used as the main resource for reconstruction. The 'cleaning tapes' offer more pedagogical information than the 1978 film. But, says Rainer (9/10/2004),

> ... it would still be a tricky business to try learning *Trio A* only from the tapes without additional input from an official instructor. Video distorts the spatial orientations, the geometric configurations of the floor patterns, for one thing.

On top of that, the tape is not easily available: currently only Rainer and Johnson own copies, moreover analogue and digital video tapes may become obsolete through continuing progression in video technology.

Rainer has become more and more concerned about the conservation of *Trio A* in the future:

> In the spirit of the 60s a part of me would like to say, 'Let it go.' Why try to cast it in stone? Why am I now so finicky and fastidious, so critical of my own performance, so autocratic about the details – the hands go this way, not that way, the gaze here, not there, the feet at this angle, not that? In the last decade I have become far more rigorous – some might call it obsessive – not only with respect to the qualifications of those whom I allow to teach the dance, but in my own transmission of its peculiarities. In the presence of the Laban notators in the summer of 2003, it became increasingly clear to me that here was an opportunity to set the record as straight as possible and forget, at least for the moment, my scruples and caveats about fetishisation and immortality (Rainer, 2005 p.7).

When Rainer was approached, she was interested in the notation project, but at the same time sceptical. In the same *Dance Theatre Journal* article mentioned earlier, she writes:

> If the thought of having *Trio A* Laban notated had ever crossed my mind, it was only with the conviction that such a venture would be quite impossible. The subtleties and dynamics of this dance, performed without the structuring support of a musical score, seemed outside the domain of any graphic notation system. But when the opportunity arose in conjunction with teaching *Trio A* at the Greenwich Dance Agency in the summer of 2003, I did not object, in fact, was curious (Rainer, 2005, p.6).

Rainer has been supportive throughout the project. A DVD of Rainer teaching *Trio A* in Greenwich is supplied with the score. The intention was not originally to distribute this footage with the score but to use it to support the notating process. If the creation of a DVD was the intention Kolff would have wanted a more suitable microphone and a camera operator, not just in the afternoons, but also in the mornings. Instead, in the mornings a camera on a tripod recorded the teaching. However, Kolff realised that the video footage was an important resource in itself. When Kolff re-edited the video and indicated chapter points to correlate with the pages in the score the DVD became part of the archiving of this work and a support to reconstruction.

The main menu of the DVD consists of three sections. One section gives an overview of the workshop. In another section Rainer introduces the sequences to students. The third section provides some information about the history of the project and about the use of the DVD. It also contains the credits for the project. In the 'introducing the movement' section, where Rainer teaches the movement to the students, all movements of *Trio A* are shown. A submenu on the DVD allows the user to jump immediately to or near to the point in the dance or score they want to watch. Page numbers at the bottom of the screen then indicate the correlating page in the score. Therefore there is a very close relationship between the DVD and the score and one can be used to support the reading of the other. A run-through of the whole dance is not included as the DVD is an aid to learning the work rather than a performance recording. Rainer demonstrated and showed more than what can be shown on the DVD (hours of footage were recorded). Further and more detailed information is contained in the score itself. What is significant about the DVD is that it records how Yvonne taught the work and can thus, inform a reconstruction process.

The process of reconstructing Trio A

Trio A is a highly prescriptive dance work that requires a very exact execution. This is exemplified by Rainer's teaching as can be seen in the DVD in that the detail and accuracy of execution is the main requirement. It could readily be claimed that the identity of the work is in the detail of the discrete actions which accumulate to form the continuing illogical sequence of events. The medium of Labanotation as a recording devise is therefore an apposite one in that the movement has been broken down and analysed in detail in order to be recorded symbolically and that detail is essential for accuracy in performance.

The performance of *Trio A* is then a process of doing it perfectly accurately. However, that is not as simple as it may first appear. Rainer's performance ethos is one in which the movements are to be accomplished rather than displayed. They are every-day, task-like, work-like, matter-of-fact and unpretentious (Sigman, 2000). There are no repetitions in the work. It is made up of discrete units, none of them a variation of the other. Their order, though set, does not seem to be important. Hence, memory is a factor as recognition is not aided by logic or any sense of ordered development. The task of performance is to execute individual actions almost like following a set of instructions to complete a complex task. In this way, using a score which is literally a set of instructions seems a fitting way to teach this work.

A criticism of Labanotation is often the fact that it breaks down and subdivides bodily actions into discrete parts – the analytical nature of the form. Translation processes from score are therefore considered to be normally one of integrating bodily actions and re-discovering phrasing, in order to bring the work back to life. The personal input and expression of the dancer and reconstructor are usually important to breathe life back into the work. With *Trio A* it is more a question of not doing that. *Trio A* is a dance to be performed in a neutral way and not in the traditional sense of performing with a sense of outward communication, presence, charisma. The performer is projecting inward rather than outward and ignores the audience. This is especially made explicit through the gaze which is never directed at the audience. At those moments in the dance when the body faces the audience, either the head is turned or rolling or the eyes are closed. Some movements can be adjusted to the flexibility of the dancer but all should be performed without a sense of display. Thus, the process of reconstruction is one in which nothing should be added to what is written in the score – but this is very difficult. The process of translating is one that travels from symbolic representation to body and the body is not merely a tool but an individuated person with his/her own expressive actions.

So, in reconstructing it seems appropriate to not hide the score but openly work from it. Through this process the reconstructor would purposely not bringing attention to herself, helping to make the dancers aware of the lack of personal expression. Feedback then would help them to be aware of their own expressive actions so that they could chose not to do them. The performer's attention should be on the embodiment of the task. It is often said that what the dancer is thinking about is what the audience sees – for *Trio A* the dancer must be intricately knowledgeable about the work through repetition and practice of all the fine detail and yet perform it as if tackling the tasks anew. Like building a wall – it is always the same process but the bricks still have weight and still need to be aligned precisely. Thus, to perform it you have to memorise the instructions so that you can then set out to complete the actions as precisely executed tasks.

One of the ways Clarke found to support this task-like involvement in each movement was to understand what the task is through analysing the building blocks of the choreography. To do this Clarke used the analysis of the

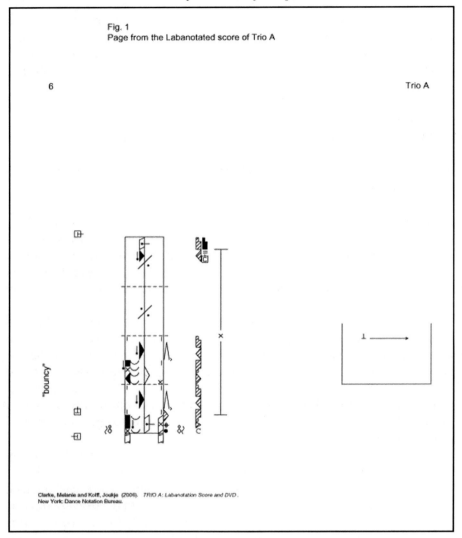

Fig. 1
Page from the Labanotated score of Trio A

6   Trio A

"bouncy"

Clarke, Melanie and Kolff, Joukje (2006). *TRIO A: Labanotation Score and DVD*.
New York: Dance Notation Bureau.

score to see the composition of actions as well as taking note of Rainer's teaching – highlighted in Kolff's DVD. One recurring feature is that the material is often constructed of layers of material in different planes simultaneously.

For example there is an action that requires a bouncy motion of the body in the vertical dimension with a simultaneous circling action of the head in the horizontal plane, whilst the foot draws a straight line on the floor (fig. 1). Thus, the dancer must do three opposing actions simultaneously.

Another example (fig. 2) is an action that includes a horizontal circling of one leg, a forward progression and a upper body motion that causes a sagittal

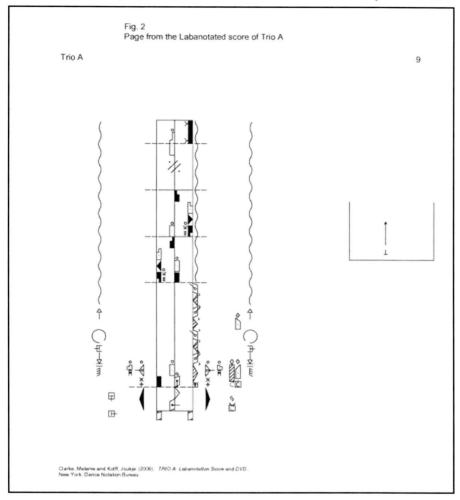

Fig. 2
Page from the Labanotated score of Trio A

Trio A

9

Clarke, Melanie and Kolff, Joukje (2006). *TRIO A* Labanotation Score and DVD.
New York: Dance Notation Bureau.

circle to be draw by the hands. At the same time the head is turned so that the focus is directed into the diagonal direction.

Focusing on these as separate entities in the body helps to keep the motion task-like rather than dancerly. Thinking about three or four different simultaneous actions concentrates the mind on the task in hand. Thus, the energy exerted is the real energy it takes to perform the movements, as Rainer wanted. One does not need to seem light or make the movements seem easy nor difficult or virtuosic. The spectator sees the actual weight and unenhanced physicality of the body (Rainer 1966).

Another major feature of the work is the lack of dynamic changes. Although some movement units should be performed in a regular counting rhythm, the dancer takes the time it takes the body to go through the movements: an actual time takes place, the dancers are never purposefully

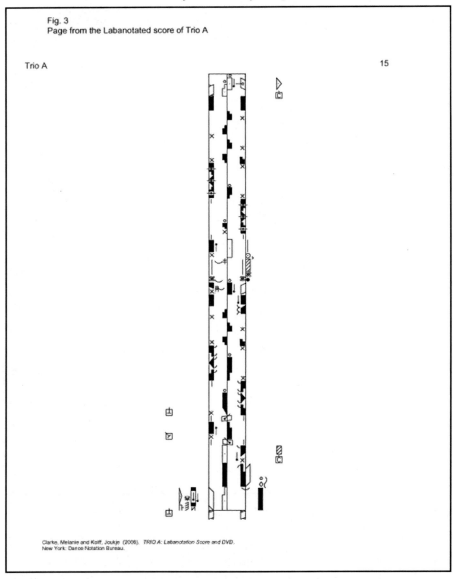

Clarke, Melanie and Kolff, Joukje (2006). *TRIO A: Labanotation Score and DVD*. New York: Dance Notation Bureau.

synchronised, each moving at his/her own tempo. Rainer wanted no phrasing or energy change through the piece, only the energy needed to do each separate action without a sense of performance. The issue of this for an accurate execution is how much energy is just enough. An example of this in the work is a jumping event (fig. 3): how much energy does it require to do this jump without over emphasising but still being able to lift the body weight off the floor? Asking these questions in the reconstruction process helps the achievement of Rainer's intentions for the work.

Rainer mentions that in much of the western dancing we are familiar with there is a maximal output of energy at the beginning of the phrase, followed by an abatement and recovery at the end (Rainer, 1966). Although one can distinguish discrete parts within *Trio A*, they are not characterised by this particular distribution of energy. Instead the various parts flow into each other without a significant pause and without emphasis, attack, or other changes in dynamics, as exemplified in the score. What does happen, As Rainer herself stated when teaching the work – is a completion of each action; a sense of reaching a destination. This corresponds very precisely with the Labanotated score as each movement is recorded through indicating destination. This is usually worked through in reading a score but for *Trio A* this is a performance requirement. So focusing on the nature of the score and what the score specifies, aids the achievement of the correct performance quality for this work.

Conclusion

Scoring *Trio A* has made it accessible to educational institutions (through hire from The Dance Notation Bureau in New York) in a form that seems to support the identity and reconstruction of the work. The physical process of embodying *Trio A*, the difficulties in execution and the embodiment of its analytical nature, gave the dancers at Laban who experienced it a deeper level of appreciation for the complexity of the work. The embodying process changed the performer's appreciation of this work and the physical performance of it gave the audience new insight into a work that they may have heard or read about but not experienced. The manifestation of the work as a live performance made the fact of performing in a manner of non-performance a very present and real reality for performers and audience alike.

Dance is an art form based in the physical and experiential. Performing dance works and seeing them live is about gaining experiential knowledge which is a more in-depth and profound form of knowledge than reading about past work or viewing videos. The Labanotation system developed from Laban's initiating formula enables the preservation and detailed analysis of dance works. Scoring in Labanotation then enables reconstructions of works which can be a powerful tool for giving current dance students and audiences' experiential knowledge of their dance heritage.

References
Banes, Sally. (1980) *Terpsichore in Sneakers, Post Modern Dance*. Connecticut: Wesleyan UP, pp. 40-55.

Clarke, Melanie and Kolff, Joukje. (2006) *TRIO A: Labanotation Score and DVD*.

New York: Dance Notation Bureau.

Dunagan, Colleen. Complicating Minimalism: Yvonne Rainer's *Trio A*, Laban Movement Analysis and Qualitative Quantities. In Tomko, Linda J. Complier (1998) *Proceedings Society of Dance History Scholars. 21st Annual Conference*. Oregon: University of Oregon. 18-21 June pp.13-19.

Hecht, Robin Silver. (1973-4) Reflections on the career of Yvonne Rainer and values of minimal dance. *Dance scope*, Vol. 8. No. 1, pp. 13-14.

Jowitt, Deborah. (1988) *Time and the Dancing Image*. Berkeley, Los Angeles: University of California Press, pp. 307-308.

Kolff, J. (2005) Recording *Trio A* in Labanotation: issues in notation and reconstruction. *Dance Theatre Journal*, Vol. 20, No.4.

Maclow, Carinda Thinking Movement: some thoughts on recreating *Trio A*. Available at: http://www.danceonline.com/news/thinking.html [accessed 2005].

Rainer Yvonne. (1966) 'A Quasi Survey of some "Minimalist" Tendencies in the Qualitatively Minimal Dance Activity Midst the Plethora, or an Analysis of *Trio A*', in Copeland, R. and Cohen, M. eds. *What is Dance?* (1983) New York: Oxford UP, pp. 325-332.

Rainer, Yvonne. (2004) [email] message to Kolff, Joukje. Sent 12/08/2004.

Rainer, Yvonne. (2004) [email] message to Kolff, Joukje. Sent 9/10/2004.

Rainer, Yvonne. (2005) *Trio A*: Genealogy, Documentation, Notation. *Dance Theatre Journal*, vol. 20, no. 4.

Sigman, Jill. (2000) *How Dances Signify: Trio A and the Myth of ordinary Movement*. Available at: http://webware.princeton.edu/active/th-dnce/mss/rainercn.htm [accessed 2005]. and Journal of Philosophical Research, Vol.XXV, pp. 489-533.

Movement and text in dialogue

Monique Kroepfli

One of my particular fields of interest as a choreographer, dancer and dance pedagogue is the use of the spoken word whilst creating or performing movement. With the background knowledge of the terminology used in Choreological Studies and having been a movement practitioner for over twenty years, I am using Rudolf Laban's methodologies in my dance practice on a regular basis. In the following paper I focus on the use of these tools in a choreographic context supported with practical examples from the workshop taught at the Laban International Conference.

The importance of shared terminology

Creating movement vocabulary and developing it further is the personal handwriting of a choreographer. Like the written word, movement can be drawn from an almost infinite vocabulary. Talking about movement and naming it is a skill that needs to be learned and practised even as an experienced dancer. The terminology from Choreological Studies has proved to be a most useful tool in my practice as a dancer as well as a choreographer. The point of the use of defined terminology is to share a common language when talking about movement; a language that is more objective. This language forms a verbal meeting point between expressing and perceiving, irrespective of the number of people involved.

Shared terminology also enables and empowers both dancers and choreographers to make choices about what they want to create and what they want the audience to see. Practitioners with experience in using the methodology of Choreological Studies have the power to make detailed and minute choices that can have a significant impact on the outcomes. These choices involve the structural components of movement: Body, Space, Dynamics & Timing, Action and Relationship and an infinite variety of combinations for these.

A practical example

Using terminology

How can this be embedded in a practical workshop? Here is one way:
Together with the participants a collection of the terminology is made and written down for all to see, for example, the vocabulary used to identify ac-

tions such as the following eleven terms: travel, jump, turn, hold, twist, transfer of weight, lean, fall, close, open, gesture. As a physical warm-up everybody is asked to perform the entire list of actions in the studio space. The participants are then asked to work in pairs and verbally give each other cues about which action to do next. In this way the vocal chords are activated and sound is created whilst moving. The terminology can be put together with the appropriate action and thereby is physically memorised. As a side product participants get to know another person and the awareness of the relationship between the movers and the shared space in the studio is activated. This can support the creative process, particularly when using the spoken word, which for dancers can still be an unfamiliar medium.

Creating a movement phrase

Before the group is divided up and dives onto more specialised areas of interest, it is led through a short process with a practical example that highlights the numerous solutions that can be found even within a relatively narrow task: eight given actions are put together in a predetermined order and at least three of them must be accompanied orally, i.e. the mover should say the word 'turn' while turning.

Looking at the twenty or more solutions to the task, its narrow frame, the strict order of the given actions, allows the viewer to recognise the almost limitless range of possibilities even within such a simple task. In a group of people who are more or less familiar with analysing movement, a sharing of the findings is a reminder of the freedom of creativity when devising movement within a narrow frame. Discussion is saved for later, when tasks get more complex.

Combining movement and spoken word

Having gone through the introduction, the warm-up and having shared the findings of a common task, the participants divide into five groups, each of them with the focus on one component (Body, Space, Dynamics & Timing, Action or Relationship). As a next step each group is divided again: one half first creates movement and then adds a given text to it, and the other half uses the given text as a starting point to create a movement phrase. The instructions concerning the movement component are identical. For example, for the participants working with 'Action', both groups follow the pattern of a certain order and number of actions such as 'shift of weight into stillness into close into open into balance into twist into fall into turn'. Once again keeping a narrow frame for the task allows the viewer to recognise the freedom of creativity within it.

Due to the short timeframe of the workshop at the Laban Conference, the groups were only given a few minutes to solve their tasks. When working with experienced dancers, time pressure can produce clear, authentic and often witty solutions and therefore appears less 'aesthetically censured'. The aim is to create raw material that can be worked on.

The text material in this instance was taken from advertisements in free newspapers through chance procedures. This is an example: 'You said you love the fruit, so we added more.'

It goes without saying that the participants using the text as a starting point automatically incorporate the rhythm and dynamics of the spoken word. At a later stage are they may drop, repeat or distort words. Those who start without text, however, are faced much earlier with choices of effort and timing.

Try it!
It is beyond the scope of this paper to go into a more detailed description of the workshop procedure and of the findings. But I cannot resist encouraging pedagogues, choreographers and dancers to draw on their knowledge of movement analysis using restricted and simple set tasks as starting points for creating and developing movement vocabulary, be it with or without the use of the spoken word. With the use of the spoken word an additional element arises: Meaning. How far does the audible influence what we see and vice versa? 'The Choreographer's Paradise' will be a workshop taught at the next Laban Conference...

Laban's methodologies in the context of Switzerland
BA course in Contemporary Dance
As an example of the positioning of the use and teaching of Rudolf Laban's methodologies I mention the start of a BA course in Contemporary Dance in Zurich in autumn 2009, the first of its kind in Switzerland. In the curriculum there is nothing to be found in the field of movement analysis. It shows that neither knowledge of Rudolf Laban (who lived and worked in Zurich less than a century ago), nor understanding of his methodologies appear to have any relevance as part of this academic dance training.

Artistically non-established
Putting my choreographic work within the context of Switzerland, I can without hesitation say that it figures in the category 'non-established'. The Swissgerman part of the country, even more the Basel area, still has a strong attachment to the classical ballet tradition. To many members of the funding arts councils the term 'dance production' stands for danced narrative. I need hardly explain the positioning within that culture of my work which is non-narrative.

When I first returned to Switzerland in the mid-nineties, I was one of the very few people who returned with a degree or an MA from the Laban Centre. Therefore I kept in touch with some of my fellow students and I am still fostering a regular exchange with dance scholars with a Laban background, mostly in London. In the meantime more Laban trained dance practitioners have taken root in Switzerland but interchange does not happen automatically. Working together currently or studying together is a more important factor for professional exchange.

As a choreographer I draw my encouragement to continue and develop my work from audience responses and some reviews, from people who are interested in dance as its own art form.

Teaching Laban in Israel

Milca Leon

In this short paper, I will locate my work within the spectrum of dance and movement studies in my country, Israel; the challenges that stand in the way of spreading Laban work, and the routes I have found through these difficulties.

I have an MA in Dance Studies from the Laban Centre, specialising in Choreological Studies, Choreography and Education in Dance since 1992. I arrived at the Centre, somewhat accidentally, as a result of my frustration with the duality that was implied in my dance studies in Israel. The course curriculum included no substantial dance-based body of knowledge. The implicit message, I sensed, was that dancing requires getting into the studio and doing 'plies', 'pirouettes' or 'contraction', while 'thinking' is done in the university. I opted therefore, for a B.A in Dance and English Litereature, in two different institutions at the same time. This split was suffocating both practically and conceptually. Intuitively I knew that there must be another way that could unite my love for movement, my desire for artistic expression, and my uncompromising intellectual curiosity. So after two years I left, studied Labanotation in correspondence with the DNB, and a year later I came over to the Laban Centre. The first four years were both hard and amazing. At last I could breathe. I felt my horizon had expanded, and I absorbed everything around me. For the first time since I had started to dance (at the age of 9) I began to read and think about dance in a conceptual way. I read half of the library and started to form opinions, not mere reactions. The most meaningful subject of study that brought the thinking into the feeling-full body was Choreological Studies.

When I finished my MA I taught Choreological Studies at the Laban Centre, and movement for actors at The Central School for Speech and Drama for a few years. In 1996, after eight years in which I half lived at the Laban Centre, I cut the umbilical cord, and moved back to Israel.

In Israel I rediscovered a vivid and highly promoted professional dance scene. The Training/Education scene was somewhat more stagnant. There are a few higher education and professional dance training bodies, in which students study dance, and dance related subjects such as Physiology, Education, Dance History and Eshkol-Wachman movement notation (EW).

Although dance training and education in Israel have changed since my time there, it still seems to have no 'inherent' theoretical basis.

The main reason for its absence, I think, is the hegemony of the Eshkol-Wachman movement notation studies within the academic dance institutions. EW is a unique Israeli movement notation, which is used to notate movement rather than dance. Its creators and some of their followers have in the past distanced themselves from dance to the extent of refusing to use dance traditions such as step-names (from ballet, for example), music, lighting, and other performance devices. They called themselves movers rather than dancers. Some of them have affined themselves with the American post-modern dance in their conceptual framework as well as in their practice. Though there are some variations between institutions, in practice these studies have a strong emphasis on reading and writing notation scores, and the physical work is often provided through contact improvisation and/or martial arts classes. Some EW people have ambivalent relationships with Laban work, and when I taught dance classes to EW BA students I was asked not to use Laban terms, in order not to confuse the students.

This hegemony, I think, creates a lose-all situation, whereas both the 'dance' and the 'movement' people are losing. On the dancers' side, because the EW was supposed to provide a conceptual basis, dance people in Israel were less desirous of exploring and developing an independent body of dance-theory. Yet, since EW does *not* have a strong conceptual basis beyond the fundamentals of its notation, in addition to its distance from dance, the dancers who study EW hardly ever use it beyond the classroom. On the EW side, the split from the dance practice and its power positions, the EW work remains relatively esoteric, and does not get to really influence the dance scene. And then, everyone loses together because this division of forces entails a lack of funding from governing and academic bodies, who know how to appreciate written theoretical knowledge but not artistic expressions. The lack of the former, results in under-funding of the latter.

Since 1996 I have been working throughout the dance education system in Israel: teaching at graduate level, at professional dance schools and at A Level programmes. I have supervised a large number of student choreography projects, co-wrote the Israeli Core Curriculum in Dance for the Ministry of Education, but taught very little Laban, except some lectures and a few intensive courses for teachers. I have offered, and still offer, Laban-based courses to most of the significant dance bodies, but have not succeeded much, as yet. Instead, I have opted for an underground version.

My ex-students at the Dance Academy in Jerusalem will testify that I brought Laban through any back door I found. Teaching mainly choreography and contemporary dance, I had to be focused on what exactly I wanted to teach – ideas, principles and skills – and find how to teach it without, on the one hand, getting too deep into the theoretical basis, and on the other, without compromising the choreographic process or the level of performance. In technique classes, I taught my students to look for the logic of their dance exercises, to see how an exercise, or a full lesson, can develop in its use of space, body, or dynamics; to think in movement terms and act through them. We have looked at inherent expressional content of movement components, so that they could find an inner connection to what they perform rather than wrap it in some external expression. I hoped I was empowering them, so they did not need to regurgitate their teachers' class to their own students, as they used to. Some of those students have later arrived at Laban, following their quest for more of that material.

In my choreography classes (in Israel they are usually called composition classes) I have emphasised Laban-based knowledge that gave the students tools to understand their creative choices, but again without supporting it enough through a theoretical basis. This is because of an additional hurdle, unfamiliar in Europe or the USA, which is complete lack of written material on dance in Hebrew. Unfortunately, there is not *one* Laban-related book translated to Hebrew, and hardly any substantial text translated or written about dance in Israel. The lack of theory-based dance practice and education results in little demand for dance theory books, and so on. It is a cycle that needs to be broken by people with vision in power positions. They, unfortunately, are not easy to find.

Four years ago I left the Academy and started to run my own Laban workshops to people of diverse backgrounds – mainly therapists of varied disciplines. The interest surprised me! People who have done any of the workshops on offer told me the Laban work was for them the most meaningful and in-depth system. The focus of my Laban teaching moved from dance into, mainly, therapy and some acting. I took psychology and group facilitating courses, I study Body Mind Centering, and I now teach Laban at some of the movement therapy and psychotherapy programmes in Israel, although I work in complete isolation. I rarely get to talk with other Laban people, not to mention do further training or research. I buy any book I find in the field, but expanding my Laban work through books is a bit like learning to dance through correspondence. The Laban conference, as you can imagine, was a breath of fresh air for me.

However, working in isolation also has its merits. I am allowed to be a bit more naïve, sometimes explorative, make my own mistakes, learn from them on my own, develop my own new ideas, and still believe I have discovered the moon.

I love teaching therapists, as it brings into my work new realms that have not been prevalent before. I shifted my emphasis from the formal-visual aspects to the experiential, emotional-based ones, yet without abandoning the former completely. To use Peter Madden's (1996) terms I shifted from – 'shape and shaping' to 'voluming', which he defines as 'space-time process that will allow Laban based thinking to move into the 4th dimension of perceiving and experiencing'.[1] I have started mixing ideas from therapy into my work with dancers, taking them through experiential work such as the Bartenieff 3D Breathing exercise. I used it to evoke feelings and images of a three dimensional inner space, that were then taken into the actual three dimensional space of the studio, developed and manipulated in accordance with Laban's principles of spatial harmony. Doing that, they were asked to keep an inner connection with the original image. This, in fact, is the project I have presented at the Laban conference. It was interesting to see the products of that process, but even more to hear the dancers' reactions. For the first time they were made to be responsible for their creative work, given tools for expressing their ideas through the dance medium (with special attention to skills of expressing through space) and were asked to remain attuned to their own inner world. Most of them said they felt challenged and empowered, a term often used in therapy work.

I personally, feel empowered by the vastness of possibilities that are there for me to explore through the fundamental, though by no mean simple, medium of Laban-based movement and dance analysis. Because it is so fundamental, it is shared by all media. For me, and I quote Madden (1996) again,

> What may probably be the most important thing about Laban Movement theory is not the codified system of movement concepts itself, but the experience of Laban based thinking and perception.[2]

I work with a strong emphasis on the experience of the movement, interweaving the theory in between the lines.

Lately, I see a lot of interest around me in Laban-based work. People in dance, theatre and therapy gradually acknowledge this work, and me with it. There is much interest in workshops. Even within some of the fortresses of dance education there begins to be an interest. It is gradual and slow, but the younger generations show great appetite for it. They, who are further from either the modern dance ethos which was imported to Israel by the Graham-based teaching that sometimes sanctified the codified 'text' over the learner, or the Puritanism of the EW founders, are looking for new ways to explore and understand movement in a more holistic way. So my horizon is wide and open, and the future is hopeful.

References

1. Madden P. 1988. 'Shaping the Spacetime Continuum' in Madden, P. 1996 *Symmetry and Harmony: Sensing, Feeling, and Moving Multi-Dimensionally* Vol.1 (unpublished collection of essays) p.22.
2. Madden P.1993. 'Shaping Motion and Movement' in Madden P. 1996 *Symmetry and Harmony: Sensing, Feeling, and Moving Multi-Dimensionally* Vol.1 (unpublished collection of essays) p.50.

Closer/quieter, louder/larger: Seeing Six *through video and the LMA lens*

Loretta Livingston

Introduction

I am watching a dancer move through a solo phrase of movement in front of a black velvet curtain. We are in a large, airy studio with a high ceiling and light grey floor. As I direct the videotaping in one area of the room, the rest of the studio is lively with the sounds of twenty-three other dancers in rehearsal. Slowly my attention is drawn to the breathing of the solo dancer. As steady and quiet as the eye of a storm, she unites each movement with her inhale and exhale. Her concentration never falters, surrounded by the noise and chaos. She pulls me in. I realise her breath is the key to her performance. We need to tape it again, in complete silence. I ask the cameraperson to pause. I ask the busy, good-natured cast to stop working. All eyes turn to the soloist. The studio, the space, the silence and the moment are hers. She begins again.

In this paper I offer my experience as an artist: Something unexpected transpired in the process of adding a new area of knowledge – Laban Movement Analysis – to my established practice of working collaboratively with dancers in creating contemporary dance theater. This conference asks the question: Of what relevance is the work of Rudolf Laban today? I answer: It serves my art making in unanticipated and surprising ways.

Incorporating LMA into my artist practice

I added an LMA certification relatively late in my dance career, initially looking for support in teaching emerging contemporary dance artists facing a daunting array of approaches to contemporary dance techniques and dance making. I wanted language that could manifest precise specificity while maintaining stylistic neutrality, encompassing and crossing generations of modern dance training without lodging in or favoring any of the almost ten decades of modern dance evolution, each of which represents distinct theories, preferences and aesthetics of the practitioners of the time.

What I did not foresee was how useful, generative and engaging the LMA framework would be for me as a choreographer, including leading me to use video as both distillation and magnification of choreographic ideas.

During 2007-2008 I created a new dance theater work called *The Vacant House*, inspired by narratives in short stories by contemporary Korean writer

Shin Kyongsuk. Attracted to the lyrical language of Shin and her themes of memory, separation and loss, I set up the parameters of the project to include my Seoul-based Korean collaborator, Dr. Sam-Jin Kim. I designed *The Vacant House* project to support a trip for Dr. Kim to come to southern California in January 2008 to create a segment within the work on my American dancers. Dr. Kim's performance practice is Korean Traditional and Buddhist dance, but as a choreographer she creates contemporary work. She and I both make dance theater – differently, but compatibly.

My interest as an artist is in movement *as* theater. I elicit performances from dancers that include voice, improvisation and physical theater beyond a conventional dance vocabulary. I am curious about how individual dancers translate movement passages designed on my body and meant for theirs. Their translations are the beginnings of our co-created theatrical events.

In particular I am interested in the small margin of difference manifested by a trained contemporary dancer, who, while working for accuracy, still manages to reveal something highly personal. This makes good theater. The differences are not those of a novice who is not able to replicate, but instead are those of a trained artist who can create simultaneous templates of accuracy and individuality.

When watching dance in performance, I know that all of us in the audience will be succumbing to inner preferences, stimulated by the unique signatures imbedded in the way the individual dancer/actors perform the choreography and inform the event. We are attracted to human movement in a very personal way. Providing a way to map these movement differences in my directing process is how LMA initially engaged me as an artist. On a sensate level my ideas of preference, control, and approach to directing live within me like a camera's aperture – opening, closing, softening or sharpening as I work. This internal aperture became differently articulate with the LMA training.

While in choreographic rehearsals for *The Vacant* House in fall, 2007, I set up a concurrent LMA investigation, examining how the dancers translated my movement. I called the LMA project *SEEING SIX*. I chose six dancers from my cast of twenty-four – three men and three women – who differed in height, body type, approaches to the kinesphere, Effort qualities and body organisation.

I asked the six dancers to rehearse a foundational phrase from *The Vacant House* as a tiny, cohesive solo – about a minute and forty-five seconds. It was material the entire cast had learned from me. With a cameraperson I set up two cameras on tripods in the studio, front view and side view. We ran the cameras simultaneously for each dancer performing the solo.

Looking with Laban eyes

My first lesson in seeing with Laban eyes came with the first video take. As I watched the solo dancer performing for the camera, I found myself leaning in, straining to hear her breath, knowing it was important. My internal aperture was opening. I needed to listen. I needed to hear her and see her in silence. My senses were differently tuned with LMA.

Working with the initial video data, I had target areas for analysis, knowing that some personal movement preferences were going to be eliminated or substantially reduced because the dancers were executing my choreography rather than their own. Having seen these dancers repeatedly in rehearsal and class, I knew that each had developed a working relationship with his/ her body structure. That internal dialogue facilitated either a highly precise or highly individualistic rendition of my choreographic work, and sometimes both. I knew that analysing these unique body pathways would reveal aspects of their personal movement signatures.

As a template for examining body organisation I referred to six fundamental 'patterns of total body connectivity' delineated by American author, educator, CMA and dancer Peggy Hackney (1998, pp.11-14, 19-24, 42-43). The Breath pattern was a crucial area of movement technique for my dancers, both with me and later in their work with Dr. Kim, who uses an extremely subtle breath technique inherent in Korean Traditional Dance. I use a full, strong, audible exhalation, with free flow at the release point. This sets up a subsequent rebound into upward motion and suspension, or a weight sensing re-stabilisation at the bottom of a falling action, as if regaining equilibrium of the senses before embarking on another action.

One of my female dancers matched breath audibly and forcefully to her strong, direct approach to each action. Another woman let the exhalations spill into her liquid use of weight. She, in fact, organised all her motion with the Breath pattern, with tremendous suppleness throughout her body. The third woman held her breath in the center of her chest and throat, constricting upward with ever tightening binding until, at the point of exhalation, she manifested a light bound flow through her upper body. The tallest man – over six feet – powerfully matched his breath with his actions, which entailed the management of his huge reach space through limbs that appeared to lengthen without limit. Another man, less tall but not without length, gave only the smallest evidence of breath, but linked elegant, light exhalations with flying and floating arms and hands that lingered and left traces in space. The third man – very small and compact – neutralised his breath as a component of motion, but found moments of softening in light free flow through his chest, arms, neck and head that signalled private moments of internal ecstatic dancing within soft exhalations.

Continuing with body organisation, I looked at their torsos. For me, the torso is key for choreographic signature. I use head-tail lengthening in order to make space for dividing my torso into quadrants, facilitating complex and overlapping isolations and directional changes through the core body. I lead with my head into off-vertical space and anchor with countertension in the pelvis. The whole topic of countertension – articulated in depth by Irmgard Bartenieff (1980, pp. 101-115) – was difficult for my dancers to reproduce. They often made a facsimile of my counter tensioned actions by deepening the legs and moving up and down in the vertical dimension rather than venturing out into the large, disc-like off-vertical pathways. Sometimes they rendered the movement as gesture, giving the phrases the look of separate tasks, staying in Action Drive and missing flow entirely.

Whatever may have been missing in these dancers' versions of my choreographic phrase material was rendered moot by the fact that their expressive use of Effort qualities in flow, weight, time and space gave me the lively, present moment of performance I seek in making dance theater.

Using video as an organisational and aesthetic tool

I began developing visual organisation – seeing with Laban eyes again – through the video data of my SEEING SIX study. I edited multiple versions of small movies. I have a visual art background, so this was natural for me, but I took note of it in my process. I selected and edited moments in the document footage in order to identify topic headings. I made a video sequence that focused on the use of the torso, running the clips in real time and then in slow motion to examine utilisation of the core body. I made a sequence that highlighted different moments of individual expression and another in which all the dancers chose the same place to fulfill, each in a unique way.

I was responding to various Effort qualities that I felt read well on screen. This was off topic for my LMA investigation but feeding my art making. Onscreen, I favored weighted free flow and anything strong, especially, but not limited to liquidity. Moments in which the dancers melted out of bound flow into free with successive phrasing, landing at the bottom of a drop with reverberations of weight sensing made me sit forward and *watch*. Returning to the measurement of the Breath pattern, I was captivated by the dancers' capacity to unite their breath with action. Equally attractive to me was their ability to shift with ease between a very public gaze – at me, at the camera, at the viewer – and then retreat into Dream State or Passion Drive, withdrawing all attention to space while knowing they were still being watched.

Lastly I noticed I was falling in love with my dancers all over again – feeling that moment of attraction as a director. This motivated me to go back into the studio with a hand held camera for a closer/quieter, louder/larger look. I wanted to respond to their dancing rather than document it. I scheduled the six dancers for another video shoot, this time using the power of the zoom and close up. My intention was to feature and frame their expressivity, informed by hours of examination and analysis of the original document footage of their dancing.

At this moment in my simultaneous processes of creating a dance theater work and running a concurrent LMA investigation, I knew that something new was emerging for me as an artist. It was related to, but not the same as, the work I was making for stage. Another framework was being shaped – architecturally – within in my thinking, prompting me to begin creating specifically for the camera and screen.

Repeating the project in Singapore

At the end of 2007 my colleague in Singapore, Tamatha Ling Wong, said she wanted *The Vacant House* for her dancers at LASALLE College of the Arts. In March 2008 I went to Singapore, acquiring 24 new dancers from China, Indonesia, the Philippines, Australia, Sri Lanka and Singapore. They learned *The Vacant House* (not including the segment created by Dr. Kim) for performances in Singapore planned for May and October 2008. Prompted by the differences I saw in the Singaporean dancers' approach to my movement and theatrical materials, I ran the *SEEING SIX* LMA investigation while there. As with my American cast, I chose six dancers, selected for their differences in height, build and inherent Effort qualities. Using the same short solo I used with the Americans, I had each dancer perform facing a fixed-position camera on tripod. And, as before, I ultimately went back into the studio to shoot with a hand held camera, working expressively and responding to my LMA discoveries.

Creating screendance

By late spring of 2008 I had created two video studies – one American and one Singaporean – using the hand held video footage. I was developing a palette for creating screen versions of my longer dance theater productions. Video representations of my live works are problematic due to the length (typically an hour or more) and the sites (often non-proscenium and public, and sometimes 'migrating' locations). The two video studies were allowing me to establish palettes of color, texture and time – the beginnings of ideas that would feed into a screen version of *The Vacant House*.

During the summer of 2008 I worked with editor Carrie Smaczny, my cameraperson in both southern California and Singapore, to create a screendance version of *The Vacant House* using our video footage from the initial choreographic period in fall 2007. I titled it *The Ghost House* to distinguish it from the stage piece.

Sifting through an overwhelming amount of raw video footage to select materials for this highly condensed screen piece was made manageable by the sensibilities I honed through the *SEEING SIX* studies. Having examined the dancers in detail using LMA I was able to quickly organise strong screen visuals and performance dynamics, condensing a twenty-minute live segment into four minutes for screen.

Fourteen narrative figures were featured in *The Vacant House* version for stage, with concurrent strands of narration running throughout the work. It was impossible to delineate all these characters in the screen version. Having practiced a more neutral stance while viewing with an LMA lens, I did not choose the dancers who most attracted me in my first video studies. Instead I moved away from my preferences and chose dancers I knew could deliver the narrative content through what I had learned about their Effort qualities.

To anchor the action in *The Ghost House* I chose a fighting trio – two women and one man. Two of the dancers in this trio were in the *SEEING SIX* study, but I didn't feature them in the early screendance study. However, by having analysed their approaches to movement, I knew that they could manifest intense emotional performances for screen in a range that could be reached through particular kinds of physical tensions and held places in the body. For the woman, a pattern of upward holding in her chest and throat gave her a poignant vulnerability. When she used strength, she used bound flow to the point of compression – in face, voice, chest – manifesting a perfect fury for angry, distraught, continuous vocal improvisations and unrelenting fighting/condensing actions. The small and compact man held an area in his lumbar spine that produced a compensatory advancing of his skull, which was perfect for the boxer-like belligerence of his role. He countered this pugilistic stance by momentary excursions into dreamy, eyes-closed reveries at the touch of the women, manifesting light free flow in his upper body.

In order to find a place of visual and emotional completion for *The Ghost House* video, I understood that my preferences for strong, weighted free flow combined with a mesmerising Spell Drive gaze would serve in creating resolve and suspension as the last image disappeared.

Final reflections

Many words could serve as final reflections for this account of my use of Laban Movement Analysis and its effect on my dance making, but I select *surprising, revealing* and *renewing* as the most resonate. Using the ideas of a man I never met, I leaned in – *closely and quietly* – and saw my art and craft differently.

I close with brief narrations of my three videos.

breath (the Americans)

She rises and appears. *Close*, the camera is *so close* we see only her. Wearing an unadorned gaze she looks at the viewer – front – with neither astonishment nor concealment. She sinks. She swims upward again and out of the frame, a fine large fish leaving a black pond. A new figure appears, blurred, then sharp. He exits on a breath – strong. Another, dreamy and weighted, sways with an inward gaze. Later, another, quick and coiled, flashes – then disappears. Hands, face, hair, skin and huge fragments of limbs fill the frame. They rise, sink, pull, drop, emerge and submerge, reshaping a black rectangular space. The camera is my eye, and I am getting closer. Here, the camera mimics the aperture in me that *opens*. I lean in and listen. (Whispered): Breath propels the motion.

light (the Singaporeans)
Hands. Gongs. A bird chirps in the background of afternoon light – tropical. I see quickness and then sharp outlines of straight, black hair flung fast into the likeness of charcoal marks on white paper. Drawings in motion, these figures do not look at the viewer. They have a private gaze, unavailable. I try to sneak in, approaching them like wild animals, the camera seeking closeness. That softness – that masterful lingering – is deceiving me. They are strong, not soft, and they vanish. I cannot hear their breath. It has become an internal chime – a secret.

The Ghost House
Whispers. A face contorted. A fight. Sounds of feet are running in the dark. This is a paper nightmare: rustling, chaotic, violent and fragile. A touch and recoil, a push, a slap – these keep the battle current. A grip on the head shifts into violence. Ghosts rise from the walls and floors of the house. Disembodied voices shout. Narrations build, fall, disappear and return. The camera is my high intensity witness. It doesn't flinch.

References
Bartenieff, Irmgard & Lewis, Dori, (1980) *Body Movement, Coping with the Environment.* New York and London: Routledge.

Hackney, Peggy, (1998) *Making Connections, Total Body Integration Through Bartenieff Fundamentals.* New York and London: Routledge.

A dialogue between art and education in Brazil: Laban and beyond

Isabel Marques

A short note on Laban in Brazil

I was 21 when I came to know the work of Rudolf Laban due to my unwillingness to keep taking classical ballet into my body and my choice to graduate in Education. Ballet at that time was taught in a very traditional way and it contradicted all I was about as an Education student in terms of seeking a more critical and meaningful education for the whole self.

I was introduced to Laban's principles by Regina Faria, a pupil of Maria Duschenes, who first brought Laban to Brazil in the 1940s. In 1988, I flew to London to deepen my understanding and practices in dance as a whole. Lonely, I was the first Brazilian to complete the MA in Dance Studies at the Laban Centre. Lonely, I came back to Brazil and followed my own paths towards developing a connection between what I had learnt in London and what I found important to Brazil.

In the past twenty years, in my very particular way, I have been developing what I think critical and meaningful to learn, to teach, to make, do and appreciate dance with the work of Laban as a sound background. My partners, however, have not been 'the Laban people in Brazil'. They have been schoolteachers, dance students, researchers from abroad, books and articles, and the dance audience.

There is no formal organisation in Brazil to enable regular meetings amongst Laban professionals in the country. Networking is almost nonexistent. My life history working by myself leads me to suggest that the development of Laban studies in Brazil could be synthesised by the headline - 'isolation and progress, dialogue when possible'[1].

I understand Laban's work as being developed in Brazil in the vertical way. Researchers focus mainly on advisees; teachers' main concerns are the students; artists seek the audience. In my personal trajectory, I have hardly met with Laban professionals to share research or to exchange views and/or experience ways of teaching. I have never met Laban peers to create a dance performance. On the other hand, I – and certainly other professionals too – have dialogued extensively with 'new comers' willing to research, to learn and to appreciate the contributions of Laban towards the development of dance as an art in Brazil. I dare say this view of 'horizontal loneliness' is probably shared by many professionals in the country and it is certainly not only a matter of choice: Brazil is a huge country and geographical communication is not always easy.

As I write this paper and think about the enormous growth and increasing interest in Laban's work in Brazil in the past years, I realise that having made a 'vertical choice', professionals may have lacked peer support and feedback that might have led to conceptual depth and precision. On the other hand, the non-specialised public has profited enormously from the opportunities opened up by those professionals.

For these reasons, in this paper I will not discuss anybody's work in Brazil but mine. I will give a short historical introduction to the main theoretical background of my work and then relate it to how Laban's work has provided a consistent basis to approach Education in artistic situations.

Theoretical background

Back from the Laban Centre in 1989 I started to teach at the University of Campinas in the field of teacher preparation. Later on, I was in charge of developing a Dance Programme for São Paulo City (1991-92). I was also responsible for writing the National Standards for Dance Education in Brazil (1997). In 2002, I received a sponsorship from UNESCO to continue this path and work towards preparing public school teachers in the field of Dance.

At a first glance, it seemed I was more involved with Education than with Dance, but I soon found out educating and dancing are inseparable. The multiple relationships between Education and Art became the keystone of my work.

As I worked with both school teachers and dance artists, I was able to unravel the common sense ideas that uncritically accepted that artists can teach just because they 'know dance in their bones'. In addition, the fallacious thought that teachers do not need to be good dancers – let alone school teachers – must be reviewed. Also, I was intrigued by the general acceptance that dance at schools should not worry about aesthetics, appreciation, technique (etc), but rather it should be taught only for the sake of personal/group development. In this line of thought, schoolteachers needed to be better pedagogues and psychologists than dancers!

Another point that caught my interest was the naivety of dance teachers and dancers towards social issues. Having had a background in critical thinking at undergraduate level and having worked under the supervision of Paulo Freire in São Paulo's Secretary of Education (1987, 1991-92), I could not bear the idea that dancers – and dance teachers – were so encapsulated and restricted to the dance world itself. At that time, critically interacting with the outer world in dance lessons was a growing theoretical research line

(Stinson, 1998; Shapiro, 1998; Anttila, 1996; Marques, 1989; Green, 2001), but not yet a comprehensive practice in schools.

Since then, my arguments have been that, 'considering that the dance world with its possibilities of creating, of having aesthetic experiences, of relating dance to society is made possible primarily by the doors and visions opened by the dance teacher, it becomes crucial that this professional is not isolated from the dance world him/herself' (Marques, 2004a, pp. 81-82). I advocated that in order to teach dance, school teachers should be able to cope professionally with the three main standpoints for the Arts in schools: doing-making, reading and contextualising (Barbosa 1991, 1995, 2002). Although obvious in some countries, in Brazil of the 80s this was crucial to develop a consistent dance programme at schools. Dance – if taught – was mainly step dances, copies from TV shows, or indulgent self-expression.

I offered the suggestion that if dancing implies knowing in the body, teachers should be able to dialogue with their own *dancing* bodies by feeling, understanding, and questioning dance in the classrooms (Marques, 2004a). In Brazil, there were/are two typical teaching situations: 1) school teachers who teach dance without having had enough professional dance experience to share. In this situation, dance is often taught 'verbally' (only appreciation, dance history, etc) or 'remotely' (only the students dance); 2) dance teachers with professional dance experience do not always allow the *artist* to enter the classroom. Many artists see dancing apart from teaching, and prefer to demonstrate, to be copied, to verbally correct, to tell how to do steps, positions, and sequences instead of being committed to *sharing* their artistic and aesthetic experiences with the students (Marques 1999, 2003). I see the second situation not restricted to Brazil, but to several dance programmes and literature around the world. I have argued this view splits the roles of the teacher and the artist: it separates Education from Art (Marques, 1996).

I proposed that the dancing body, the artistic active body of the dance teacher should be the main loom to 'weave' dance knowledge in the classroom. In 1996, I started working – in theory and practice – on the role of the artist-teacher: the artist that knows *and* teaches 'in the bones', by *dancing/ performing*. One of its developments is the dance performance 'Coreológicas' which will be discussed further.

However, *knowing* and *sharing* dance as art to me was not enough to become an artist-teacher: I often argued that 'a closer and more direct relationship between education and society [was] needed so that our students [could] learn the tools to critically engage with technological, social and political changes [in contemporary society]' (Marques, 2004a, p. 76). As Freire (1982, 1983, 1996) argued, we need 'an education that is focused on human praxis – the thoughtful and conscious struggle to reshape our world into one that is more just and compassionate' (cited by Shapiro, 1998, p. 9).

In 2001, I systematised a triangulation of my thinking practices: the context-based dance education (Marques 2002, 2004b, 2007). I drew up a dance teaching methodology based on the tripod dance-education-society. The main principle of this tripod was/is grounded on the non-hierarchical, multifaceted, and inter-related web of mutable relations I believe desirable to know dance in the bones, to share the art of dance with the students and to relate it all to the world we live in.

The educational/artistic approach to dance via the context-based dance education tripod conveys the idea that 'by sharing and experiencing bodily possibilities of construction and transformation in dance classes we can also feel empowered to interact with people in different ways. So, by dancing and in dancing we should be able to make a difference in the society we live in' (Marques, 2007, p. 146).

The work of Laban was crucial to achieve these inter-relations between dance-education-society and it became the main thread to sew together the theory and practices of my research, teaching and dancing.

Laban comes in
The work of Laban did not come into my work after I had developed the core of it. On the contrary, working with Laban's principles helped me to better understand my proposals and to make them plausible and consistent. In this paper, I will focus only on three topics as they relate to Laban's work: teaching dance, dance and social transformation, and the interactive dance performance.

Laban dialogues with Ana Mae Barbosa: relating dance to teaching
In the 1970s Ana Mae Barbosa, a Brazilian researcher, gave the first critical input to the field of art education that became an internationally recognised theoretician on the teaching of Art. She called for a more comprehensive art-education process which should include not only doing-making, but also reading and contextualising art in the classrooms. By reading/contextualising she meant not only formally appreciating and criticising artworks, but also understanding the several layers of the artwork in its aesthetical historical heritage. Barbosa's work (1984, 1995, 2002 et al) focused on a historicised art-education process that allowed for a critical understanding of society.

As I translated Barbosa's theories into dance actions, I understood we should be able to do-make, read, and contextualise dance *articulating* it to the practices of the *artist*-teacher. In other words, I pointed out that Barbosa's triangulation should be closely related to 'teaching by dancing'. Thus, I needed 'bodily tools' to inter-act doing-making/reading to the several articulated layers that juxtapose a dance performance. Above all, I needed *dance* tools to make possible the contextualisation of the artwork as proposed by Barbosa.

Laban comes in – the main tools available to me were the strands of the medium as developed by Valerie Preston-Dunlop (1980, 1998, 2002 et al). In order to contextualise the art/dance work as proposed by Barbosa, it is necessary to go beyond description, it is necessary to understand dance works by articulating doing and reading.

Laban's approach to the inner and intricate elements of dance allow us to feel, think and do/make dance, deeply understanding the interwoven meanings of the artwork. I found in Laban's proposals a support to do-make/read/contextualise dance in an articulated way. Mostly, his ideas and practices help the dance teacher to be in the body, in the *dancing* body. Laban's work allowed the artist-teacher proposal to take place in the classrooms: the teacher, by dealing directly with the medium of dance, reclaims *dancing/performing* – rather than talking and exercising – as his/her main commitment in the classroom (Marques, 1996).

Laban dialogues with Paulo Freire: relating dance to social issues

The contributions of Paulo Freire, Brazilian educator, are countless and known worldwide. Freire advocated that Education should relate to freedom, to political and social consciousness. Education, as he understood it, is only possible if availability for dialogue is in the root of a teacher/student relationship. Moreover, he stated that 'dialogue is the encounter of men for the pronunciation of the world' (Freire, 1983, p. 160).

Critical awareness has been an important and necessary key for Freire's dialogical Education towards social transformation. To be critical, he said, implies problematising[2] the cultural, political, and social realities we live in. Implicit in Freire's critical pedagogy is the will to seek for different viewpoints and to understand there is no universally correct truth. Freire's lessons are lessons of belief, diversity, and humbleness made possible by socio-political consciousness and participation.

Laban comes in – connecting Freire's dialogue to dance practices, I suggested verbal interaction was only part of it (see also Anttila, 2003). Considering that dance ideas, narratives, and themes are embodied in the dance medium (Preston-Dunlop, 1998), I proposed that dance dialogues must be born from and rely on the intrinsic components of dance. To me, if Laban's principles are understood, chosen, and openly shared, the dialogical relationship suggested by Freire might become a bodily – dancing – dialogue.

As I connected Freire's critical pedagogy to dance, not only did I understand it was necessary to know/describe/interpret the strands of dance (Preston-Dunlop, 1998) but also to deconstruct the master narratives of dance embedded in them. By doing so, we could understand dance in its

multiple layers and manifestations. As I related Laban's work to Freire's critical thinking, I understood that problematising, articulating, and criticising
the strands of the dance medium was necessary to understand contemporary society and to educate the critical citizen (Marques 1996, 2004b,
2007).

Laban dialogues with contemporary society: the interactive dance performance

Considering that contemporary society has been overwhelmed by deep conceptual transformations of the body-time-space relations (Harvey, 1992;
Jameson, 1991; Lyotard, 1993; et al), I asked: what changes must there be in
the teaching and performing of dance? Further, how could dialogues between Laban-Barbosa-Freire be linked to contemporary society? (Marques,
1996).

My artistic response to it was the conception of the interactive dance performance 'Coreológicas'. My interest was to integrate in *one* single dance
performance the major concerns of my own research: the role of the artist-
teacher and the critical dialogue between dance and (contemporary) society.
At the same time as 'Coreológicas' was created, due to my personal interest
to teach Choreology in an artistic/aesthetic format, I was seeking new ways
to perceive, understand, and teach the movement components proposed by
Laban (1960, 1988 et al).[3]

'Coreológicas' is a choreography based on Laban's principles and Preston-
Dunlop's structural model (1998, 2002). The performance is divided in five
short choreographic pieces – each one dealing with a different movement
component. The set choreography, performed by the dancers, is transformed
into an invitation for the audience to join in by dancing. Based on the choreography, the audience is asked to re-create the dance by improvising and
collectively relating.

My proposal as a choreographer is that the audience can learn by relating
reading and *doing*: doing (joining in) depends on what and how members of
audience read (as in Barbosa) each choreographic piece. In other words, appreciation is directly connected to doing and making during the dance
performance.

Participation in 'Coreológicas' is an invitation for critical dialogue (as in
Freire): not compulsory, not intimidating, not cathartic or indulgent. Rather,
participation depends on the critical reading of the dance piece and on
choosing how to respond to it. There is in the dancers' invitation/participa-
tion proposal the acknowledgement of audience's personal histories, body
differences, personal needs and experiences. The audience is bidden to enter
the performing space, to *re-create* the dance and to bodily dialogue with the
dancers and amongst themselves. Considering the core for dialogue are

Laban's movement components, as the bodily dialogue occurs, teaching and learning Choreology also take place *through the dancing bodies*.

The call for participation is also grounded on the critical dancer. The choreographic pieces are carefully composed not to be presented or delivered onto the public, but to be dialogically *shared* with the dancers. The dancers' bodies convey a call for understanding, choosing, and dancing basic social issues embedded in the choreological choices I make as a choreographer.

Laban's work, in dialogue with Barbosa and Freire gave me the support to challenge the connection between Dance and Education in an artistic situation, the conception and production of 'Coreológicas' was a response to it. In 'Coreológicas' I met my proposal not to split the dance teacher from the artist she/he should be. The audience, by learning Choreology in their bodies, are also educated to read, to do, and to contextualise dance. In the dialogue established between the choreographer/dancers and the audience, choices are made and the social context reshaped, transformed.

References

Anttila, E., (1996) *Dance education in theory and practice*. Licentiate's Theses. University of Helsinki.

Anttila, E., (2003) *A dream journey to the unknown: searching for dialogue in dance education*. Helsinki: Theatre Academy.

Barbosa, A. M., (1991) *A imagem no ensino da arte* [Image in art teaching]. São Paulo: Perspectiva.

Barbosa, A. M., (1984) *Arte-educação: conflitos/acertos* [Art education: conflicts/making it right]. São Paulo: Max Limonad.

Barbosa, A. M., (1995) *Modernidade e pós-modernidade no ensino da arte* [Modernity and post-modernity in art teaching]. *MAC Revista*, 1 (1), pp. 6-15.

Barbosa, A. M.d ed., (2002) *Inquietações e mudanças no ensino da arte* [Inquietudes and changes in art teaching]. São Paulo: Cortez.

Freire, P., (1982) *Educação e mudança* [Education and transformation]. Rio de Janeiro: Paz e Terra.

Freire, P., (1983) *Pedagogia do oprimido* [Pedagogy of the oppressed]. Rio de Janeiro: Paz e Terra.

Freire, P., (1996) *Pedagogia da autonomia* [Pedagogy of autonomy]. Rio de Janeiro: Paze Terra.

Green, J., (1999) Somatic authority and the myth of the ideal body in dance education. *Dance Research Journal, 31*(2), pp. 80-100.

Green, J., (2001) Socially constructed bodies in American dance classrooms. *Research in Dance Education*, 2 (2), pp. 155-173

Harvey, D., (1992) *Condição pós-moderna* [Postmodern condition]. São Paulo: Loyola.

Jameson, F, (1991) *Postmodernism or the cultural logic of late capitalism.* London: Verso.

Laban, R., (1960) *Mastery of movement.* London: MacDonald & Evans.

Laban, R., (1988) *Modern educational dance.* 3rd ed. London: Northcote House.

Lyotard, J. F., (1993) *O pós-moderno explicado às crianças* [The Postmodern explained to children]. Lisboa: Publicações Dom Quixote.

Marques, I, (1989) *Dance in the curriculum: the Brazilian case.* Master Theses. London: Laban Centre for Movement and Dance.

Marques, I., (1996) *A dança no contexto: uma proposta para a educação contemporânea* [Dance in the context: a proposal for contemporary education]. Doctoral Dissertation. São Paulo: University of São Paulo.

Marques, I., (1998) Dance education in/and the post modern. In: S. Shapiro, ed. 1998. *Dance, power and difference.* Champaign: Human Kinetics, pp. 171-185.

Marques, I., (1999) *Ensino de dança hoje* [Teaching dance today]. São Paulo: Cortez.

Marques, I., (2003) *Dançando na escola* [Dancing at school]. São Paulo: Cortez.

Marques, I., (2004a) Giving meaning to dance education in Brazil. In: R. Mason, & L. O'Farrell, eds. 2004. *Issues in arts education in Latin America.* Kingston: Queen´s University Press, pp.75-86.

Marques, I., (2004b) Metodologia para o ensino de dança: luxo ou necessidade? [Methodology for teaching dance: luxury or necessity?]. In: R. Pereira, & S. Soter, eds. 2004. *Lições de dança 4* [Dance lessons 4]. Rio de Janeiro: UniverCidade, pp. 135-158.

Marques, I., (2007) I see a kaleidoscope dancing: understanding, criticising, and recreating the world around us. In: L. Rouhiainen, ed. 2007. *Ways of knowing in dance and art.* Helsinki: Theatre Academy, pp. 144-158.

Preston-Dunlop, V., (1980) *A handbook for dance in education.* 2nd ed. London: Longman.

Preston-Dunlop, V., (1998) *Looking at dances: a choreological perspective on choreography.* London: Verve Publishing.

Preston-Dunlop, V. ed., (2002) *Dance and the performative: a choreological perspective – Laban and beyond.* London: Verve Publishing.

Shapiro, S., (1998) Towards transformative teachers: critical and feminist perspectives in dance education. In: S. Shapiro, ed. 1998. *Dance, power and difference.* Champaign: Human Kinetics, pp. 7-22.

Stinson, S., (1998) Seeking a feminist pedagogy for children's dance. In: S. Shapiro, ed. 1998. *Dance, power and difference.* Champaign: Human Kinetics, pp. 23-48.

1. Thanks to Maria Mommenshon, professionals who work with Laban and kept apart have had the opportunity to meet in some events she organised in São Paulo City. The last ones were held in Rio de Janeiro, 2002/2008, organised by Regina Miranda, bringing the international community together.

2. Freirian's term from the Portuguese 'problematizar': to ask, to pose questions, to investigate further, to dialogue about, to see from a distance.

3. 'Coreológicas' was a development of my Doctorate (University of São Paulo, 1996) performed by Caleidos Dance Co., under my direction. The first 'Coreológicas' was presented in 1996, followed by 'Coreológicas Duets', presented nationally and internationally; in 2005 'Coreológicas III' was produced and in 2006 'Coreológicas IV'. In 2007, in research collaboration with the Theatre Academy, Finland, 'Coreológicas Brasil-Finland' was shown in Brazil and video-discussed in Helsinki. In 2008, the Caleidos Co. premièred the performance 'Coreológicas V' awarded the 'Fomento à Dança', a renowned prize in São Paulo. Invited by Acupe Dance Co. from the Northeast of Brazil, I choreographed 'Coreológicas-Recife' which won the public acclamation prize for the best dance performance in 2008.

Transcending cultural and contextual specificity: posture-gesture mergers in movement pattern analysis

James McBride

Abstract
This paper introduces the physical and conceptual basis of Movement Pattern Analysis (MPA), with focus on its sole object of observation: Posture-Gesture-Mergers (PGMs). After briefly introducing MPA and the general connection between cognition and bodily movement, we'll look more specifically at the core concept of PGM, which, when observed with sufficient repetition (i.e., in a two-hour interview), allows MPA to transcend cultural and contextual specificity.

Based on the disciplined analysis of nonverbal behaviour, MPA is probably the most comprehensive system available for assessing an individual's core motivations in decision-making processes. MPA has a wide range of applications, from management consulting to career guidance, and over 30,000 individuals – primarily those involved in senior management – have made use of MPA-Profiles over the last 50 years.

MPA maps out – in very practical terms – how people are intrinsically motivated to take action and interact throughout all stages of a decision-making process. For example, some people are most motivated to get results, while others would rather research or explore ideas – alone or with others. Still other people are most driven when they believe in a cause or see the relative importance of a particular action. Understanding individual motivation ensures the best fit between people and areas of responsibility – leading to greater personal- and work-satisfaction for individuals and teams.

While each individual is different and unique, teams need a certain balance in order to make decisions and achievements in accordance with required tasks and strategies – so as not to have blind spots or an excess of emphasis in one particular area. Teams function most effectively by identifying and profiting from differences, so that potential strengths complement or compensate for potential weaknesses.

MPA establishes guidelines and a shared framework – tailored to each individual and team – for effective team-leadership in practical, easy-to-apply terms – at all levels of management.

In sum, MPA functions as:

- • a *tool* for individual and team analysis – how to optimise existing strengths,
- • a *framework* for understanding human diversity of motivation and interaction (the big picture),
- • a *guideline* for planning and development – from meetings to team-strategy to succession.

Professional MPA-Practitioner training has allowed MPA to spread to a wide range of fields, although its main application has been in management consulting, spanning over more than 30 countries. Some companies and multinational corporations have continued their success with MPA for over three decades, which is rare in the trend-seeking private sector.

Typical applications of MPA in Management Consulting include:

- • Personal-, leadership-, and team-development,
- • MPA-Coaching and self-management,
- • Recruiting and (re-) definition of roles,
- • Planning-structures for meetings and work-strategies.

MPA was developed by Warren Lamb in the 1940s and '50s, building upon the innovations of Rudolf Laban and one of the UK's first management consultants, F. C. Lawrence. Warren Lamb assisted Laban and Lawrence in their groundbreaking research within British industry – first among factory workers – then focusing on management.

Already in the early 1940s, Laban and Lawrence were working from the premise that '...thoughts have speed, strength, direction, [and] flow' (R. Laban, F. C. Lawrence 1943, cited in C. -L. Moore, 2005: 31). Indeed, thinking is a dynamic process. Thinking is movement.

Laban and Lawrence realised early on that certain aspects and qualities of thinking are echoed in other kinds of bodily movement – and vice-versa.

Warren Lamb went on to synthesise these and his own findings and develop a solid framework and unique method – now known as MPA – for analysing core initiatives in decision-making.

Despite Laban and Lawrence's early insight into the link between cognition and bodily movement, 'scientific attempts to understand [movements accompanying language] have for the most part focussed on their social value – the meaning that gesticulation adds to the verbal message which it accompanies' – as Deborah Du Nann Winter notes (1992: 153).

Such 'social meanings' are of course highly complex, with infinite variations, both culturally and contextually. 'For instance, one of the most common nonverbal behaviours, smiling, may express...contentment, ecstasy, approval, or seduction, but it may also express contempt, submissiveness, or anxiety.' (Philippot, et al. 1999: 3). Not only are the social implications of gestures culturally specific, the possible links to emotion (for example in Ekman's study of facial expression) are links to *transitory* states – again varying from one context to another.

If we want to find more *enduring* patterns of nonverbal behaviour – as is the focus of MPA – we have to find links at a deeper, cognitive level. And if we want to transcend cultural specificity, we have to abstract from individual or cultural movement-styles and identify underlying, panhuman characteristics, based on basic human functions. This is where Laban's taxonomy of *physical* movement becomes relevant – as it relates to *mental* movement.

We make sense of the world by comparing the unknown to the known – to an established reference. Our most fundamental reference is our bodily experience of the world, as it relates to forces in space and time, and is perceived through all the senses and proprioception. These primary experiences and their interconnections make up a schematic structure on which to base subsequent experiences. This is how we come to know the unknown.

As neuroscientist Antonio Damasio explains, '...our very organism...is used as the ground reference for the constructions we make of the world around us... ...Our most refined thoughts and best actions...use the body as a yardstick.' (1994: xvi).

Or as Merleau-Ponty so aptly puts it:

> For us to be able to conceive space, it is in the first place necessary that we should have been thrust into it by our body, and that it should have provided us with the first model of those transpositions, equivalents and identifications which make space into an objective system... ([1962] 1998: 142).

The fundamental yet complex understanding of space, 'at the level of bodily perception and movement,' becomes the primary basis of schematic structures for understanding all other abstract concepts, including those underpinning language (Armstrong, Stokoe & Wilcox 1995: 51-52).

For example, in most sign languages, and indeed many cultures, forward is associated with the future – where we are headed – and what is behind us is associated with the past – where we have already been. This timeline also ties in with Laban's proposed affinities between advancing/retreating and decelerating/accelerating.

According to W. J. Mitchell, spatial form is:

> ...the perceptual basis of our notion of time...we literally cannot 'tell time' without the mediation of space. ...We speak of 'long' and 'short' times, of 'intervals' (literally, 'spaces between'), of 'before' and 'after'—

all implicit metaphors which depend upon a mental picture of time as a linear continuum (1990: 274, cited in Bauman 1998: 217).

Like Armstrong, Stokoe & Wilcox (1995), B. Rimes (1983) points out that movement is not only essential for understanding our world and giving it meaning, it is also essential for expressing these meanings. Not only do we use movement to communicate, '...the intrapersonal process of articulating these meanings is aided by gesticulation.' (Winter 1992: 153). The same phenomenon of spontaneous gestures accompanying speech also exists in sign languages, by the way, serving the same cognitive functions (Liddell, Metzger 1998).

David McNeill's extensive and cross-cultural analysis demonstrates how gestures not only complement speech in its linear, sequential form, but also display imaginative (cognitive) schemata of a multi-dimensional, spatial nature, which are otherwise impossible to convey in spoken language. For example, specific areas or entities in space might be established for reference or relational comparisons: 'on the one hand, and on the other,' so that '...abstract ideas have a physical locus' (McNeill 1992:18).

While the above-mentioned research reveals a tendency or need for the movement of thinking to be accompanied by (or indeed in a gestalt with) movement of the body, the kind of bodily movement examined is limited to gesture. Like postural poses, isolated gestures have proven to be transitory in nature and potentially culturally specific.

While developing the grounded theory that underpins MPA, Warren Lamb discovered important distinctions to be made between gestures, postures and what he dubbed 'Posture-Gesture Mergers' or 'PGMs'. While isolated gestures and certain postures could potentially be controlled or even faked, PGMs could not. These '...unselfconscious moments of postural adjustment, when a fleeting congruence of posture and gesture occur' reveal the 'essence of a person', at least in terms of preferences in decision-making (Moore 2005: 39).

While gestures can vary from context to context and from culture to culture, the relative proportion of an individual's PGMs remains constant over time – indeed throughout adult life (as far as the MPAs over the last 50 years have demonstrated). As mentioned before, MPA-Profiles have been made of over 30,000 individuals in over 30 countries, and individuals vary as much in one culture as across cultures. In other words, each individual MPA-Profile is a unique composite of the same universal factors, relating to basic human functioning (expressing effort and shaping in three dimensions).

For this reason, MPA focuses only on PGMs or 'Integrated Movement'.

Serious analysis of an individual's integrated patterns of movement requires not only the identification and categorisation of PGMs, it also requires a statistically sound number of repeated observations within one interview. The usual period of time for an MPA interview is therefore two hours. We all do a little of everything, so it takes time to distinguish what we do most from what we do least.

While brief observations or those of mere gesture or posture may have some cultural or semiotic significance, they give no basis for serious analysis of enduring, authentic characteristics of an individual's decision-making process.

Warren Lamb's unique contributions (and notably, the identification of 'Posture-Gesture Mergers') are unprecedented in the field of nonverbal behaviour and have had – and continue to have – tremendous success in management consulting for over a half a century.

References

Armstrong, Stokoe, and Wilcox (1995). *Gesture and the Nature of Language.* Cambridge: Cambridge University Press.

Bauman, H.-D. (1998). *American Sign Language As a Medium For Poetry: A Comparative Poetics of Sign, Speech and Writing in Twentieth-Century American Poetry.* Ph.D. dissertation, Binghamton University, State University of New York.

Brandt, P. Aa. (1998). 'Domains and the Grounding of Meaning.' Paper presented at the AELCO, First Congress of the Spanish Cognitive Linguistics Association, Alicante; published by (ed.) R. Dirven: LAUD, Linguistic Agency, Series A: General & Theoretical Papers, no. 464, University-G Essen.

Davies, Eden (2001). *Beyond Dance: Laban's Legacy of Movement Analysis.* London: Brechin Books.

Farnell, B. (1999). Moving Bodies, Acting Selves. *Annual Revue of Anthropology.* 28: 341-73.

Farnell, B. (1996). Metaphors We Move By. *Visual Anthropology, Vol. 8, pp. 311-335.*

Johnson, M. (1987). *The Body in the Mind: The Bodily Basis of Meaning, Imagination, and Reason.* Chicago: University of Chicago Press.

Laban, R. and Lawrence, F. C. (July 31, 1943). 'The Rhythm of the Office Worker' NRCD Laban Archive, ref. no. E(L)/66/13.

Lakoff, G. and Johnson, M. (1999). *Philosophy in the Flesh.* Chicago: University of Chicago Press.

Lamb, Warren and Elizabeth Watson (1979). *Body Code: The Meaning in Movement.* London: Routledge.

Lamb, Warren (1965). *Posture and Gesture*. London: Gerald Duckworth & Co. Ltd.

Liddell, S. K. and M. Metzger (1998). Gesture in Sign Language Discourse. *Journal of Pragmatics* 30: 657-697.

McNeill, D. (1992). *Hand and Mind: What Gestures Reveal About Thought*. Chicago and London: University of Chicago Press.

Merleau-Ponty, M. ([1962] 1998). *Phenomenology of Perception*. London: Routledge.

Mitchell, W. J. T. (1990). Against Comparison: Teaching Literature and the Visual Arts. In J. P. Barricelli, G. Gibaldi, and E. Lauder (eds.) *Teaching Literature and Other Arts*. New York: MLA of America.

Moore, Carol-Lynne (2005). *Movement and Making Decisions: The Body-Mind Connection in the Workplace*. New York: Rosen Publishing Group.

Philippot, P., R. S. Feldman, and E. J. Coats (eds.) (1999). *The Social Context of Nonverbal Behavior*. Cambridge: Cambridge University Press.

Talmy, L. (1988). Force Dynamics in Language and Cognition. *Cognitive Science, 2*.

Turner, M. and G. Fauconnier (1995). Conceptual Integration and Formal Expression. In M. Johnson (ed.) *Journal of Metaphor and Symbolic Activity*, vol. 10, no. 3.

Winter, Deborah Du Nann (1992). Body Movement and Cognitive Style: Validation of Action Profiling. In S. Loman (ed.) *The Body-Mind Connection in Human Movement Analysis*. Keene, NH: Antioch New England Gratuate School.

Winter, Deborah Du Nann, Carla Widell, Gail Truitt and Jane George-Falvy (1989). Empirical Studies of Posture-Gesture Mergers. *Journal of Nonverbal Behavior, 13* (4).

The education of young children in dance and creative movement: dance-pedagogics, how to recognise and practise it

Gisela Peters Rohse

Let me start with a German phrase:

Wachsen will ich, um jeden Preis!
About learning and teaching, growing and developing

One should accept and honour the life of a child, as being as important as one's own. Perhaps then another kind of school would arise, a school without exams and without competition that would not shun life but would constantly stride towards it. This is the only kind of school that would not hinder but help and would not nip personalities in the bud but give everyone the opportunity to achieve their deepest ambitions. As the poet Rainer Maria Rilke (1875-1926) attested, a teacher must aim to develop many different people from the starting point with which he was entrusted. It is better if he errs and divides someone into two conflicting personalities, rather than following the traditional path of forming all his students into one kind of being. That is what I aspire to, in our special field of teaching dance to young children.

But let me nevertheless outline how in my view the education of teachers specialising in creative children's dance and alternatively training for professional practice should be done. Discussion of each of these two fields could take more than just one paper, but I propose to clarify different points of view, to point out absolute necessities, to discover weak points and to search for more and better ways.

Whenever I have to put down in a written form what I have been occupied with for more than forty years I notice how much I changed in the course of time, how much my mentality and my opinion, my views changed and my standards, in reference to myself as well as my student teachers. Those moments demonstrate that not only is dance a permanently changing art but the pedagogics of dance are constantly changing too. These changes could be understood as a continuous development, an evolution. That does not mean that the old values should be thrown out, but it means that these values nowadays occupy another place. We have to realise this in order to find our own place in the abundance of traditions, the well-established experiences as well as innovations.

In order to demonstrate my method in creative children's dance I would like to invite you all to go back with me to the year 1944 to a little village in the north of Germany where I had the first day of my thirteen years of learning at school. Fitted out with a big old slate and slate-pencil I was eager to learn. Our teacher asked us to sing well-known children's songs and at the same time draw with the pencil over the lines of our slate. Each song had another and different 'writing-script': we went up and down in zigzag, made two loops down and two loops up, bows and curves, wavy lines – full of eagerness we sang and drew – and I had the happy feeling to be writing. I did it, I could do it, I knew how to write! It was very easy afterwards to add real letters and orthography. Not for a single hour did this teacher let us feel our incapacity and lack of knowledge. Because of the singing we were relaxed and our hands drew the writing bows in a rhythmical way. Very much later I realised that on this day our most elementary feelings had been touched, that we put together singing (breathing), rhythm and movement (albeit in the hand) in order to approach an unknown field.

What else does a child do with respect to its fields of experience? And this is the starting of my method of teaching dance to young children: through the interaction of rhythm, speech, self-made noise and movement I teach them to explore their body, to become acquainted with it and to occupy themselves with it. By this way the child has the feeling: 'I know how to dance' already after the first lesson.

Starting with its birth the child is permanently learning and discovering. It discovers its surroundings, its own body and languages (the language of the parents and the language of the body). All these discoveries are experienced through the body movement and sensuality. In Germany we have the same word for understanding by learning and for touching with hands: begreifen (in English to grasp/ in both senses). That suggests that there must be a connection between body-learning and cognitive learning.

Children develop their verbal language, testing it, playing with it and thus accruing later language repertory. With this repertory of sounds of words, bits of words and whole words children associate an event, a feeling, a vision or an idea – and after having conquered a word in that way, children start to improvise with it. I base my method of physical dance-education and early instruction for children on the method of the sensual acquisition of their native language. In this way the child will get to know its body in a sensual way and start to improvise with it in order to reach in the course of time a conscious control of its body.

By considering the free and unhindered expansion of the children's soul as the first responsibility in my work with children, I want to work from the very beginning against any restriction of movement. Children's dance, in which preverbal mental processes and feelings are expressed, later gains its special meaning and shape. Children who are impeded in their development through the incapacity of their parents or unfavourable circumstances in their environment often show us frightening deficits in their physical constitution and movements that also have effects on their mental condition. Children's dance in this way should correspond with the natural wish of the child to move, because the movement is the very first and the most intensive medium of the child's expression and will.

By experiencing this expressive medium from and by themselves children get into contact and relation to space and their environment. The mimic and spatial play gives rise to spontaneous action, play-like exercising and trying out and the final discovery by the child of its own body-instrument through self-guided discoveries of the rules of dance. In the sense of Maria Montessori's[1] principle 'help me to do it by myself' I offer the instructions to children in order to help them to conquer their bodies by themselves in all the possibilities, to handle their bodies in space, in time and in a group knowingly and purposefully, to use their bodies in a self-creative way and to transfer these self-creative experiences into other fields. The more children proceed in the self-exploration of their bodies the more they will have the desire to increase and improve their technical abilities. Out of this greater knowledge the wish arises in them to reach new fields and possibilities. This steady wish, this desire, this impulse of the child will be very sensorily orientated, something I try never to forget during a dancing lesson. Only later understanding, reason and the abstraction of these events and occurrences will be possible. Nowhere is the reciprocal effect of the psychical and the physical conditions as obvious as in the dancing class with children; they show us differently motivated movements and simultaneously changing emotional states.

A great deal of my teaching results from observing how the children present themselves in their natural behaviour of movement. The very important aims for them are to become stronger, taller and faster and the most important is to do all newly explored things totally by themselves. If educational projects or impediments in the natural environment did not change or limit their elementary expression and influence the children's behaviour, we could almost read in observing them the schedule for the methods and didactics of how to teach them. The child normally uses its body in a total way; if their body is intact, it will move totally. For us teachers this means that one of the teaching aims has to be the re-finding of the total-movement during improvisation in order to preserve this natural ability. In an ideal world that would mean harmony.

Children's play, which is equivalent to the daily work of the adults, from time to time brings forth patterns of movement which make them forget their original motivations so that after a while they only enjoy the delight of movement: hopping games, rocking of the body, swinging with arms or legs, spinning around, circulating, turning around. This phenomenon is equivalent to the former work dances in the adult world, in which the original movements of work were translated into pure dance, rhythm and sometimes mime. Only when children understand, in childlike logic, the reason for repetition, they will do the movements once more and repeat them more and more often until totally exhausted. We can observe this in children's games. Who does not know a child's happy cry: once more please! We have to know this 'logic' and also this desire for the repeating impulse in order to use it during body-shaping and technical exercises.

In summary this means that we have to know about, to recognise and to make use of the child's natural motivation to move freely and intensely. As teacher's our knowledge about the technical details of dance (to whatever style it may lead one day: ballet, modern, jazz, hiphop or folkdance) and about psychological behaviour must supplement this in order to help the child in its development. The instructions for children of about five to seven years are primarily a big adventure, which means that they follow a very lively lesson, which stimulates their fantasy, which satisfies their instinct to play (work) and which stands in relation to their capabilities. But, conducted by their teacher and almost unnoticed by themselves, they will also do a lot of real work. Beside a light training (we call it Körperbildung) of the whole body, in accordance with their anatomical abilities, they will do exercises, fine-motor skills, studies related to space, they will, consciously at times, move in one of all three dimensions and learn from the very beginning the qualities of movement. It is obvious that at this young age the child is not aware of all the aims which the lessons have, because for the child the happiness and delight in dance-movement, the joy of being and moving in a group and the jubilation of and with their body come first.

But after a while children will also discover their progress in dance technique, that means the ability to influence their motoric movement, and will also enjoy this. If the lesson has the character of various newly-motivated actions, just like many movement-games, the child will normally also accept the uncomfortable exercises for its body in an intensive manner, because these exercises are a continuation of the whole 'story' of the lesson. For example: in order to sensitise as well as to train the feet, these feet (we are sitting at the floor, the legs stretched out in front of us) can in the first lesson be two puppets in a puppet show who are making nonsense, who are bending and turning, leaning far out over the parapet and hiding under a hedge; in the following lesson these feet are possibly slippery fishes, who slip out of the water, who are fighting in a fisherman's net and can slip away; and in another lesson two moles are coming out from the ground, they feel so cold and decide to go back, but they are curious and come once more ... and so on; or two impudent mice are teasing the hungry cat, but of course! they are quick enough to flit away. Of course the children want to do it again and again, because they (or rather their feet) are the winners. And here we have one of the most important 'tricks': if an exercise or an expressive movement contains the wish of repetition, we can really work with our pupils.

While children carry out these training-forms, sometimes also done in qualitatively orientated forms, and observe them, they see – in the way I described for the feet – in miniature what afterwards has to be done in the big way, in the whole-body improvisation. I call this the microcosm of the body, from where – having watched and felt – children will later take their knowledge into the macrocosm, their whole body. In these small exercises children perceive and realise what it feels like to be fast or slow, big or small, to be full of tension or relaxed. This body-feeling will be adapted to the total movement of the body.

Normally, the fragments of free movement and improvisation join with technique during a lesson to build a big whole. They are ordered in a way, that the whole body can be reached in its specific functions thus securing, over a period of about two years or more, that the children learn more and more to discover and to conquer their bodies; and if we give to the child through creative dance teaching the competencies for exploring, acting and conflict-solving, they are eager to discover and improve the body but also the space and all possibilities for quality filled movements.

Each lesson has a special aim for the last part, which builds the main focus. The whole lesson with its division into

1. tuning the communal mood = Einstimmung
2. movement technique   = Bewegungstechnik
3. movement development   = Bewegungsentwicklung
4. creation of movement   = Bewegungsgestaltung

will always lead to the big event at the end. The main focus can deal with: 'changes of tempo' (children normally want to be faster; they will bear also the very slow movements because they know it will return to 'quicker time'; 'expansion and confinement'('largeness and closeness') – this corresponds also to the elementary wishes of children: at first they want to become taller, but they love to hide in little holes); 'tension and relaxation' (they love this feeling of being full of force and they remember how one feels with a fever or fatigue), and there are various more main focuses.

In order to demonstrate how a simple 'change of dress' can keep the child's motivation alive – although the movement remains the same – let me use the example of the next focus, which is 'staccato – legato': one day it is popcorn which drops in a bucket filled with water, another day it can be salad-oil which flows around the fresh and crunchy lettuce leaves. Or in another lesson a ball on the Christmas tree will break into a thousand pieces because it looked with too much vanity into the candle-light... In these cases it is not important that the children repeat certain movements, but it is important that they create from their own body-feeling and body-knowledge movements and qualities relating to the theme – and this is absolutely possible at this age in the dualism of consciousness and sensuality. Normally children will reach the total movement in dancing these inspirations because they are prepared and so they involve the whole body. This is possible because the children have received and now possess the competence to decide on their own what to do and to find their very own way of how to dance the theme.

I see it as one of my responsibilities to make those pupils who are reserved lose their inhibitions and to lead the ('brimming over with foam') exuberant-ones from a movement which is guided by their own will into a self-moderated movement. In each case I try to make sure that during the improvisation everyone reaches his or her very own event and feeling of success through this self-creative action – even if the child's treatment of a theme runs against my opinion or if I can only recognise it very obscurely.

The curriculum of the (as we call it in Germany) pre-school dance-education has to be as complex as possible. Through the total movement in improvisation the quality of movement and the dynamics have to be developed; through the different forms of exercises the knowledge of the body, and also the trained body has to be achieved, inside the group social contacts, the sensibility for a group and the readiness for partnership with another child have to be achieved as well as self-esteem, and last but not least the self-confidence: everyone can speak and comment through his movement!

We all know how strong, vital and important rhythm can be and how our breathing is connected to it. It is therefore easy to imagine how much rhythm, spoken words or rhythmical breath can inspire a movement. That's why my credo is: the children's dance is not limited to a single field, the children's dance includes all other forms of art and, most importantly, the whole individual human being! That's why I think that dance for children is such an important and essential part of children's development, because nowhere else can the ideal in the equal development of body, soul and spirit be achieved in such an extensive way through feeling, developing, improving and discovering. Nowadays the sound relation of body and mind is increasingly obstructed, we can say blocked by the change of environment and circumstances. With the progressing industrial technologies and high tech, human beings are progressively going away from their bodies. The less we use our bodies the less we are able to understand our body-signals or to send them out. In my lessons I want to teach and to help the children to re-understand their body-signs. If the children's self-knowledge later leads also into a self-responsibility for the body, then the dance-education has achieved a very important goal. This education is not only cultural or artistic teaching, but, beside all the other aspects, it also gives human beings back their very own instrument, their own body – and that can be of inestimable worth on the way to humanity.

1. Maria Montessori, an Italian doctor and pedagogue, 1870-1952).

Developing choreological maps of the processes of creating multimedia works of dance theatre referring to *William Forsythe's* The Loss of Small Detail

An AHRC sponsored research project

Valerie Preston-Dunlop

The maps in this project are available for study as a web file at Trinity Laban Library, with the archive material associated with it.

The background

As research director of this project I was already familiar with the work of Forsythe since our first meeting in 1989, not only from performances but by observing workshops given by him at the studios of Frankfurt Opera and at LABAN. In 2006 I went across to Dresden where Forsythe was remounting *The Loss of Small Detail* to open the season. I saw the company at work, talked to them and to the technical staff on their roles in the creation and performance.

Resources

The Forsythe Foundation had donated the archive materials on *Loss* to LABAN in 2005. These consisted of unique paper and moving image materials on the making of the work from its first version in 1987 to a performance of the third version in 2002. This archive offered a privileged insight and documentary evidence into Forsythe's working methods, which led to the decision to undertake the creation of a way of documenting the making process. I was already aware that Forsythe was interested in finding ways to capture the process adequately as an aid to remounting his own work.

From studying the moving image footage of rehearsals it became clear that they did not reveal sufficient evidence on how the dancers were working. To fill the gap Forsythe dancer Ana Catalina Roman came to LABAN, to work with professional dancers. Her sessions on Forsythe's methods for generating and modulating the movement for *Loss* were filmed and this footage became an additional archival resource for the project.

Articles were located and studied and added to the archive. Thom Willems visited LABAN and his discussions on 'the sonic environment' were recorded and used.

Background to choreological perspectives

Choreological perspectives provide methodologies for practical dance scholarship (see Preston-Dunlop and Sanchez-Colberg)[1]. Briefly, they deal with the complex mix of *process and product* that a work of performance contains, the *concepts* embodied in it, the transformative and symbiotic *procedures* used to connect concept with media, the particular *nexus of the strands of the media* used by an artist for each work, the collaborative *ways of working* as a creative team, the *vocabularies* of movement and sound chosen, the artists' expectation and manipulation of the *audience's engagement* with the work, the mix of *phenomenal and semiotic* content created and received. The strength of these methods is that they start from the viewpoint of the makers, looking at what is going on from the inside. For investigating creative procedures these methods are ideal as such a task cannot be achieved by extrinsic analysis.

Why mapping software?

The difficulties of documenting performance on paper are well known. You can write about performance but you cannot show it or quote its visual or oral content. Film alone is problematic as it provides images of a product and not of the procedures that gave rise to the image. In order to get a fresh insight into possibilities I set up a brainstorming event between the Forsythe Foundation, specialists from LABAN and the Institute of Digital Art and Technology of Plymouth University, the leading research unit on digital technology. After discussion standard mapping software was selected as the way forward.

The criteria for the mapping process focused on the need for the output to be in a format that would be accessible to the greatest number of users. It was for this reason that a specialist design company[2] was employed to transfer the multi-media materials into an HTML universal format. The use of HTML allows for a normal web browser to be utilised as the key interface and any material becomes accessible to a world wide audience, over the internet, or locally in say a library environment.

Copyright issues

Rights in performing arts are complex and had to be sorted out before work could begin. It was already known that films of performances and rehearsals of Ballett Frankfurt were not available for public showing or for viewing via the internet. What could be achieved was an overarching agreement from Forsythe that we could proceed in the manner we intended. We also had to set up a study facility for the finished maps that did not infringe the company's rights. This has been done by creating a web file on the internal web of TRINITY/LABAN available to students, faculty and visitors.

Making the maps

The mapping is achieved by constructing a graphic that links one concept to another by means of 'blobs' and arrows. Selecting data in the form of quotations and film clips forms a significant part of the mapping process. The original film clips were extracted and converted to Adobe Flash files. At no time does the mapmaker hazard a guess or have an opinion. The responsibility lies in taking clusters of data from the archival resources, stating the ideas contained in a logical and easy to read form in the 'blobs', and identifying images for precise illustrations of the ideas.

The order of the map making was dictated by the documentation in the archive. Ultimately twenty eight maps were clustered under four topics Concepts, Movement, Characters, and Sound/Space. While readers can start anywhere I started with David Levin's article on the making of *Loss* in 1986[3]. At the time Levin was acting as dramaturg to Forsythe, along with Patrick Primovasi and this article discussed essential concepts that underlie *Loss*. The article shows the complexity of Forsythe's thinking but also his playful element. The sheer fun in translating a hyperbolic text in German romantic prose into New York's wacky vernacular could not be missed. It became clear that the researcher should stay away from looking for how art embodies concept when Forsythe's process is far more lateral and idiosyncratic.

The tripartite perspective

How, for Forsythe, making, performing and appreciating interact, the first two from the inside, the third from the outside, is a prime choreological issue. Map 1 investigated what he and the company expect from one another in the creation, rehearsing and mounting of a new work. The map shows that the roles overlap copiously but only up to a certain point in time, then 'Bill' takes control.

Process and product works

Forsythe does not regard 'the work' as complete and final in its premiere. He relishes the ephemeral nature of dance; it disappears at the moment of living. Forsythe makes performances not a repeatable product and is particularly interested in the procedures that he devises to create the performance. The second version of *Loss* in 1991 had apparently different movement, costumes, sound, texts than the 1987 first version. It was nevertheless *Loss*. *Loss* for him has a chronology from version 1 to 2 to 3 with differences of outer form but each made of the same stuff by the similar procedures that are specifically *Loss* procedures. To capture that perspective I

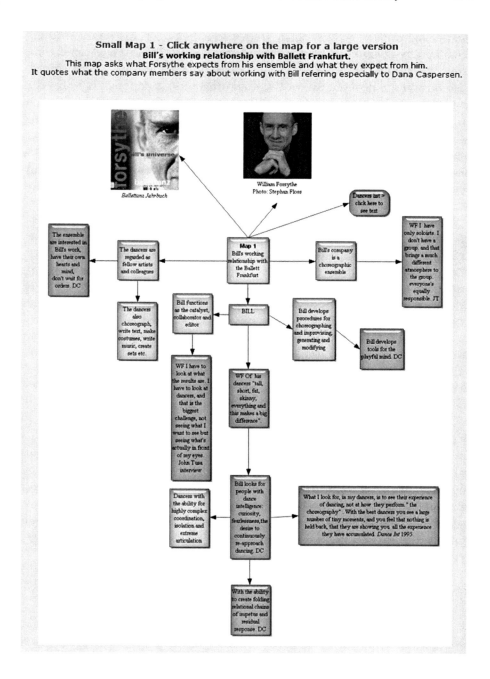

Small Map 1 - Click anywhere on the map for a large version
Bill's working relationship with Ballett Frankfurt.
This map asks what Forsythe expects from his ensemble and what they expect from him.
It quotes what the company members say about working with Bill referring especially to Dana Caspersen.

made Map16 which contexts the procedures of *Loss* version 1, 2, 3 in the other dance theatre works Forsythe made between 1 and 3.

Idea, procedures and media

Choreological perspectives look at these three areas as being interconnected simply or in a complex way. The strong idea coming into *Loss* is translation, from one text to another, from one movement to another, from text to scenography, and so on. But in *Loss* the translation is doubled. Bill likes the phrase 'it will have been', not it will be or it has been but it will have been, a two stage process. How is dance a language he asks himself, can linguistic concerns explain the complexities of what dance represents? This is the basic idea of *Loss*. It is not a narrative idea or style idea or medium idea but a procedural idea. There will be symbolic elements that suggest meaning but they are not the stuff of the work in the way translation is. Maps 3-6 unravel these issues.

Further concepts are shown in maps 10-12, some common to Bill's work as a whole, such as structuring temporality, some peculiar to *Loss* such as collapse, playing with positive and negative, 'walking through a museum'. These ideas are not given to the audience in programme notes, some are just suggested in the thought provoking title and contained in the overhead brief and occasional Supertitles (Map 27) but the dancers know them and work with them.

Binocular vision

Choreological method looks at 'binocular vision', a term from theatre studies that discusses the need for spectators to engage with a work of dance theatre on two concurrent levels, phenomenological and semiotic.

With an inside perspective the researcher is asking how is Bill taking account of the binocular vision? Does he work on phenomenon? Does he provide semiological clues? Clues for the dancers or clues for the spectators? Bill talks about it straightforwardly. For him dance expresses itself, nothing more, and the context he provides throws up signs that may lead an attentive spectator to structure their own meaning. Turning dance from familiar movement to an unfamiliar phenomenon is what Bill's method does. Getting the balance and shifting the emphasis, layering it, from phenomenon to sign is the artistry that is traced in Map 21.

The nexus of the strands of the dance theatre medium

The basic choreological concept of the medium is the mix of performers, their movement, the sound, the space they engage with. The nexus between them provides a kind of spider's web map of ways of working that constitute the style of the artist or of one work.

For Forsythe and the ensemble some performers both dance and speak (Map 17), others only speak, others only dance. His movement material is ballet-derived (Maps 7& 8) but with radical translations and transformations

(Maps 14,15). The sound score written by Thom Willems integrates the texts spoken, whispered, argued, distorted (maps 18,19 & 22). The space is lit by Forsythe himself, the stage is covered with snow falls, films appear briefly, strobe lighting flashes with thunderclaps and blackouts. (Map 23). The space is filled with props, tables, stools, microphones, projectors, skulls, a snow shovel (Map 24). The dancers move the props around, effect scene changes. They turn stools into walls for projecting a film. As they do it they combine phenomenon with sign, you understand what they are doing and you appreciate the way they do it for itself, moving with fully rehearsed, timed and choreutically organised action.

So far as the resources reveal, these maps look at the creative time line behind the action in all these areas, connecting references with embodiment, concept with transformational procedure.

The work

How does Bill put in place a new work? Map 2 looks at the schedule he has for making, what comes first, what last. Forsythe does not start to make the work until everything is in place as a resource, solos, trios, quintets of move-ment material to select from, concepts sorted out, texts written and rehearsed, all to be used or not, with lighting design in place, sound score there (not always but it was for *Loss*), films made, props sorted and in place. Then he starts in the last three weeks to structure the work as a work, pulling down what he needs from the assembled resources. Map 2 gives an overall look at this schedule. Subsequent maps look at each of those parts in detail. Map 9 looks at how he brings the company along with him into the world of the new work and its innovative procedures, preparing them for what he requires from them. He draws sketches and asks the dancers to write cap-tions to them in quite specific lateral and double-translation ways, helping them into the double-removed-from-the-mundane world of *Loss*. Then he generates movement for the dancers to double-translate (Maps 14 & 15).

Movement heritage

Where does Bill's movement come from? What are his core combinations made of? Every choreographer starts with a heritage through their training and early company work. For Bill that is ballet, through his training and his early career with the Joffrey company. So why doesn't *Loss* contain ballet steps? In map 7 Bill speaks about his attitude to ballet, his love for it and his moving on into a new form of ballet. He had to find a new way of looking at ballet beyond the ways of artists like Balanchine and he found it through Laban. Bill read Laban's book on movement as living architecture, *Choreutics*, and Map 8 details what his response was and how it enabled him to make his now well known CDRom *Improvisation Technologies*, with illustrations from *Loss*. Moving image clips of the company in rehearsal show how Bill can start with a ballet combination and, applying modalities to it, come up with material that no spectator would believe was ballet-based.

The reality of applying modalities

Modalities are Bill's particular trademark, distinct ones for different works. Here in Maps 14 and 15, Ana Catalina Roman is seen working with professional dancers at LABAN, teaching them the combination Bill taught her for 1987 and giving them the *Loss* modalities. We see them working on it and see examples of the solos and trios that they came up with.

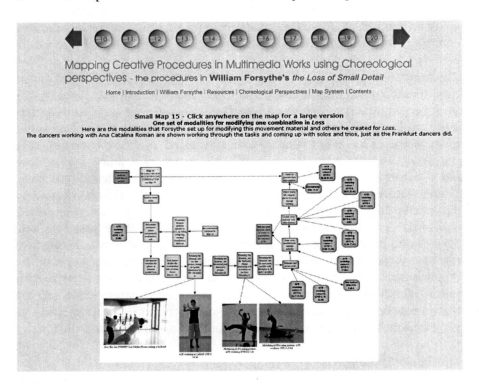

These two maps show crucial issues for Bill and for *Loss* and for archiving performance procedures. While analysis and documentation of a product can only be done with footage of the actual event, documenting procedures requires another kind of archive, taken in the studio during rehearsals or, as here, created afterwards. This may have significance for how professional archive holdings of performance works curate their materials and how working artists prepare their own archives of their working processes. The 1987 combination given to Ana Catalina, never appeared in the performance but the modulated material did and is still there in the 2002 and 1996 performances. In one performance she is seen dancing it while sitting on a stool and the same duo material she made is passed on to another dancer for the 1996 performance. The economy of Bill's method is superb as shown in Map15. One combination produces an astounding array of fresh material which is nevertheless coherent, for the dynamics set for the piece with which the original is made was always maintained.

Speakers

Map 17 details the characters in the work. The two men's characters are a positive and negative of each other, both nude and spotted from head to foot, one black on white, the other white on black. The origin of this is clearly the snow, a translation of snow to costume and translation again from white on black to black on white. One of the films is a short loop of a spotted Dalmatian dog. Here Bill is translating across media.

The female characters are subtly differentiated while the male characters are individual. The Primitive Person is silent and simple in his walking and running. The Dalmatian man by contrast is raucous with virtuosic distorted speech and wild gestures. They follow through the procedure of negative/positive across what they do and how they speak as well as how they look.

Texts and their sources

Text is an integral part of *Loss* and it is a mixture of text written and modified by Bill and Levin, and other text taken from his named sources, straight with no modification. The translation of hyperbole to vernacular is direct in *Loss* 1986 but by version 3 the change of style is from one whole piece of text to another whole piece. The opening is spoken with serenity at a table as of one giving a lecture. She speaks of 'the sublime' and of a 'ludicrous dust' that will settle on it. She is anticipating 'what will have been' as the snow which is already there will come again and settle on what was. Bill has marked in a Roussel text a reference to 'a table and some one sitting behind it'. One cannot tell whether the marked source material is indeed the inspiration for some incident but there are enough instances where individual moments appear to have had a starting point in marked texts. Hoisting the skulls on to the legs of an upturned stool, a foot writing on a parchment, thunder, over-cast sky, primitive communities in Africa, kissing, these are moments that pepper *Loss* with inexplicable phenomena all adding to the sense of amorphous loss.

Space, lighting, props, films and supertitles

Maps 23, 24, 25, 27 show the ideas and the means that Bill uses to provide the visual context for the dancing. The choreological theory of the significance of the nexus of the strands of the medium is brought into prominence in these maps. The lighting, designed by Bill and experimental in the way he diffuses the light to avoid shadows, adds to the otherworldliness of *Loss*. Excerpts from his discussions with lighting designer Jennifer Tipton are included. The film loop *Hund im Schnee* of the Dalmatian dog and snow links across to the costumes of the two male characters and to the projections of sparkling snow on a duo and the falling snow in a down spot on The Primitive Person. The second film is deliberately difficult to decipher. It appears in the storm, its erotic and corporeal content, its colours and sharp editing adding to the mayhem of sound and sight. The supertitles are unusual for dance theatre, but as Bill says the work was presented in an opera house where they are a familiar device. They address an unspoken but anticipated query: what does *Loss* mean, by offering short, occasional sentences, some descriptive of events, some enigmatic. How the sentences for the 1987 supertitles came into being is documented. It is the dancers who act as stage hands but, as one states, they are both carrying, positioning, switching on and off while simultaneously being an art object. Map 20 looks at what it takes to function as a creator/performer in a work such as *Loss*. Performing is as multilayered as the work itself.

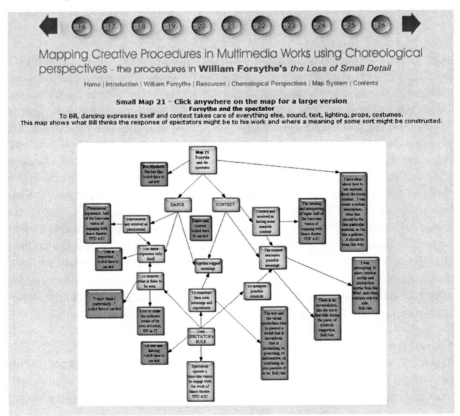

Communication and transaction

The choreological methodology includes issues of communication and transaction between artists and spectators. The injunctive function or way in which the artist gets a response of some sort from the spectator is shown to be one of Bill's strengths. He says little about it but the texts he uses have startling or enigmatic or serene content with potential effect through the way they are presented. The question and answer section is quite brutally sexual. The trio interrupting each other in casual chatter and lack of understanding conjure quite other responses. The German speaker declaims quietly and calmly while partially hidden behind a rectangular form. She is saying a ridiculously complex description of the opening of the curtain at the beginning of the show, so complex that the 'detail' has 'lost' the meaning. She immediately stands up and dances a solo of immense quality, stops and observes the Dalmatian man as he gesticulates and vocalises wildly while balancing on a stool. This is all highly injunctive theatre.

Bill does not speak of the metalinguistic function, or the phatic or the performative, so these terms do not appear in the maps, but the way he creates his pieces shows beyond doubt that he is in total control of the communicative aspects of his work, and Guiraud's theory helped me as mapmaker to know what to look out for.

Conclusion

The project shows that map-making of this sort helps to reveal and display the underlying layers of the making of complex works of theatre. A clearly focused methodology was essential and the choreological methodology was not only adequate to the task but was sufficiently flexible to accommodate the innovations offered by William Forsythe. Adequate archival resources were essential to give access to the past and they had to be archives of the practitioners and events active in the making process. Forsythe and his individual dancers ensured that film footage of rehearsals was made, for very practical use in remounting the piece.

The map-makers of process will always have to be practical scholars and a good knowledge of choreological method will help them to navigate through the archival data.

Could this method be used for other works and other artists? There is every reason to believe that it could. It would have to include the making or collecting of adequate archive materials as part of the project. It could encourage artists to be deliberate in making adequate archives as they undertake their creative work

Has it produced worthwhile information? While most of the information was there in some form, it was largely hidden. Teasing it out and organising it through a comprehensive method does give the reader access to a leading artist's way of working in an accessible and vivid form. The unique process undertaken at LABAN in the Roman workshops, in preparation for the project, has produced remarkable material and pioneered a new way of archiving procedures.

Because there are 29 separate maps, clearly named and introduced, readers can navigate their own routes through the maps. In this way the project can attract readers from several disciplines, scenographers, dramaturgs, text writers, choreographers.

Documents in the Loss Archive at LABAN or in the LABAN Library that are referred to in the maps by initials

DL   Levin, David J. (1992) 'Moving to Language: Ballet and/as Text in *The Loss of Small Detail*.' Bauschinger, Sigrid and Cocalis, Susan L. eds. *Vom Wort zum Bild: des neue Theatre in Deutschland und den USA.*

RS   Sulcas, Roslyn in conversation with William Forsythe. (1995) 'Kinetic Isometries'. *Dance International.* Summer pp. 4 – 9.

RS2   Sulcas, Roslyn. 'How William Forsythe has both subverted and enlarged....'. *Ballettanz Jahrbuch.* 2003-2004.

DC 2   RS3 in Roslyn Sulcas. (2000) Watching from Paris. *Choreography and Dance 5(3).*

OJ   Odenthal, Johannes. (1994) 'A conversation with William Forsythe.' *Ballett International* 2/94 pp 33 – 36.

PB   Boenisch, Peter M. (2007) 'Decreation Inc.: William Forsythe's Equations of "Bodies before the Name"'. *Contemporary Theatre Review.* Vol 17 (1) pp 15 – 27.

DC   Caspersen, Dana. (2004) 'The company at work'. *Forsythe: Bill's Universe.* Ballettanz Das Jahrbuch.

JB   Forsythe, William and Caspersen, Dana. (1998) 'Ballett Frankfurt 6/3/98'. Burrows, Jonathan ed. *Conversations with Choreographers.* Royal Festival Hall.

YM   Yukio Mishima. (1969) *Runaway Horses.* Penguin Books.

RR   Roussel, R. *Impressions of Africa* (fragments).

SD   Driver, Senta (ed). (2000) *William Forsythe.* Choreography and Dance, Vol 5 part 3.

JB   Burrows, Jonathan (1998) William Forsythe and Dana Caspersen. *Conversations with Choreographers.*

JT   BBC Radio 3. (2004) *Transcript of the John Tusa Interview with William Forsythe.*

PB & HG Baudoin, Patricia and Gilpin, Heidi. (1987) *Proliferation and Perfect Disorder.*

RL   Laban, Rudolf. (1966) *Choreutics*. MacDonald & Evans.

DC3   Caspersen, Dana. The Body is Thinking in G. Siegmund. *William Forsythe Denken in Bewegung.*

PL   Prue Lang. Thinking, Motion, Language. In G. Siegmund *William Forsythe Denken in Bewegung.*

GS or DC4 in Gerald Siegmund. Interview with William Forsythe. *Dance in Europe 8/9.*

JT   Jennifer Tipton and WF. (2000) In *Choreography and Dance 5 (3).*

CS   Chris Salter. *Timbral Architectures.* (2008)

VP-D Valerie Preston-Dunlop and Ana Sanchez-Colberg. The binocular vision. *Dance and the Performative.* (2002)

1. Preston-Dunlop.V. & Sanchez-Colberg. A. 2002. *Dance and the Performative: a choreological perspective. Laban and beyond.* London: Verve Publishing.
2. IDM Ltd www.idm.org

Green Clowns 2008
Recreating Rudolf Laban's Die Grünen Clowns (1928)

Valerie Preston-Dunlop and Lesley-Anne Sayers

Die Grünen Clowns (1928) responds to dehumanising aspects of modernity following the first World War. Rooted in Expressionism and drawing on aspects of Dada, Rudolf Laban's radical and challenging approach to movement and dance-theatre involved improvisation with an emphasis on the corporeality of the dancers and their experience in the creative process. Re-created in 2008 as part of the Trinity Laban historical project, directed by Alison Curtis-Jones.[1] *Green Clowns 2008* was performed at the Laban International Conference by undergraduates and members of Transitions Dance Company alongside the launch of a documentary film[2] about the work's re-creation.

Valerie Preston-Dunlop, who originally re-sourced and re-created *Green Clowns* in the 1980s, explains the background to this work and Lesley-Anne Sayers reflects on her documentary about its re-creation.

Valerie:
Die Grünen Clowns was a suite for Laban's Kammertanzbuhne, his Chamber Dance Theatre, with a premiere at the 2nd Dancers Congress in Essen in June 1928. Of the original six scenes we include four in *Green Clowns 2008*. As for the premiere, the dancers wear simple green overalls, are masked with white skull caps to emphasise their anonymity. The opening scene *Maschine* (Machine) draws on the dreaded conveyor belt system, newly introduced into factories. The belt moved at a pace that demanded continuous speed from the workers, causing physical stress and anxiety. This scene is the only one with music, deliberately there to impose tempo and beat on the performers. The movement is designed to be uncomfortable so that the dancers may experience the workers' stress. The second scene *Krieg* (War) reminds the viewer of the horrors of the Great War, so fresh in the minds of all in the 1920s. The confrontation is improvised on a strictly organised structure, demanding intense concentration and group awareness plus belligerence, the dancers accompanying themselves with breath and vocal cries as the conflict rises. To achieve this scene while masked, barely able to see or breathe, is frankly virtuosic. Its climax resolves into a War Memorial tableau choreographed in a typical Laban spatial canon group form. In the *Procession of the Dying*, each dancer explores what it might feel like to be mortally wounded with the life

Green Clowns, 1928. Courtesy Laban Archive.

force ebbing away. The rehearsal director, for this performance Alison Curtis-Jones, develops and moulds their contribution as a choreutic/eukinetic canon, mainly impulsive rhythm and formed in the three spatial planes, the sound score emerging from their sighs. *Romance* is a duo posing the question: can/should people who have been killing each other fall in love? It is built on the relationship categories in Laban's notation system. The watching Clowns function as a choric commentary. *The Club of the Eccentric People* is the finale, where the dancers play with the oddities and scandals of the human race, with all manner of vocal contribution.

This is a re-creation not a reconstruction. It never was fixed as Laban enjoyed live improvisation. This poses an ironic question as on one and the same day he presented his new notation system to the assembled dance world in the morning and this un-notateable work in the evening.

Music had to be found. I drew on Adda Heynssen's piano works, her *Machine Dance* and improvisation on her *Pastorale* for the *Romance*, sometimes sung and at other performances played on a wind instrument.

The re-creation method is a sophisticated mix of studying archival resources on the work itself, good understanding of the culture of the period, the Weimar Republic, understanding where this work came in Laban's oevres and priorities, knowledge and skill in using his rehearsal and production techniques for contemporary performers. So much of this work was new for audiences in 1928, much of it is music-less; dancers speak and vocalise, behaviour is the movement material, rough, tough, rude, full of pathos. It is designed to elicit shifting attention from the spectator, from laughter and surprise to empathy. Laban was a consummate man of theatre at this period of his career and the re-creation team have to consider what that might mean for today's theatre practitioners.

Lesley-Anne:
The performance of *Green Clowns 2008* was a highlight of the Laban International Conference and it was the first time I had seen the work in performance since making a documentary about its development earlier in the year. It was also the first time I had seen another cast (a mix of BA students and Transitions 2008) dance this work. Knowing the work as well as I have come to know it – through making this documentary – it was fascinating to see a slightly different interpretation, a different nuance here and there, subtly different qualities; – the work had changed – lost something – gained something – as works invariably do – as casts and audiences and contexts change. When you know a work well – 'from the inside out' – as Valerie might say – what you can see and find in performance is of course not only enriched but also expanded. What we see in a performance after all, while it is of course the vital artistic output, is what Valerie terms the surface form' of a work, and a 'work' is a broader entity involving creative process and much more than is seen on stage.

Making a documentary about the re-creation of *Green Clowns* attracted me for several reasons. I wanted to try and record, document, capture – something of the creative process – that is otherwise unseen by the work's audiences; I wanted also to understand the processes involved – the sources – the methodologies. Making a documentary gave me access to this wider 'work'. So with limited funds but enough for one cameraman[3] I followed the re-creation of this remarkable work during a few intense weeks in February 2008. The annual historical project at Laban is a special time for our BA2 students; since joining the academic team at Laban in 2006 I have witnessed how this experience of re-creation richly involves the students in their dance heritage to an extent that is difficult to equal in the lecture theatre. One of the things that interests me about the potential of re-creation is how we access works in our dance heritage when there is no notated score, no living work in the repertoire, no video recording, and perhaps few visual or other records of its existence. All of this is the 'presence of absence' that amounts to the historical *Green Clowns*. Yet, when one begins to research a 'lost' work, so often what is there to be 'found' amounts to a lot more than 'absence'; there may be an absence of surface form, but rich resources in relation to the 'work' in a wider sense. Aspects of a work's original conception and developmental progress may have survived in forms that are accessible to study, interpretation and rediscovery. These might include a scenario, critical accounts, letters between the collaborators, sketches, designs, music, photographs, etc. and not least their relationship to the contexts, discourses and artistic outputs of the day. But I was continually reminded by Valerie not to think like an 'outside eye' and to engage with the creative process – for therein – she insisted – lies the 'work' – and the means to accessing the historical *Green Clowns*.

Valerie's methodology for the re-creation of Rudolf Laban's works is rooted in making creative use of his principles and working methods. She may not have very many sources relating to the original surface form of his *Green Clowns*, but she knows very well how he would have created it and the basis and nature of his 'language'. She uses therefore the principles that are in the notation as well as her knowledge of the work's original context. As such she has passed on to Ali (Alison Curtis-Jones) and a new generation, the means of re-creating this work afresh – and potentially for generations to come. Ali's version introduces variants of Valerie's original re-creations in the 1980s, worked out through improvisation with the dancers. Ali used Laban's effort and spatial principles enabling the students to become aware of and articulate their movement in relationship to space and dynamics, to choreutics and eukinetics. Laban's way of using groups in spatial canon for example, (as in the movement choirs) was used as a basis for the War Memorial section, and Ali describes finding the harmonic opposites in the movement to find the depth in the space. What Valerie has given us therefore, is not a reconstruction of a surface form, but the invaluable gift of a methodology to access the 'work' and realise it in many different variations. As such *Green Clowns* remains very true to its original conception as a living process work, formed afresh each time through the interaction of developing principles steeped in on-going research, sources relating to the original *Green Clowns*, and an individual cast of dancers.

What enables contemporary engagement with this work, however, is its avant-gardism – its politics and the attitude towards the body. Herein, it seems to me, is something fundamental to the original work that – whatever happens to the music or choreography – has to be at the heart of its re-creation. In keeping with Laban's working methods – as passed down through Valerie, the students worked through guided improvisation to find the movement in response to the ideas of the piece. This was an extraordinary experience for many of these dancers. As dance students they expect to study a variety of dance 'techniques' but of course there is no codified Laban technique as such – the movement has to be found from the dancer's interaction with the ideas of the work. The opportunity to engage with dance theatre – with socio-political and identity issues – relating to war, politics, love, mechanisation and loss of humanity, created an extraordinary and ex-

Green Clowns 2008. Photo: Peter Sayers.

citing sense of creative involvement for these students – and the movement gradually became their own, motivated from within.

Classes of all kinds and studio rehearsals were filmed... and the footage grew and grew. I subjected Valerie and Ali to lengthy interviews as we tried to articulate what is involved in all the processes taking place. We captured on film wonderful moments as the students creatively engaged with the processes, transforming materials through their own individual qualities. I watched expert teachers, Ali, Rosemary Brandt, Trinity Voice Coach Linda Hurst, Musicologist Robert Coleridge, and Valerie herself, passing on great treasures to a new generation, and I began to understand archeo-choreology and *Green Clowns* – (historical and in-progress) – that bit better. I invited historian Ramsay Burt to come down to Trinity Laban and see what we were doing and interview Valerie – hoping he would, as he did, come up with interesting angles I hadn't thought of. Archivist Jane Fowler, historian Anne Daye, and dancer/choreographer Gary Lambert also helped me interview Valerie, each bringing something different out of her extraordinary and invaluable memory bank of experiences and knowledge of Rudolf Laban's work and approaches. More and more footage developed containing wide ranging discussions from Rudolf Laban through to Rudolf Steiner.... I began to realise just how many potential documentaries there were here... and the challenge of finding the 'right' 50 mins. (Not 'right' or 'wrong' perhaps – to paraphrase Marion North once more from the conference – just *'different'*).

I felt that elucidating process, and *Green Clowns* itself, was facilitated by dividing the documentary into parts that followed the sections of the work itself ie *Maschine, Krieg, War Memorial* (really an extension of *Krieg*), *Dying Procession, Romance* and *Club of the Eccentics*. In fact the process of development, as Ali explains in the documentary, began with *Krieg* to facilitate the student's entry into this work. The documentary imposes from the outset a particular kind of 'narrative' approach – one of many possibilities provided by the recorded materials. As a historian with an interest in re-creation, and a relative outsider to Laban based work, what emerged for me was both a strong sense of how *Green Clowns 2008* is rooted in Rudolf Laban's principles and approach to creation, and how invaluable is the student experience when working in this way.

One example of how sources and principles and contexts are all involved in this re-creation, occurs with the development of *Maschine*. The original phrase of workers on the 'line' was lost so something else had to be found. Working with the students in rehearsal Valerie explained how one of the central movement phrases came from her experience of working in the Pilkington's Tile factory in the 1940s. In the 1940s Valerie was as a student, along with Warren Lamb, assisting with Rudolf Laban's observational and corrective methodologies for combating the inhumanity of factory work and its impact on the body. She was also working with him in the studio creating dances with themes – *Chaos, Fight* and *Liberation* – that she now realises were connected with his earlier dance theatre works. Contacting Pillkingtons Tile Factory today we discovered there is an archive, and Pilkingtons kindly supplied us with images of female workers making tiles back through history, much as Valerie described. In giving the dancers the basic movement phrase Valerie then asks them to imagine having to do it 5,000 times a day and to feel the discomfort in their bodies.

However, the emphasis in *Green Clowns* of course is not realism, but expressionism – *feeling into form*. As Valerie points out in the documentary, there were numerous machine dances around at this time, not least in Soviet Russia where the machine was idealised as a comrade and co-worker. The important difference is that Rudolf Laban did not want to *depict* the machine, he wanted to show its dehumanising and oppressive affects on the body. The work's avant gardism can be defined not only through its critique of the contemporary socio-cultural fabric and political situation in Germany during the 1920s, but also in opposition to the abstracting, formalising nature of modernism found at the Bauhaus and across the arts at this time. Satiric in places, soul baring in others, *Green Clowns* points to the deformities that underlie adaptation to oppressive and destructive modes of existence. *The Machine, War, Romance, The Club of the Eccentrics* – all the sections of this work – explore aspects of distortion and inhumanity in the modern world. For dancers today performing such a work, it is vital – as Ali and Valerie both

Courtesy Pilkington's Tile Factory.

stress in the documentary, that they get under the surface of the work, that its issues, oppositions, contexts and perspectives become meaningful to them. But of course the process of creation was very much about Ali and Valerie getting them to expressively form their responses – to channel and contain their expressive responses so that it would be visible/readable to an audience, rather than something simply 'felt'. It was a search for expressive form – but always coming from experienced content. Sometimes there would be the feeling without the form, sometimes the form without the feeling – but gradually the students developed and experienced their authentic expression of the given scenario – leading them into a deeply felt connection with the work.

What the students say about *Green Clowns 2008*, at the end of the documentary, is that it's the experience of feeling connected to the original ideas, concerns and issues of the piece, that made the work come alive for them and will, in their view, keep it alive for future generations to rediscover. They did not talk about the work's expressive *form* as such – but about its emotionally experienced content.

Re-creation is invaluable I think, not simply for what it produces – but as a process, as a mode of exploration and discovery that can bring huge insights, not just onto the past, but onto how we are working today and how that relates to and departs from our cultural heritage. If reconstruction can be defined as seeking to repeat the surface form of an original performance, re-creation has a freer relationship to the original work producing a dialogue with the past that has always been a rich source of creative inspiration. For example, Beethoven's *Diabelli Variations*, Picasso's re-workings and transformations of Manet's paintings, David Hockney's 2003 version of Picasso's *Massacre in Korea* (1951), Matthew Bourne's *Swan Lake* (1995), are all re-creations of various kinds, and contribute to discourse and artistic innovation through exploration, transformation and renewal. They also contribute to the development of the artist – as he/she explores his/her heritage and evolving language and formative ideas in different and changing contexts.

Something Valerie said during one of her many interviews stuck in my mind throughout the making of this documentary – the students had to dare, '*they have to dare*'. With Rudolf Laban's *Green Clowns* they certainly do have to dare, because even for today's dancers it is challenging to explore the crude, the rude and the grotesque, to scratch each other's bodies, spit, indulge in same-sex kissing, and make strange noises – all of which is demanded of this kind of avant-garde theatre with its connection to dada as well as to expressionism. In a sense though, in any recreation we have to dare – dare to get beneath the surface form of a work and really engage with its raison d'etre – including its artistic and socio-cultural contexts; in other words to get at the life-sources of its original innovations and the source of its many potential versions. We have to dare to question, take apart and explore the identity of the work and explore its resources and potential versions today.

1. See Alison-Curtis Jones: Historical Recreation and Current Practice...what is the relevance of Laban's work for today's dance artist? *Movement and Dance*, Magazine of the Laban Guild, Vol.28 No. 1. Spring 2009.
2. Re-creating Rudolf Laban's *Die Grünen Clowns*, (performance 15 mins: documentary 50 mins.) Directed by Lesley-Anne Sayers. Produced by IDM Ltd. 2009. wwwdancebooks.co.uk
3. Peter Sayers. With thanks to Trinity Laban for a research grant to make this documentary.

Laban's Art of Movement; a basis for a creative, holistic movement programme for individuals affected by complex needs, ASD (Autistic Spectrum Disorders) and behaviour which challenges

Dilys Price

Touch Trust is a pioneering charity which runs an Art of Movement programme for adults, children and babies with complex needs (that is profound and multiple disabilities, including challenging behaviour) and profound autism. Our guests are isolated because of their severe disabilities from the usual activities that society offers, adapted and other. We do not turn anyone away, our sessions are for those adults and children who are failing in the programmes offered them.

We have been a formal organisation for only ten years, without funding or premises. Our rise has been quite meteoric because today we are one of the seven Arts organisations in the iconic Wales Millennium Centre, in Cardiff the Welsh capital. This centre for the Arts aims to reach out to the whole community. The organisations range from the elite Welsh National Opera, Diversions Dance Company of Wales, through to Academi (literature in Wales), Ty Cerdd (community music in Wales), Urdd, (youth movement for Wales), Hijinx (community and special needs drama) and us.

We run a full programme in the Centre. As well as our daily creative movement sessions, we have special events when we can bring in the other organisations for more ambitious collaborations in creative movement activities. This has led to exciting DVDs and ambitious sharing of integrated projects.

We are highly successful, so much so that we have;

1) Daily group and individual Touch Trust creative movement sessions in the Centre.

• 10.0 - 6.0 Monday to Saturday throughout the year in our beautiful Centre for schools, families, social services, Community Houses.

(This means that each carer with their guest is dancing as well, so weekly we have two hundred people experiencing the benefit of participating in art of movement activities!)

2) Week long creative projects.
• Exploring extended themes and creativity.
• Extending collaboration with other artists.
• Extending expression and form.

3) A training school.

- We train education and care staff and other professionals in our method.

This is a nationally validated qualification ; OCN Level 2 (6 units) & Level 3 (6 units).

4) We have licensed the programme.

- We have copyright of materials and the Touch Trust programme.

- We have a Membership (mentoring and monitoring scheme to ensure the continuing integrity of the programme) for those who have completed training.

5) A Pilot College of Touch Trust and Arts.

- This is for post nineteen-year-olds with complex needs.

- The Touch Trust programme and philosophy underpin its curriculum making it unique.

Our success is validated by the fact that the local special schools send classes to our Centre every week; Social Services regularly use our services; we have lectured to local NHS hospitals on dementia and babies and Estyn (the Welsh Education Inspectorate) praises our work.

Our many success stories of individuals also build up our evidence that this programme is valuable. Here are three typical stories.

Gill has profound and multiple disabilities including autism and learning disability. Her achievements include happiness and an interest in others and her environment; her self-harming has stopped. Her mother says Gill is no longer clinically depressed. She enjoys creating expressive movement and voice activities and she is regaining her walking ability. Gill can enjoy the group creative movement activities now (after having to be in a one to one situation only.)

To quote her mother, 'This Christmas was the best we have ever had; Gill is able to cope with change now. For the first time ever I can cuddle her, she is learning that the world can be a beautiful place.'

The Professor of Learning Disabilities at the Welsh Centre for Learning Disabilities, Michael Kerr, who is her Consultant and Clinical Psychologist at University Wales Hospital, validates our achievements with Gill and with other guests whose Consultant he is. He says we are making a significant difference to the children with complex needs who are his clients and that 'the only problem is that I want more to have your programme'.

Lily had 80% brain damage at birth and the doctor told the parents she would remain in a vegetative state. After many one to one holistic creative movement sessions she has sight and hearing, plays and interacts and involves herself happily in exploration and mastery of movement skills. She is a joy and starting school as a happy little girl, learning and making connections socially.

Debby has severe cerebral palsy. After intensive sessions with her over several years her achievements now include: relaxation, focus, happiness, body awareness and movement development leading to awareness of breathing, centre and midline, controlled limb activity and even fine motor control as well as gross motor and effort control. Debby can now hold a pencil and write her name and she can even sit without bindings to restrain her arms and legs.

The Touch Trust Programme is entirely based on Laban's philosophy and movement analysis and teachings. I was at the Art of Movement Studio in Addlestone, Surrey from 1955-57. Lisa Ullmann and Marion North were my main teachers, Valerie Preston-Dunlop and Geraldine Stephenson also taught us and Laban took special sessions.

I cannot describe what a wonderful experience those two years were. I felt as if I was under a fountain of gold. I was able to immerse myself in the flow of movement. Along with the other students I was nurtured, respected for my creative movement expressions and inspired to believe in life and myself in a world made beautiful by dance.

I was fortunate enough to have had group and individual sessions with Laban. He was electric when he taught us. I was 'pole-axed' by his power, his energy, and his charisma. It was as if he switched on a light in me, it was unbelievable and I have been driven ever since by his vision, his humanity, his belief in the beauty of the ordinary person and their potential for wellbeing and spiritual fulfilment through being immersed in the flow of expressive art of movement, in ritual dance, in circle dance, in the cosmic dance of the universe, in the Art of Movement. He believed movement and art change people and are central to a 'good' fulfilled life.

Laban so believed that there is beauty in the ordinary individual's rich movement life that much of his energy went into his many Movement Choirs in Germany, (these being a practical expression of his philosophy) and later into the Modern Educational Dance programme he and Lisa Ullmann introduced into British Education, also expressing his loving and optimistic vision for people.

Here I would like to refer to Laban's writings:

Few people realise that their contentment in work and their happiness in life, as well as any personal or collective success, is conditioned by the personal development and use of their individual efforts (Laban and Lawrence, 1947. p.x).

The inhibition of the freedom of movement and its degradation to the role of a means of production only is a grave error which results in ill health, mental and bodily discord and misery, and thus in a disturbance of work. Movement has a quality, and this is not its utilitarian or visible aspect but its feel. One must DO movements in order to be able to appreciate their full power and their full meaning, but this is carried out in our civilisation in a very scanty, very casual and insufficient way... (Laban and Lawrence. 1947. p. 65).

In Mastery of Movement he writes:

Man moves to satisfy a need. He aims by his movement at something of value to him. It is easy to perceive the aim of a person's movement if it is directed to some tangible object. Yet there also exist intangible values that inspire movement (Laban. 1960, p. 1).

I immersed myself in Modern Educational Dance and Laban's Art of Movement for fifty years. It is his analysis which is the basis of all the movement work at Touch Trust. Laban's book *Modern Educational Dance* (1948), is inspiring and provided the analysis of Body, Space, Effort, Relationship which guides our work, although we only touch on Themes 1-5 of the 16 Themes. We immerse our guests in the healing flow of movement, carrying them into different dynamics and moods, building relationship skills, enriching their movement life in every way we can. We build up self esteem and body awareness and we are always ready to move them into further development in the Art of Movement. But essential always is that their movement is authentic.

Laban believed that children need opportunities to choose and develop their own efforts through play and then dance,

...but whatever is danced should be executed with full inner participation and clearness of form. The creative stimulus and the awareness of the enlivening and freeing influence of dance movement are all that is desirable. The cultivation of artistic taste and discrimination in general cannot be furthered better or more simply than by the art of movement. Yet the dances which are produced must never originate from the wish to create outstanding works of art. Should such a miracle occur once, everyone will be pleased, but in the schools we should not attempt to produce external success through effective performances (Laban. 1948. p. 50).

In conclusion, the creative and movement needs of those with complex, profound and multiple disabilities had been held back in the past by both the failure to find appropriate dance styles and the failure to find a suitable and fundamental analysis of movement and creativity and expression. Laban gave us the tools to redress this. His analysis of movement and his understanding of the creative process of the ordinary person and their need for expression made it possible for us to connect meaningfully through the Art of Movement and bring about development for our guests.

Laban believed in art as a transformer, and that the most fundamental and effective art is the Art of Movement. He believed in the dignity and beauty of the human being and the necessity for us teacher/leaders to become skilled observers of people and movement, to see ourselves as explorers and advocates for joy, life and humanity through the Art of Movement.

He showed the way, he made it possible to bring joy and development to our guests who have complex needs and who because of the accidents of fate had been isolated from life. He helped us to become a community (of guests and 'carers') all celebrating diversity and dancing together with joy into life. That is what the Touch Trust does, that is what the Touch Trust Programme develops and that is what Laban gave us.

References
Laban, R. (1948) *Modern Educational Dance*. London: MacDonald & Evans.
Laban, R . Lawrence, F.C. (1947) *Effort*. London: MacDonald & Evans.
Laban, R. ed. Ullmann, L. (1960) *Mastery of Movement*. London: MacDonald & Evans.

Unlocking the closet: using Laban analysis as key to interpreting and staging Seneca's Phaedra

Annabel Rutherford

'Anxieties when slight, one can express in words, when great, they remain strongly silent' (*Phaedra* trans. Ahl 1986, p.72).

Comedy is, perhaps, the genre that immediately springs to mind when one thinks about the dramatic tradition left to us by the Romans. In large part, this is because of our familiarity with such musicals as *A Funny Thing Happened on the Way to the Forum* or, for those of us old enough to remember, the long-running television series of Frankie Howerd's highly comical *Up Pompeii*. But Roman tragedy, too, through adaptations, plot borrowings, and re-workings, is just as influential and prevalent on stage today as the comedies. Shakespeare's *Titus Andronicus* and Caryl Churchill's *Thyestes* are good examples, as, indeed, is Sarah Kane's *Phaedra's Love*, which, as the playwright admits, is directly influenced by Seneca's tragedy *Phaedra* as opposed to the earlier Greek (Euripides) or later French (Racine) versions of the tale. But while the Greek and French plays continue to be staged today, a production of Seneca's *Phaedra* would be a rarity. Indeed, the majority of scholars believe his plays not to have been written for production at all, but instead, for performed readings and, it is thought, most likely spoken by just one voice. In other words, Seneca's tragedies are considered closet dramas and, taken as such, seriously neglected today.

Research into Seneca's play reveals two particularly interesting issues about *Phaedra*: Classics and theatre scholar Frederick Ahl is of the belief that the play may well have been staged in private theatres such as those that existed in the ample well-to-do homes of the Romans (1986, p.27). Secondly, while the play is generally accepted as an adaptation of Euripides' *Hippolytus*, its true source play is believed lost. Scholars are of the opinion that Euripides wrote an earlier version of *Hippolytus*, which was banned for being too scandalous. It is this lost play that is considered to have been Seneca's source.

Literary analyses of Seneca's drama may well provide valuable insights into the contents of the lost source play, but since *Phaedra* was written as a play and not a myth or legend in prose, any literary analysis proves insufficient and, thus, inadequate. Indeed, the physicality inherent in the lines of the play demands movement analysis – and who better to turn to than Laban? Space-movement analysis proves enormously useful when attempting to understand the workings of this comparatively obscure play, which, whether acted out or not, requires recognition of its status as drama. (Drama here is defined as a genre through which characters are physically brought to life through movement in space, as opposed to the static black word, of other literary genres, which lies heavily on the white page.) An exploration of *Phaedra* through Laban movement analysis elicits a far richer and more compelling play than has previously been acknowledged by scholars. Furthermore, it suggests that, when considered in terms of its inherent physicality, *Phaedra*, as Ahl believes, must, surely, have been written with the intention of it being staged, even if that was an unusual occurrence in Roman times (1986, p.26). In light of time constraints and the concern of confusion for those unfamiliar with the play, this paper will focus solely on the two leading characters, Hippolytus and Phaedra, and explore their scene together – the pivotal act in the play – applying basic movement analysis. Although no attempt will be made to reproduce the scene choreographically, it is hoped that an exploration into the inherent physicality may suggest that *Phaedra* is highly stageable and entertaining as a fully produced drama.

First, a brief reminder of the plot of Seneca's Phaedra

Phaedra, wife of Theseus, is passionately in love with her stepson, Hippolytus, who is Theseus' son. During Theseus' lengthy absence, Phaedra expresses her love to Hippolytus who rebuffs her, having chosen instead a chaste life. Theseus returns home. At her Nurse's suggestion, Phaedra, distraught and revengeful at being rebuffed, feigns rape by Hippolytus. In a burst of uncontrollable anger, Theseus uses his ancestral power of the gods to place a curse of death upon his son who, having escaped Phaedra's clutches, is racing away from the palace in a chariot. A raging bull rises up out of the sea and savages and brutalises Hippolytus, smashing his body on the rocks and scattering it across the countryside. Upon discovering Hippolytus' fate, the guilty Phaedra confesses to her husband before committing suicide. The remorseful and grieving Theseus curses his wife in death, denying her body burial rites.

The forces and message that drive the action of the play, then, are unattainable desire, uncontainable passion and the resulting serious consequences. While Phaedra's love is unrequited and taboo, Hippolytus' love for chastity is unnatural. Nonetheless, Hippolytus is an unwitting victim, while Phaedra, aided by her Nurse, is instigator of the entire tragedy.

The physical characteristics with which Seneca provides Hippolytus and Phaedra are immediately apparent from the beginning of the play. Of Hippolytus' striking figure and handsome looks, there can be no doubt. But surface appearances aside, most intriguing are the descriptions of his physical abilities. Ironically, perhaps, (from a dancer's perspective,) the first reference is to his feet – 'agile feet', feet with which he scales the jagged cliffs bare-footed (Ahl 1986, p.56). Despite his youth, his muscles, we are told, 'match the embedded muscles of powerful Hercules' (p.80). When hunting, his 'well-skilled hands', too, are commented upon as 'more agile' than any ever before seen (p.80). His great strength is not just of the body but also of the mind. For, we are told, it is virtually impossible to 'flex and bend' such a fierce and beastlike mind (p.58). Not only does this young Adonis have extraordinary strength and agility, he also has speed. When he runs, he is compared to a strong 'nor'wester spinning the clouds' in its wake (p.77). Hippolytus' actions are direct and strong. He operates predominantly in the vertical plane. His flow is bound. Most striking is how Seneca deliberately points our initial focus to his agile hands and feet before describing his limbs, torso and head (mind). Indeed, all his physical action begins at the outer extremities before progressing towards the limbs and torso.

In stark contrast, Phaedra, consumed by passion, is described as lacking both strength and radiance. She 'walks unsteadily', even 'staggers', and her feet move aimlessly (p.62). Seneca emphasises this point farther by having the Nurse inform us that '[c]oncern cripples her joints and limbs' (p.62). Phaedra has indirect and weak movements. She moves aimlessly through space and her body is in continuous flux. A more different image to Hippolytus it would be difficult to create. By presenting such opposites, Seneca deliberately draws our attention to the importance of the characters' physicality and, by extension, their movement. Indeed, such detailed physical description strongly suggests how vital this is to a full appreciation and understanding of the key scene in the play: Phaedra's confession of love for Hippolytus.

While Hippolytus might be in continuous flux outdoors, inside the palace the image conjured is of an Adonis, still, taut and very straight: As the Nurse observes 'Like granite headland, so unwavering against the waves he stands' (p.71). In the image of his father, 'his arms are soft, / but muscles are embedded in them...his head is high' (p.74). And when he strikes blows, 'they leave no obvious gashes / yet penetrate deep and clean into hidden hollows' (p.59). Hippolytus, then, is identifiable by his strong, direct, thrusting movements, virtually all of which occur predominantly within the vertical door plane. And when he moves with speed, his action is compared to the force of a 'raging hurricane' (p.77).

Phaedra's movement in space, on the other hand, conjures an image of a semi-hysterical woman either 'lying prostrate at [Hippolytus'] knees' (p.74), or feigning a faint into his arms: 'look your Hippolytus / is using his own arms to hold you up', exclaims the Nurse (p.71). Phaedra's gestures cannot be contained. They continuously spill into Hippolytus' kinesphere. Her strength is all but sapped by consuming passion as her pain tosses her from side to side, 'this way and that' (p.62). In physical space, she rarely rises above the horizontal or table plane and her movements are indirect, soft, and pliant. Whereas Hippolytus hair is described, like his father's, as 'taut', on his 'upright head' (p.74), Phaedra's 'flows down [her] neck', a neck that can 'hardly hold her head straight'(pp.63, 62). While Phaedra associates herself with 'water's vastness' and sea swirl (p.48), Hippolytus promotes his image as a hunter, 'glistening and lustful', who controls his weapons 'with taut, unerring bowstring' (p.59).

The true erotic nature of the scene becomes apparent only when physical action replaces words. And Seneca goes to great length to explain this, for he has Hippolytus tell Phaedra: 'Anxieties when slight, one can express in words, when great, they remain strongly silent' (p.72). The Nurse, too, informs us of Phaedra's inability to 'talk about' her predicament, adding, 'she keeps it locked within herself' (p.62). She adds, however, that her expressions/gestures betray her. And a little later, Hippolytus urges her to 'speak openly', arguing that she is merely "tossing words about all intertwined" and making little sense (p.73). Thus, Seneca emphasises his reliance on visible patterns of movement and action in space to convey a meaning deeper than is verbally expressible. Indeed, movement infuses the vitality missing from what could otherwise be dismissed as a very dull scene that, arguably, would have a negligible impact on the listener.

In Hippolytus and Phaedra, then, Seneca presents two strongly contrasting body types: The one taut and erect, inhabiting the vertical plane, the other soft and pliant, functioning primarily in the horizontal plane. Hippolytus' energy is strong, and he is in complete control of every muscle as he moves directly through space from one position to another with great precision. Phaedra, as we have seen, spills across into his kinesphere, which makes perfect sense, given that she is the one attempting to initiate bodily contact. Her energy is weak and her movements are lacking in control. Her path through space is curved and her body is in continuous flux with gathering and scattering movements before dissolving into an attitude of self-indulgence. Whereas Phaedra, whose hair is described as flowing down her neck, 'tossed as it will... till it blows behind in the breeze', is likened to water, Hippolytus is compared to a strong pillar of granite rock 'unwavering against the waves' (pp.63, 71).

If the movements of these two characters mirror their inner state of mind, their characteristic postures, taut, controlled and erect versus soft, fluid and pliant, reflect their sexuality. As two images placed side by side, it is not difficult to perceive them as a sexually aroused male and female. The rhythm of the scene is set by the delivery of the words: Lying prostrate, this time at his feet, Phaedra speaks in short abrupt phrases going so far as to explain, 'a great force prompts my voice; but a greater force restrains it' (p.72).

Hippolytus responds succinctly: 'Trust your anxieties to me' (p.72). The combination of movement and phrasing heavily suggests the rhythmic ebb and flow of the tide as the water gently laps against the strength of a promontory, and that rhythm slowly picks up pace and builds to an extraordinary climax.

From the perspective of movement, then, the climax of the scene is highly sexual and dramatic. Fully aware of Phaedra's desire, Hippolytus' initial outrage and anger turn to violence. He draws his sword to stab her. Phaedra remains 'prostrate upon the ground' and Hippolytus, with drawn sword, stands over her, erect (p.76). Not only does the sword, then, symbolize the idea of male penetration, but the association of the image with death can be understood as *le petit mort*, or orgasm, a frequent reference in Roman poetry. Realizing how dangerously close he has become to engaging in sexual intercourse, Hippolytus 'cast[s] away' his sword 'contaminated by / [Phaedra's] touch' and runs, out of the palace in his characteristic straight and direct path: 'faster than a stellar comet racked with flames, driven by winds, extending far in its wake a fiery trailpath' (pp.76, 77).

The implicit eroticism of this scene, which is all but lost when merely spoken as words, is contained in the movement. Indeed, Seneca has constructed his text in such a way that it is quite possible to glimmer an underlying movement text throughout the play. And that the playwright is clearly aware of the vital importance of movement to our understanding of his work is evident through the frequent references to the inadequacy of speech to convey the inner profound meaning. But what is most intriguing is this Roman's appreciation not only of the power of movement and action in space, but in the physical interrelationship between two characters who, in reality, never actually touch each other.

Whether the play was ever staged is no longer possible to know. But given the immense physicality inherent in the work, Ahl's claim that it may have been performed in private indoor theatres is more credible than that made by other scholars: that the play was written to be read aloud by one voice. And yet this raises many questions. In burying the eroticism of the play in a choreographic subtext, was Seneca perhaps attempting to outwit any possibility of censorship? After all, the Greek source play had been banned for being too scandalous. Was it perhaps this specific scene, missing from the surviving version of the Greek play, that had caused the problems for Euripides? In which case, we could draw certain conclusions about that missing play. Such questions may never be answered with any certainty but the question still lingering: If *Phaedra* was written as a closet drama, then why would Seneca have deliberately included so much physicality? Would his audience of listeners (if you like, the equivalent of a modern radio audience) have grasped any sense of the movement inherent in these lines? If so, and one assumes it must be so, what could this inform us about those Ancient

Roman listeners if they were able to understand the physicality without see-ing it in action?

That this and other ancient plays have been largely dismissed today as closet dramas and, therefore, considered too difficult to stage is unfortunate. As we have seen through a swift and brief exploration of a key act in *Phaedra*, the richness of the play lies in its physicality. That Seneca, the stoic, has written a simultaneous movement text is quite remarkable. That this ancient play lends itself so readily to Laban analysis is fascinating. And that this play could be readily staged today as a dance drama is, surely, enticing.

Reference

Seneca. *Phaedra*. Translated from the Latin by F. Ahl (1986). Ithaca: Cornell University Press.

Creating personally meaningful ballet through co-authored choreography

Paula Salosaari

In October 2006, choreographer Michael Klien visited Finland and gave lectures in the Zodiak – Centre for New Dance. Talking and giving examples of his work, he said amongst many other things: '… dance always points towards the possibility of change… towards the unknown…' (Klien & Vast, 2007). My dance form is ballet. It is often thought of as a rule-governed and pre-determined set of steps executed to precisely timed musical beats. Would it therefore be possible at all to understand ballet as dance in the way Klien mentions, pointing towards the unknown, towards change? Where is the change? Is ballet dance, dance as art?

Over several years I have developed and put into practice in ballet education the concept of multiple embodiment in classical ballet (Salosaari, 2001). During my teaching and workshops I have collected students' experiences of dancing ballet and co-authoring ballet-based choreography by discussing dancing with them and asking them to write about their experiences.

Roughly, these experiences can be divided into two categories. One of them emphasises the repetition in ballet as routine, expressing the stagnation in the dance. Dancers talk about this experience with expressions like 'business as usual' or 'feeling pretentious', or 'putting on a form' and the like. For me this experience became boring, as I began to need in ballet the experience of creating something new in my own art form. To contrast this routine way of experiencing ballet, dancers have found another way, which in their words gives 'soul' to the dance. It surprises them with the freshness of it, facilitating dancing and being joyous.

In my work I have found that the dancer's feelings during performance are indicators of whether they are repeating the tradition in a pre-determined, routine fashion, as if looking backwards to the past without giving fresh insights to the previously known steps. It is also possible to experience the joy of fresh insights in the same performance, that is, dancing the same dance in such a way that in the here and now moment in one way or another something new is revealed to the dancer in his or her creative moment of dancing.

In my teaching and co-authoring of ballet with dancers, I treasure and try to bring about these magic moments, where something new and meaningful is revealed to the dancers in their experience and is thereby immediately expressed in their performance. In my earlier work I have explained the tools to bring this about: understanding ballet vocabulary as open qualitative form and intending it, using perceptual strategies and choreological imagery. These tools help the dancer to open out the dance to new experiences and change. This process can still be enhanced by the teacher-choreographer's open tasks in the ballet studio (Salosaari 2001).

In a ballet class I can suggest that the dancers change their usual way of perceiving the dance. If they do they will get new and sometimes very surprising information from their dancing body. An example of this would be when a dancer has been used to thinking of the precise execution of ballet vocabulary, its precise timing and rules, perhaps being competitive or ambitious in this fashion and then changes his or her attitude into an open quality or new perceptual possibility in the dance. For instance, if the dancer then changes her perspective to being aware of touch and the body surfaces while dancing, this may change her experience miraculously. This was one of my first surprises when trying this out by myself in a ballet class. I felt how my feet touched each other in the fifth position, how the bottom of the foot glided on the floor, how my arms felt the air while moving. All this gave me a miraculous balance, something out of the ordinary. At the same time I became aware of which parts of my skin were visible for the audience enhancing the presenting of my body to an audience. It was not only being seen or looked at as an object, but also a very meaningful presentation coming from myself. I was not a victim of the audience but an agent, deciding about the meaning of my body being seen. Becoming aware of the skin also brought to my attention which surfaces of my body led the movement and which followed, and the changes that happened. It is difficult to describe the experience in words as it is a way of describing the experience second hand. It is first of all expressed in the dance right there, right then. However, this experience is different for each dancer even in the same movement as well as different for the same dancer during repetition of the same dance. Fresh performance possibilities emerge with the dancer's awareness and change the dancing event.

The choreological perspective of dance as Preston-Dunlop & Sanchez-Colberg describe it (Preston-Dunlop & Sanchez-Colberg 2002) is another tool for paying attention to the qualities of ballet in a new way. With this vast array of possibilities discussed in this text dancers can pose questions to their dancing bodies and reveal fresh insights in ballet. While performing an adagio in ballet class paying attention to balancing and falling off balance a student wrote afterwards: '*While dancing the adagio, I always looked forward to the moment, when I can perform a fall, an impulse or push that takes me to something totally different.*' I have described more of these experiences of the dancers elsewhere (Salosaari 2001). Klien also points out that 'we need looseness in the structure' and that ballet amongst other dance forms has closed its structure. Looking at ballet through the choreological perspective, through its dance qualities in an open-ended way, gives it this necessary looseness for creative play. This was clearly demonstrated in the conference in Preston-Dunlop's presentations of the width of Laban's work from the esoteric to the dancer's creative performance possibility. In performing arts it is also important to see the whole picture of dance with its nexus in the strands of the dance.

In this way choreological imagery and change of perceptual strategies has enhanced the dancers' experiences of ballet and brought about freshness and meaning to the routine of the ballet class. The dancers' feelings talk about whether their dancing is pointing more towards the past tradition as a pre-determined routine or whether they are re-vitalising the tradition with fresh insights. In this sense I would like to answer my previous question prompted by Klien's words. Yes. Ballet can point towards the future and change and thereby be dance, dance as art.

The dancer's revelations and multiple performance choices can be seen as interpretations of the ballet combination. It was inevitable that at some point of the work, the dancers' interpretations started to change the balletic form in one way or another and perhaps stretch the borders of their understanding of ballet. Choreological imagery can also be a way to create your own movements with the multiple qualities found in ballet. Putting these ideas together we were on our way to creating dances. They were first performed only in the studio, but soon enough we were invited to create dances for the stage. The open tasks lead the performers to create their own movement material in the performance.

If the dancers have experienced the surprise of creation, the emergence of new creation from the hidden reservation of their own bodies and beings, the emerging dance has the kind of meaningfulness to the dancer that is difficult to match. As Ana Catalina Roman said in the Forsythe Event of this Conference, choice gives her autonomy as a dancer. Bringing their own dance to performance means that the dancers (in this case dance students) are negotiating their ways of performing the tradition and the possible changes they experience with the dance community. Thereby they become agents of their dance culture.

I would like to finish with a few recent comments by the dancers of the process they have experienced during the co-authoring process and performance of our mutual dance works.

A young dancer very much tied by balletic conventions says in her feedback writing:

During the three weeks of working I learned to free myself from 'ballet's tentacles' in a totally new way and I learned a lot of new things about myself.

And another dancer's comment speaks strongly about the personal meaningfulness of the dance to her:

The moments when in the dance studio something wonderful beyond words happen, leave one mute. ... One could have touched the atmosphere in the room. During the peak moments I almost cried looking at the others dance.

References

Klien, Michael & Valk, Steve. (2007) Choreography as an Aesthetics of Change in Ojala, Raija & Takala, Kimmo (Eds) *Zodiak – Uuden tanssin tähden.* LIKE

Preston-Dunlop, Valerie & Sanchez-Colberg, Ana. (2002) *Dance and the Performative, A Choreological Perspective – Laban and Beyond.* London: Verve.

Salosaari, Paula. (2001) *Multiple Embodiment in Classical Ballet, Educating the Dancer as an Agent of Change in the Cultural Evolution of Ballet.* Acta Scenica 8. Helsinki: Theatre Academy.

A theoretical and formal introduction to DirectorNotation

Katia Savrami

Introduction

DirectorNotation is a symbolic language intended to express the form and content of film much as Labanotation provides a language for documenting dance. It thus constitutes a new approach to the creative process of filmmaking as it provides a pre-record of a complete description of film content. Musicians, and also choreographers, have long been able to express, clarify and share their intentions or document an artistic creation, using logical symbolic structures (music notation and dance notation). Yet, those working in the movie industry have to rely on storyboards and verbal description, and the only record of their artistic 'object of appreciation' is the final film itself. What is essential in DirectorNotation is that a film Director can record a complete description of his conception that assists him in the selection and decision making process so as to clarify his intentions for a film, both in terms of form and content, at the pre-production stage. The appropriate preparation and the pre-visualisation of the shots through a created software, before going actually to the field of filming will not only conserve time and money but will also assist the process of montage in the post-production phase.

Artistic characteristics

Concrete: The purpose of an artistic notation system is to describe a concrete conceptualisation of a performance. While performers must have their own interpretative freedom, a film notation must allow the Director to preserve his creative contribution with considerable accuracy in a written symbolic form.

Formal: The artistic notation can formalise completely objective statements that a creator makes about his work. The aim of this artistic notation is to be defined as the technical model that it is transformed into by formally specified software tools. For the creation of a new artistic notation system, we propose that the design of the notation and the creation of its technical model should be carried out in parallel, in an interactive, collaborative, iterative process.

The notation must record the artist's conceptualisation while avoiding irrelevant details of actual performance. What constitutes such an 'irrelevant detail' often depends on the specific piece being notated, so abstraction is required at various granularities. For instance, rather than recording precise coordinates or numerically defined camera parameters or actions, the author must be allowed to manipulate abstract concepts such as 'near' and 'far', 'fast' and 'slow' movement, or directions such as 'stage forward'.

Symbolic: The notation should be based on a vocabulary of abstract graphical symbols. This is similar to music and dance notation. Icons are flexible structures: graphical symbols can be modified (e.g. elongated), connected to each other, put through subtle variations (offering grammar), or have complex spatial relationships (e.g. inclusion or overlap), which is necessary for spatial layout

Spatially laid out: The physical space on the page or screen where the notation is laid out should be exploited to encode the syntax of the notation. This allows the artist to read notation very quickly, which is not a mere convenience, but allows the speed of visualisation, intuitive understanding and internalisation to not be impaired by a slower speed of deciphering representation: thus, notation becomes a transparent carrier of conceptualisation.

Economical: The notation should allow minimal complexity of representation. The right levels of abstraction should be available as discussed above. Additionally, there is an entirely practical need for a significant amount of information to be able to fit in the limited space available on paper or on the screen. A simple means for economy is to define default interpretations that allow symbols to be omitted in common situations where their meaning can be unambiguously implied in their absence. For example, a simple symbolic representation should be available to specify that an actor appears in a close-up shot in the centre of the picture frame, avoiding the need to specify exact spatial position and orientation for both actor and camera.

Non-minimal: The notation should allow multiple approaches to defining the same performance. Such formally redundant expressive mechanisms should allow economy of description, emphasis, and selective attention to detail, rather than being merely superfluous. For instance, in a notation for film, we should similarly be able, to emphasise the relation between actor and camera by explicitly specifying it, or to de-emphasise it by specifying independent conditions such as spatial positions and the trajectories of movements and allowing the relationship to emerge indirectly. 'Non-minimality' is particularly important for the description of changing relationships, as it allows the cause of the change to be written clearly, rather than requiring the effect to be denoted in mechanical detail. As an example, we should be able to choose between specifying a 'medium shot' and the location in space of an actor, or the location of the actor and camera together with the latter's lens settings, or the actor's location and the region in the frame the actor occupies. To then write that the shot distance changes conveys qualitatively different information from writing how exactly actor and camera move in space, or from writing how the actor's location in the picture frame changes, respectively.

Declarative: The notation should be able to denote the desired actions, effects or situations, rather than just the procedural means to achieve them. It is then a means for the artist to define the envisioned performance itself rather than a particular process that might achieve it. It is a direct record of the artist's conceptualisation of the salient features, without needing to be explicit about all the related details, the expressively significant constituent elements of a creative achievement.

Hierarchical: A notation system should offer a multi-tiered descriptive capability that allows its user to express ideas that have been developed to different extents of accuracy, detail and scope, at corresponding points in the creative process. It should also support the transitions between these tiers, that is, it should help and guide the author in the process of elaborating a set of sketchy initial ideas into a fully worked out result. In dance, when working with Labanotation a choreographer can use Motif Writing to describe the overall Action of movement, then use Structural Description to detail the actual steps that dancers are to perform, and finally add notation in Effort Description to describe qualitative elements of interpretation that are to be determined at the level of choreography rather than left to the dancer's choice. In developing an artistic notation system in parallel to software tools that support it, we should provide a closer link between the different tiers of a hierarchical description.

Easy to use: In reference to the 'user needs for DirectorNotation' we have found that Directors are happy with the idea of a 'week long seminar' in order to learn to use 'practical, notation-based software tools' that will offer even an initial level of capability to better plan and understand. Then, the Director can fine-tune the actor's actual movements in real space, rather than trying to describe small differences as they appear on the screen; such a representation is advantageous because, not only is it more detailed, but also, once actual real-world movements are described, the notation becomes robust to changes, and e.g. multiple cameras can be set to film the actions of the same actor.

Technical characteristics

Fully formally modelled: The notation must be completely elaborated at a technical level, as well as artistically. This means that a precise, machine-processable representation of any text given in the notation must be automatically derivable from the user input. The technical requirement is stricter than its artistic counterpart, as computational formalisation is extremely rigid. The technical formal model will be much less economical and intuitive than is acceptable to a human user, so a process of translation between the artistic and technical domains will be required.

Unambiguous, Deterministic: The artistic notation needs to avoid all reliance on a human reader's intuition for the extraction of its formal meaning (as opposed to the interpretation of subjective expressive ideas, as discussed above). It must leave no choices open to the reader. Instead, any notation text must formally correspond to a unique semantic and geometric specification. This requirement does not imply that every possible detail must always be written down explicitly by the notation author. Rather, the notation has a unique finite meaning including explicit recognition of unspecified parameters. There must be a deterministic process for resolving how to deal with any such unspecified parameters.

Tractable: The computations that must be performed in order to parse the artistic notation into a technical model, and to evaluate this model into a detailed semantic and/or geometric representation, must be tractable and, in practice, efficient enough to allow reasonable performance of notation-based software tools. Thus semantic models must be definable, geometric constraints must be solvable using efficient algorithms, e.g. processing time.

Complete: Notation-based software tools must be able to produce concrete output.

For instance, for the automatic generation of animated previsualisations/ storyboards, the notation must correspond to a technical model that is detailed enough for an animation to meaningfully represent it.

Incrementally useful: It is important that we do not expect a new artistic notation system to fully mature before it can be of any practical usefulness. It is thus obvious that a notation should be useful long before it can be confidently called mature or be standardised to the extent that it is no longer allowed to change. For this reason, we currently focus on example applications such as 'generating animated pre-visualisations'.

DirectorNotation development process

Stage 1: Knowledge and understanding of film domain is essential and is gained by collaborating with film directors so as to study existing film terminology and by discussing and evaluating with film experts. The reverse development process is also important and is achieved by observing films and extracting/categorising vocabulary (e.g. by analysing scripts).

Stage 2: We observe already-made film content (e.g. Million Dollar Hotel –

Wim Wenders) and identify cinematography elements (e.g. camera movement, camera angle, movement for actors, spatial orientations etc). The way that these elements are specified and used by film directors will guide what needs to be written in the form of notation.

Stage 3: We apply so far created notation to analyse other scenes (e.g. Patio Scene – Notorious). Analysing various films, we confirm commonalities in the use of cinematography elements. Scene analysis also gives us feedback for identifying new needs/finding new symbols.

Stage 4: necessity to create a team comprised of engineers and artists (film directors, labanotators) in order to approach the film domain both artistically and technically (technical modeling for creating notation-enabled software tools)

Stage 5: expand notation for other film aspects (acting, lighting etc) – through the interaction of different aspects more information is available. The aim is to develop a second layer of representation either through symbols or defaults that will be added on to the existing notation or modify the first layer of representation namely individual symbols for each element.

At the artistic level, we have received concrete feedback from several professional Directors that the notation so far is very interesting and would be very useful in practice if completed and if supported by practical software tools. Of course, the very partial notation available now cannot yet be used in applications, and no working software tools are available yet. There is no risk of our current prototype notation being unsuitable to be used as a basis for the project, because the project work is fundamentally based on a process of iterative self-evaluation and gradual improvement that is perfectly suitable to correct any problems the prototype might be found to have. Nonetheless, the prototype is considerably mature for the part of the application domain that it addresses, so there is low probability of changes.

Current status – future work

Current research has included the following:

- *Camera Work*

Often camera work will be determined indirectly from something else we want to achieve, e.g. composition, or narrative idioms, acting, etc. It has been suggested that we don't start the project by perfecting the notation for camerawork, but rather explore other aspects first.

- *Acting*

DirectorNotation - Camera Work

- Movement – Orientation
  - Body (e.g. travelling)

  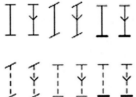

  - Facing (e.g. panning)

- Shooting
  - Framing (e.g. center-frame)

  ▰ ▯ ▭ ▱

  - Shot distance (e.g. full shot)

  ✳ ✕ ▫ ⋈ ⋈

DirectorNotation - Acting

- Actor's Spatial Movement
  - Body

  - Head

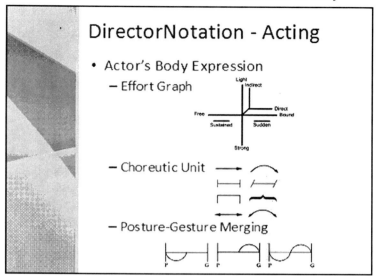

Future Research will include:

— *Lighting*

This must be declarative!

— 'At *x* moment Tom's face becomes lit in *y* manner' or 'area over right diagonal is lit/...', not 'place a light of type *z* in location *w*'

Again, there is a need to find the right abstractions, to avoid having to describe all possible ways light looks

— *Set & Location*

• Non-functional props can be thought of simply in terms of their locations

• Functional props

— When inactive: could still have its own 'actions', e.g. changing size/shape

— When active: they have their own type of actions

• Interesting to see declaratively within the action

• Need whole new set of abstractions

• Can initially get away with great simplification

— *Montage*

This may simply define sequences of shots by giving a list of sections of camera shootings. On some occasions we must have the mechanism to apply transitions when moving from one shot to another. Sophistication is when constraints on montage are given and other aspects must be inferred. This is necessary for some idioms

Penguin example

1. The example notation we present here is founded on some basic assumptions (e.g. stage boundaries, the 'downstage' orientation etc) which would normally be written as a key signature in the notation, but is omitted here for simplicity. The step that we start with is to write notation to declare the elements (camera(s), actor(s)) that take part in the scene. We define a new staff by creating a relation symbol for each object. In the example we only deal with one actor (Devlin) and one camera (Cam1). Both the objects are placed by default at the centre of the stage, looking in the downstage direction (as no position or orientation has been notated for any of the objects yet).

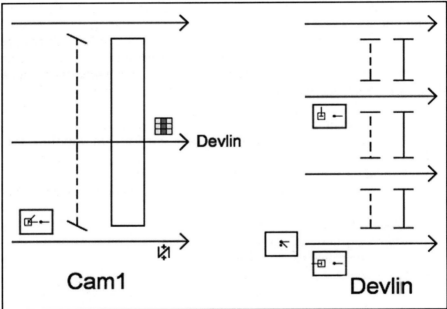

2. A single relation symbol denotes the presence of the object that it refers to at a specific point in time. In practice, we actually describe objects through time within a film. To add the dimension of time, we introduce more relation symbols for each object. The vertical distance between any two relation symbols represents the time between the moments represented by each

symbol. The duration is simply analogous to the vertical length. Notation is read bottom-up! In order to simulate this new notation visually, we animate the video preview of the notation shown to the right with a flickering effect reminiscent of old movies.

3.   Here we specify that Cam1 frames Devlin. Devlin is specified as the target of the relation symbol describing the camera. The camera's position and orientation are now inferred to be appropriate so as to meet the new requirement. The inference process applied here adjusted the camera, because this was the object constrained, while no constraints were directly applied to the actor, so his default position was maintained. Also, we did not specify the shot distance, so by default the camera frames Devlin in a precise, (non-realistic) full shot, and many other defaults have also been applied, like the choice of lens. (We can now mention explicitly that this example is a simplified description of the famous Patio scene in Hitchcock's film Notorious.).

4.   By placing a magnitude symbol in the slot of the camera's relation symbol denoting shot distance, we specify the shot distance of the camera. The result is that Devlin is now framed in a realistic full shot. In order to achieve this shot, the camera had to be moved backwards: this change is inferred, without a position for the camera needing to be explicitly notated.

5.   Here, we place an orientation symbol in the slot of Devlin's relation symbol, to specify his body orientation. As no facing orientation has been specified for him, his facing orientation follows his body orientation (a default, when describing actors). Once again, the camera's position changes, not because this was explicitly notated, but because the framing constraint that was specified earlier for the camera must still be satisfied.

6.   The next step is to define Devlin's initial position in the scene (which was so far unspecified), by adding a position symbol in the slot of the relation symbol denoting position. Consequently, the camera's position also changes in order to maintain the framing constraints (target and shot distance) already specified. This description is coarse, referring to a roughly positioned point along the stage boundary.

7.   In this step, we fine-tune Devlin's position in the scene, by adding detail to the previously placed position symbol. The camera's position is, of course, also changed correspondingly.

8.   After completing Devlin's positioning in the scene, we start defining his motion activity. As a first (simplistic) approach (to be refined), we place a single action symbol between the two relation symbols on Devlin's staff. Recall that each relation symbol defines a point in time; as such, their combination defines the duration of any action symbol placed between them. This particular action symbol denotes a straight-line forwards movement. We have not specified Devlin's speed, so this is implied by default to be a

constant, natural walking speed (recall here that all these defaults may be defined explicitly in the key signature).

9. The straight-line forwards action symbol is now replaced by another action symbol that denotes a forward movement on a curved trajectory towards the right. By default (and unless explicitly specified otherwise), the trajectory is circular (but not necessarily a full circle). Devlin is here shown to traverse a semi-circle, yet another default, more complex now, as it depends on the speed and duration of the movement. We have done this to illustrate two different action symbols, but the reader may also imagine this as the Director experimenting with different actions, in order to find the right one.

10. Adding another level to Devlin's movement (but still not having reached the final configuration), we divide the motion activity specified so far in two segments: a straight-line forward movement at first, followed by a curved movement. Note that the two movement segments are not of equal duration. This is the first case in our example where three relations appear in a staff. In general, any number of relations symbols may be written.

11. In this step, we specify Devlin's desired body orientation at the endpoint of the curved movement, by placing a body orientation symbol in the upper relation symbol (i.e. the relation symbol that defines the end-point of Devlin's movement). Consequently, the curvature of the trajectory in Devlin's turning movement is adjusted so that the body orientation constraint at that point in time is satisfied.

12. Here we finally achieve a correct description of Devlin's motion activity in the scene (to the degree of accuracy to which we intend to approach the actual film being used as an example). The curved movement segment is subdivided into two new segments: the first one is the same as the curved segment as notated previously (but of a shorter duration). The second one denotes a new straight-line forwards movement.

13. So far, the camera has not followed the actor, but this will now be changed. Two action symbols are added to the staff for Cam1, to specify the camera's motion activity. This is an initial attempt (by writing a simple pan) to be refined in the next step. The camera's position does not change throughout the scene, which must now be explicitly specified to avoid ambiguity, and is represented as the camera's body not moving. This is notated using a rectangular body action symbol. The dashed facing action symbol on the left denotes that the camera pans from right to left. The pin placed in the middle of the facing action symbol further specifies that the camera panning will cover one quadrant. By default, the speed of the panning is constant.

14. By attaching a maintained relation symbol, with a framing symbol placed on it, to the action symbols in the Cam1 staff, we define a constraint on the panning movement of the camera. Specifically, we force the camera

facing to keep Devlin 'in frame'. The exact way in which we want Devlin to be framed is represented by the framing symbol. In this case, Devlin is to be centred. The speed of the panning is no longer constant, as it must be adjusted in order to satisfy the framing constraint. The size of the panning movement is also no longer explicitly given as a quarter-circle, but follows from the need to keep Devlin centred. [Finally, a notable deviation from the film appears here, as we omit the notation to specify that Devlin enters from screen right, as happens in the actual film. This will be included in a later version of this tutorial.]

15. In the final step, we accurately specify the camera's position in the scene. This is not attempted directly (i.e. by adding a position symbol for the camera, as we did for Devlin), but indirectly. Specifically, the camera positioning is achieved in two steps. First, we fine-tune the shot distance of the camera by adding modifiers to the shot distance symbol (which results in the camera moving a little backwards to achieve the new shot distance). Second, we change the facing orientation of the camera (i.e. the angle at which the camera faces Devlin). These new constraints require the camera to be displaced, creating the desired relationships within the scene. We have gradually built a reasonable film scene, lasting several seconds, and requiring only a small amount of notation.

DirectorNotation – Acting
- Effort Graph (Laban)
- Choreutic Unit (V Preston-Dunlop)
- Posture, Gesture Merging (Laban, Lamb, Savrami)

DirectorNotation – Labanotation Commonalities
- Notation layout (bottom to top)
- Time bars (in DN they are in form of arrows)
- Action symbols – Paths
- Magnitude symbols
- Phrasing bows
- Orientation symbols – Pins

Conclusions

Our effort to create DirectorNotation so far has addressed two areas of activity. Firstly, creating the artistic notation itself, i.e. the visual language. Secondly, creating test implementations of tools to process the notation. Due to limited resources for research work before acquiring the support of a full research project, these results are by no means fully successful or exploitable; indeed, the limitations we encountered in our prototyping work have shown us clearly what is needed by a large project like ANSWER[1] in order to get together the critical mass that can make DirectorNotation a real success.

Development of a successful Director notation becomes appropriate today because of its dependence upon the parallel development of effective notation-based software tools to support the artist in the visualisation of their intention, communication to other members of the production team, and analysis of the production process, whilst still maintaining control of his creative intention. Bringing DirectorNotation to full maturity and high industrial impact will surely take many more years of research and development. The work we present here is a first attempt at the problem. We therefore concentrate equally on the actual notation developed so far and on its underlying principles. These principles not only motivate and validate our current achievements, but also pave the way to realising our long-term vision. Technical implementation issues, however, are postponed to later publications. The novel content- representation mechanisms that we introduce in this paper can in the future enrich applications for searching, repurposing and semantically analysing media databases. However, our current approach is to focus strongly on our core application, that is, the planning and deeper understanding of the filmmaking decisions and tasks of an otherwise conventional film production before it begins.

1 A new approach to the creative process of film and game production
  • Exploits DirectorNotation to create and develop notation-based tools that:
  − support the artist in pre-visualising his intention (through 3D animation)
  − enable the artist to communicate his intention to production crew
  − Facilitates a detailed description of the production process (affects the production cost)
  • Funded by the European Union, in collaboration with:
  − University of Southampton IT Innovation Centre
  − Fraunhofer IGD, Germany
  − Larian Studios, Belgium

The weathering body: composition and decomposition in environmental dance and site-specific art

Nigel Stewart

Still Life

I want to explore the different ways in which Laban Movement Analysis (or LMA) can be integral to the creation, and not just the documentation, of environmental dance, and in doing so I want to consider the kind of ecological knowledge and values that can be generated by environmental dance in general.[1] To do this I want to focus on *Still Life*, a collaboration between Sap Dance and The Lou Wilson Company that was developed over 12 days at Far Arnside, a stretch of coast between Lancashire and Cumbria overlooking Morecambe Bay, the largest intertidal area in the UK. I begin with a straightforward description of one of several performances of *Still Life* last September.

It is early evening. Spectators rendezvous at the entrance of a luxury caravan park. They are met by The Guide (Derek Tarr). He conducts them to the southeast edge of the park, down a thin winding path, then through a gate to a promontory at the top of a cliff overlooking a long beach with a panoramic view of the Bay. Beneath is a rivulet bubbling up through shingle half way up the beach. From the promontory The Guide plays a recording from a small hand-held digital recorder. It is a speech about painting composition. The Guide then gives binoculars to spectators and points towards a figure afar on a rocky outcrop at the far southeast end of the beach. Through the binoculars, they see The Woman (Lou Wilson) in an eighteenth-century dress, her arms arched place high as if she is drowned and suspended in water. The Woman disappears behind the rock's far side then reappears, splashing as she sprints along the edge of a sandbar towards the rivulet. Abruptly, she stops and stares.[2] Straightaway The Man (Nigel Stewart) spasms to life. Until now he has been unnoticed, dressed in a grey suit and slumped over a lump of mud at the end of the rivulet. What follows is 'Crab', the first of two choreographed dances: barely rising above the rivulet's water, mud and shingle, he arches, coils and scuttles up the rivulet. Reaching its source, he staggers to his feet then drops into a corkscrewed shape. He is still. A beat later The Woman runs north along the sandbar's edge.

Spectators are ushered down the steep cliff to a line of plastic bottles that mark a path past The Man and along the beach towards a large limestone crag at the northwest end. Before they reach the crag they stop by a scattering of white feathers and hear another recorded speech, this time about the biomechanics of bird flight. They then follow a trail of small apples over slippery sand between the waters edge and a limestone boulder. Climbing up through a gap onto a rocky platform, they turn to see The Man perched precariously at the top of the limestone crag. 'Gull', the second set dance, follows: The Man commandingly carves open and contracts, folds and elongates his arms and undulates his torso like a slow motion bird in flight whilst all the time stretching, spinning, staggering and side-stepping, halting, teetering, tipping and hastening down the crag's steep side. Finally leaping onto the limestone boulder, he claps his hands urgently as he follows the flight of a flock of birds and screws his body into a crouched shape.[3] Far out on the sands behind the spectators, The Woman echoes The Man's claps before running, again northward, into the setting sun then around the curving edge of the sandbar to disappear behind more rock.

The Guide then shows the spectators a series of small installations. They are taken to a little beach with a ship drawn in sand and a map made from shards of eighteenth-century pottery; then through a gully, where they see two A4-size photographs of a dead seagull in different states of decomposition, onto a plateau of spongy grass, pock-marked with pools and gouged by gullies. Led to the edge of this plateau, they see just below, on the topmost tier of seaweed-caked rock, two lines of A4 photographs, held down by stones, of waves lapping that same rock. They are then steered around the grass plateau to view a sequence of roughly-made A4-sized white cardboard frames placed over flowers, other flora and man-made debris (here a shoe sole, there a sock). Finally, they find a pool at the north end of the plateau. There they see the Woman, for the first time up-close, head-down and in a corkscrew shape reminiscent of the Man at the end of 'Crab' and the form of the rotting seagull.[4] The Guide plays the third and final recording: a scientific explanation of decomposition. The Man walks up from behind the spectators, looks over the Woman, and says: 'I had a sister, Whom the blind waves and surges have devour'd'.[5] Man and Woman are still. Spectators depart, exiting through a gate at the edge of a shingle beach north of the grass plateau.

Composition and spatial perception

In order to reflect upon what I have just described, I want to offer two contrary arguments about the environmental values of *Still Life*. The first argument is that the work accords with the view that human culture has dominion over and control of the natural world through artistic and scientific frames of description. Most obviously, all of Lou Wilson's installations involved the aesthetic framing of objects found *in situ*. On the grass plateau, she literally placed frames around all manner of plants and objects as she

found them. In other instances, she collected and deliberately arranged objects – even her own body – without an actual frame but in the manner of a
Still Life painting. But in either case the effect was partly self-referential: her
installations drew attention to how humans draw attention to natural phenomena in an effort to make them scientifically or aesthetically intelligible.

Indeed, the installations were strongly influenced by our visit in September 2008 to the *Still Life* exhibition at the Hamburger Kunsthalle, but also by plant ecology, in which the composition of communities of flora are mapped though a comparison between samples of species analysed within quadrants placed over areas of land (Rodwell 1995)[6], and, less obviously and on a much larger scale, by scientific cartography where geographical features are mapped according to abstract grid lines.

A similar point can be made about the prints, again on A4 paper, of photographs of disappearing phenomena. The two photographs of a rotting seagull were placed in the very spot where the actual sea gull was found and photographed at three day intervals, and from where that real seagull was subsequently washed away. The photographs of the sea were arranged at low tide on the very spot where the sea was photographed at high tide. In both cases the permanent digitised record seems to triumph over an ephemeral originary that has since vanished with the tide and can only be verified though photographic re-production.

Ostensibly, then, these installations were instances not so much of the natural world *per se*, but rather human points of view *of* the natural world that dictate *how* the natural world is to be perceived. To pursue this line of argument, the whole performance consisted not of an unmediated experience *of* nature but a sequence of points of view *over* the natural world. Quite literally, *Still Life's* dramaturgy was plotted by the route that spectators took to vantage points from which they could view human action on land and sand – and, it could be said, from which a landscape and seascape were constituted. Points of view were also presented through speeches associated with key vantage points. Arguably, those speeches were given greater authority because they were pre-recorded and played from a digital recorder, and they were deliberately designed to determine the spectators' perception of what they saw. For instance, the first recorded speech lists eight 'elements of design' in the composition of paintings, namely, the elements of *line, shape, colour, texture, direction, size, perspective, space* (Dunstan 1979).[7] Accordingly, spectators were predisposed to see exactly those *painterly* elements in the wider environment, and in particular how The Women, in running along the edges of the sandbar and other land forms, delineated the geometric *shapes* from which the landscape is apparently composed.

Crucially, it can also be argued that even the choreographed dances arose from this tendency to impose an alien human system of description upon an impermanent autochthonous phenomenon – that is, a biological, geological or physiological phenomenon indigenous to and formed in the spot where it is found. Firstly, this can be seen in my strategy of what I will call *metonymic transference* whereby I attempted to avoid autochthony by evolving my solo movement material not at the spot where I knew I would eventually perform it, but rather on the very different terrain immediately north of that spot. Thus I choreographed 'Gull' on the plateau of soft grass and then transferred it south and imposed it onto the steep, dry, sharp limestone crag, and my 'Crab' material was originated on that crag and then transferred south to the beach and imposed on the flat stony rivulet.

Secondly, it could be said that LMA provided yet another example of a human system or frame of description that was imposed upon natural phenomena, for I used LMA to analyse the flora and fauna that inspired my movement. This can be detailed in my development of 'Gull'. Not only did I derive a basic movement phrase from biomechanical studies of bird flight, but the variations I made on that phrase were directly informed by an effort analysis of the flight patterns of birds as they descended and arose from a lake at Leighton Moss, a large RSPB Nature Reserve at Silverdale. Looking out on the birds through the window frame of a hide by the side of the lake, I notated what I observed using distinctions made by Ann Hutchinson Guest in a 1985 paper on dynamics. Specifically, I observed that differences in the ways in which birds took off, flew and landed could be defined not just in terms of bound or free flow, but the way in which bound or free flow was differently combined with the spatial direction and focus of flow. For instance, I noticed that the wing tips of some birds moved in even carving arcs and in proportion to the sustained articulation of the proximal joints, not just on the downward pull but also on the upward return of the wing. I was reminded of the sagittal motion of an experienced long-distance freestyle swimmer who pulls evenly through the water right from the shoulder to the tips of her or his flat hand then stretches forward above the water without seeming to increase or decrease the speed of motion, or else a rower who engages her or his core to follow through the pull of the oar and then, with the same even resolve, lifts the oar backwards over the water to the insertion point. The effect is of a sustained and direct surge in which bound flow of movement is combined with outward flow of energy and outward focus and projection of attention. By contrast, other birds combined an outward projection and free flow of energy on the sustained upward action of the wing, but this was followed by the inward and bound flow of a jerking downward pull. And by contrast to both of these examples, other species seemed to combine an extended peripheral flow of energy and outward projection of attention with long downward pulls and shorter upward returns, then abruptly brought their focus and direction of flow inward as they engaged in a frantic, freer faster flapping.

To summarise this first line of argument, LMA in particular, and indeed *Still Life* in general, fits what aesthetician Malcolm Budd terms the *object model* of environmental aesthetics. According to this model, which is espoused by analytic philosophers such as Hilary Putnam, it is unfeasible to come to terms with nature as a whole, but it is possible to make nature comprehensible in human terms by 'cut[ting] up the world into objects' (Putnam 1981: 52). According to Budd, we do this by 'remov[ing aspects of the world], actually or contemplatively, from [their] surroundings' (Budd 2000: 130), and, crucially, we do that, says Putnam, through either aesthetic or scientific 'scheme[s] of description', of which, then, LMA would be one example amongst many others (Putnam 1981: 52). In short, by using LMA to study the dynamic qualities of natural things I am not experiencing nature *qua* nature but a human construction of nature.

Furthermore, our strategy of giving vantage points to the spectators from which they could survey the design of the landscape, and my attempt, from the vantage point of the hide by the lake, to survey designs in the movement of birds and then to let those designs inform my own choreographic designs, both seem to fit the closely-related *landscape* model of environmental aesthetics. According to this model, nature is 'constituted as nature' by 'scaping' it from a position of surveillance – a masterful vantage point over nature typified by the facility that humans have to observe, and replicate what they observe, in scientific experiments and horticultural practices, or to reduce a multifarious land mass into a landscape painting with a singular perspective. Thus:

> before it can ever be a repose for the senses, landscape is the work of the mind. [...] What lies beyond the window pane of our apprehension [...] needs a design before we can properly discern its form, let alone derive pleasure from its perception. And it is culture, convention, and cognition that makes that design (Schama 1995: 6–7, 12).

Decomposition

There is an argument running counter to all this. This alternative argument is rooted in an experience of the natural world through which the object and landscape models begin to unravel. Significantly, in my case this unravelling was engendered by, and occurred not in spite of, my very attempts to describe the appearance and motility of things according to LMA. A key moment was when I noticed how the dynamic designs I have described were radically disturbed by abrupt changes to phenomena beyond the control of the birds, most especially abrupt fluctuations in the degree of resistance provided by air currents. All of a sudden, birds would plummet like stones or were pinged upwards before gaining some kind of equilibrium. This was especially the case when birds came into land on the lake. Birds whose on-drive had been to glide commandingly towards a destination suddenly flapped wildly to cope with gravity's pull as they cambered nose down then chest out towards the water. Out on the sands, we saw how oyster catchers powered *into* sudden gusts of wind then banked their bodies to be whooshed far away on the wind's pathway.

Soon it seemed as if everything everywhere – leaves, branches, water, rock, sand – was affected by these giddy fluctuations in the wind's weight, and, under this influence, the longer I worked the more I surrendered myself to such unpredictable and uncontrollable fluctuations. For instance, on several occasions when I started 'Gull' at the top of the limestone crag, my body was suddenly buffeted by the wind as my arms carved open laterally from place high. Rather than merely carry on according to the count and effort quality that I had first predetermined, I learnt to use my arms to sense as precisely as possible the incremental increase in the wind's resistance to that movement, and to persist only with the phrase as the wind subsided.

Even the mellow warmth of the balmy late summer early evening sun, as it beamed out of a blue gap in the clouds, exerted a delicate pressure against which I wanted to press back and which thus affected the dynamic quality of my movement at that moment, in particular sagittal undulations of my torso as I descended the crag. Of course to descend such a steep crag whilst performing my solo meant that, far from merely imposing material onto the crag, the crag itself was imposing its conditions upon me, claiming me, sculpting my material to its own peculiarities of footholds and precarious edges as I fought against gravity to prevent myself from falling and injury.

Indeed, I have learnt to consider the whole piece not as an *intervention into* a place but a *yielding* to the place's own gravitational force which has, then, profoundly affected my sense and knowledge of that place. At the end of the process I wondered why I felt so called to deploy my aforementioned strategy of 'metonymic transference', and then, right at the end of the process, I had an epiphany: I realised that it was all to do with the outgoing tide. At Far Arnside a large sand bar, which is exposed at low tide, stretches parallel to the shore line so that water in between the shore line and that sand bar cannot go directly eastwards out to sea, but rather is drained south to circumnavigate the sandbar. This was the very sandbar along which The Woman ran. Thus my pre-conscious experience of water sucking south informed my decision to transfer my movement south, and, since 'tides are caused by the effects of gravity in the earth-moon-sun system' (Natural Environment Research Council 2008), it seems that this strategy was influenced by my intuition of gravity's effects.

Forensic Science confirms that gravity affects the way in which things decompose (Haglund and Sorg 2001), and we witnessed gravity in many different decompositional processes: in the rotting seagull; in our costumes which, with successive performances, became weightier with water, sand, mud and salt; in our bodies that became heavier as they grew colder; in our wind-beaten, sun-burnished faces; in the leathery-skin of the tramp who sat like a shrub in the place from which I eventually began 'Gull'; and in the limestone, formed from the decomposed remains of millions of sea creatures and an array of chemical and meteorological forces, which continue to decay. Even the paper on which the photographs of the seagull and the sea were printed became weathered by the stones that held them down, by splashes of sea, sand and rain. Like everything else, our being there was being remade by that place.

Crucially, to recognise things as decomposing things is to neither isolate them as discrete and stable entities as in the object model, nor to survey them as in the landscape model, but rather to engage with and yield to the temporality of forces through which things arise and dissipate in an environment of which they are a part. This is central to what David Wood (2003) calls 'liminology' or the 'boundaries of thinghood'. For Wood, the *making* of boundaries is necessary to the lived experience of place – but then so too is the *breaching* of boundaries caused by a deconstrual of space and time. Most obviously, space is deconstrued through the cardboard frames because, in forming a boundary around things, they did not just heighten the quality of what they contained but also drew attention to what they could not. Time was deconstrued through the photographs of the absent seagull and waves because, in having nothing in and of themselves of the fragility and weight of the rotting carcass or the spill and slap of the sea, they defer to the onlooker to imagine those sensations and thus engender an *ekstatic* consciousness of time in which past ghosts present.[8] In similar vein, the juxtaposition of the recorded speech about the biomechanics of bird flight with the splattered feathers which suggest an Icarus-like fall after flight, indicates the impossibility of talking about the aesthetics of bird flight in such a way. That job is left, if not to The Man dancing as a gull on the crag, to the birds themselves which fly unpredictably above. Thus, if our very attempts to frame Far Arnside in different ways were always exceeded by processes beyond those frames, we needed those frames precisely to register the forces through which they were breached.[9]

In Dance Theatre, like most theatre, human action is framed by the proscenium arch or some other means of demarcating the edge of the performance space, by lights which isolate objects, bodies or body parts, by rules or conventions of style and genre, and by conceptual frameworks such as the kinesphere (which demarcates the boundaries of the abstract human body). This follows a binary logic which dictates that whatever is outside of those frameworks is, often literally, put out of sight and out of mind. Environmental dance, however, follows an *ecological logic* of interdependence in which any single thing becomes inextricably part of and increasingly subject to unpredictable forces of the environment. And this is exemplified in the altered consciousness of weight and gravity experienced in environmental dance. Arguably, our experience of gravity is literally central to our sense of place. Certainly, in LMA *place centre* is the individual's 'centre of gravity', defined as 'the dividing point between the two directions of each dimension. Thus this point becomes, as well, the centre of our kinesphere' (Laban 1966: 11). If my sense of self is coterminous with my centre of gravity and coextensive with my sense of kinesphere, then my sense of place is no more than a self-contained and set apart sense of self. Whatever the case, in environmental dance any contained sense of self is undone – joyfully or otherwise – as the human body is pulled beyond itself by the gravitational force of an expansive, heterogeneous, unpredictable and ever-changing other-than-human world. To thus experience this world's gravity is to feel its *alterity*. This, then, is the kind of environmental knowledge that environmental dance can make available. It is knowledge of environment peculiar to and registered through bodily experience but beyond bodily control. To know environment in this way is to have a kinaesthetic feeling for environment ontologically different from seeing it instrumentally as an exploitable resource. It is to respect environment as other and as that with which we have a 'natal bond'.[10] The dancer who yields to environment to become a yield of environment knows this. So does the spectator through her or his sympathetic intuition of what happens *to* the dancer as much as what the dancer *does*. As we teeter on the brink of a global environmental catastrophe that we may yet have the courage to avoid, the worth of this bond with the world and experience of its alterity cannot be underestimated.

References

Barba, Eugenio and Savarese, Nicola (1991) *A Dictionary of Theatre Anthropology: The Secret Art of The Performer*, ed. R. Gough, tr. by R. Fowler, London and New York: Routledge/Centre for Performance Research.

Berry, Philippa (1994) *Of Chastity and Power: Elizabethan Literature and the Unmarried Queen*, London and New York: Routledge.

Briginshaw, Valerie (2001) *Dance, Space and Subjectivity*, Basingstoke: Palgrave.

Budd, Malcolm (2002) *The Aesthetic Appreciation of Nature: Essays on the Aesthetics of Nature*, Oxford: Clarendon Press/Oxford University Press.

Chodorow, Joan (1991) *Dance Therapy and Depth Psychology: The Moving Imagination*, London & New York: Routledge.

Dunstan, Bernard (1979) *Composing Your Paintings*. London, Studio Vista.

Fraleigh, Sondra (2005) 'Spacetime and Mud in Butoh', in Gabriella Giannachi and Nigel Stewart (eds) *Performing Nature*, Bern: Peter Lang.

Guest, Ann Hutchinson (1985) 'Dynamics', *The Labanotator*, 40, London: Language of Dance Centre.

Haglund, William D and Sorg, Marcella H (2001) *Advances in Forensic Taphonomy: Method, Theory and Archaeological Perspectives*, CRC Press.

iLAND (2009) *iLAND: Interdisciplinary Laboratory for Art, Nature, Dance* [Online] Available: www.ilandart.org (accessed: 6 April).

Innes, Christopher (1983) *Edward Gordon Craig*, Cambridge: Cambridge University Press.

Laban, Rudolf (1966) *Choreutics*, London: MacDonald & Evans.

Laban, Rudolf (1988) *Modern Educational Dance*, 3rd edn., rev. L. Ullmann, Plymouth: Northcote House.

Manning, Susan (1993) *Ecstasy and the Demon: Feminism and Nationalism in the Dances of Mary Wigman*, Berkeley: University of California Press.

Merleau-Ponty, Maurice (1968 [1964]) *The Visible and The Invisible*, Evanston, Ill.: Northwestern University Press.

Monson, Jennifer (2009) *Birdbrain Dance: A Navigational Dance Project* [Online] Available: www.birdbraindance.org (accessed: 6 April).

Natural Environment Research Council (2008) 'Questions and Answers about tides', *Proudman Oceanographic Laboratory* [Online] Available: http://www.pol.ac.uk/home/insight/tidefaq.html#3 (accessed: 21 October).

Putnam, Hilary (1981) *Reason, Truth, and History*, Cambridge: Cambridge University Press.

Rodwell, John (1995) *Handbook for Using the National Vegetation Classification*, Joint Nature Conservation Committee.

Roth, Gabriella (1997) *Sweat Your Prayers: Movement as Spiritual Practice*, Dublin: Newleaf.

Schama, Simon (1995) *Landscape & Memory*, London: HarperCollins.

Sheets-Johnstone, Maxine (1979) *The Phenomenology of Dance*, 2nd edn, London: Dance Books.

Stewart, Nigel (2002) 'Actor as *Refusenik*: Theatre Anthropology, Semiotics and the Paradoxical Work of the Body', in I. Watson (ed.) *Negotiating Cultures: Eugenio Barba and the Intercultural Debate*, Manchester: Manchester University Press, pp. 46–58.

Stewart, Nigel (2005) 'Introduction', in Gabriella Giannachi and Nigel Stewart (eds) Performing Nature, Bern: Peter Lang.

Thomas, Helen (1995) *Dance, Modernity and Culture: Explorations in the Sociology of Dance*, London and New York: Routledge.

Waterton, Claire (2003) 'Performing the Classification of Nature', in Bronislaw Szerszynski, Wallace Heim and Claire Waterton (eds.) *Nature Performed: Environment, Culture and Performance*, Oxford: Blackwell, pp. 111-29.

Wood, David (2003) 'What is Eco-Phenomenology', in Charles S. Brown and

Ted Toadvine (eds.) *Eco-Phenomenology: Back to the Earth Itself*, New York: State University of New York Press, pp. 211-233.

1. I use the term environmental dance as a kind of catch-all phrase. I mean by it the plethora of dance and somatic practices concerned with landscape and the environment, and with the human body's relationship to place, site and the natural world, including the other-than-human world of animals and plants. Most obviously, this includes site-specific outdoor choreographed and improvised performances. Historical antecedents include the prearranged dances and choreographed combats between mythical figures which surprised Queen Elizabeth I as she walked through the woods of Kenilworth and Woodstock in 1575 (Berry 1994: 98); to the film of Mary Wigman's 'Wandering', the second section from her 1924 work *Scenes from a Dance Drama*, in which Wigman explores patterns of gathering and scattering across a rural setting with her pack of acolytes (Manning 1993); to Lea Anderson's *Out on the Windy Beach* of 1998 in which, at a number of seaside locations, a sextet of dancers, costumed in luminous lime green body suits, performed dances derived from mermaid poses, beauty contests and films of reptilian aliens (Briginshaw 2001: 59-62). This category of Environmental Dance also includes the site-specific work of a host of Butoh performers, including Takenouchi Atsushi, committed to dancing over places where large numbers of people have died, such as the killing fields of Cambodia, Poland, Japan (Fraleigh 2005: 336); Min Tanaka's *Dream Island* in which Tanaka danced over a rubbish tip in Tokyo Bay; and the work of companies associated with Tanaka's Body Weather Work, including Tess De Quincey's De Quincey Co, Stuart Lynch's Perfume Collective and Frank van de Ven's Body Weather Amsterdam. Other examples include events led by Welsh-based movement artist Simon Whitehead; and Jennifer Monson's iLAND projects (iLAND 2009), most notably her multi-year Birdbrain Migrations in which Monson and her flocks of dancers improvise over beaches, bridges and bird sanctuaries as they follow the migratory patterns of whales, ospreys, ducks and other birds up and down the whole North American continent (Monson 2009).

Another category of Environmental Dance consists of indoor works designed for the stage in which choreography and scenography have evolved from environmental field research or which seek to capture natural forms through movement. A rough guide of such works would include Loïe Fuller's evocation of flames, lilies, butterflies and other natural forms in her early twentieth-century skirt dances (Thomas 1995: 55-60); to Isadora Duncan's obsession with the wave form and concern for 'biological dance' (Innes 1983: 117); to Merce Cunningham's *Beach Birds* (1991) and *Pond Way* (1998); and, much more recently, to Rosemary Lee's *Beached* (2002), Celina Chaulvin's *Phos* (2004), Sap Dance's *Lune* (2005), and Jacky Lansley's *View from the Shore* (2007).

Just as importantly, environmental dance includes approaches to movement training that develop the dancing body in and through the exploration of environment. I'm thinking of the workshops and courses run by Whitehead, Monson and other aforementioned artists, and the Body Weather Work training system. Finally, Environmental Dance arguably includes different *choreological* systems which each attempt to enumerate primary qualities of motion manifest in all moving things, particularly in the natural world. These includes Laban's eight basic efforts (Laban 1988: 52–84) and 'four fundamental trace-forms' (Laban 1966: 83), Gabriella Roth's Five Rhythms (Roth 1997); Theatre Anthropology's five transcultural laws of scenic bios (Stewart 2002: 47–50; Barba and Savarese 1991: 56); dance phenomenology's four components of virtual force (Sheets-Johnstone 1979: 49–58, 112–28); and Jungian dance therapy's seven archetypal affects (or emotions) exhibited by humans and other animals (Chodorow 1991: 71–84).

2. Spectators wrote to us afterwards. They felt that 'Lou [Wilson's] haunting stillness was quite ominous and powerful. It was as if she was part of the surroundings, a presence that is always there and always watching – much like nature itself. [...] Perhaps the most engaging impression for me was the sense of movement through space and thinking in very large compositional terms. [But] I cannot get the sound of Lou [Wilson's] feet slap, slapping through the water's edge, out of my mind.'

3. One spectator said that 'Nigel [Stewart's] dancing on the rocks [...] opened up the focus and eye line of the audience to take in the enormity of the space. [...] The environment as a whole felt very

charged. There was a freedom and honesty to his movement that achieved absolute attention from the audience.'

4. Another spectator commented on this 'final tableau. Shocking, shocking. She is dead, her hair in the water, the [...] wildflowers in her hand yet also in the water. Drowned? Almost certainly. Washed there and left by the tide? Maybe.'

5. The line is Sebastian's from Shakespeare's *Twelfth Night* (V.i. 226-7).

6. The size of samples can vary from 2 x 2 metres for short herbaceous vegetation to 50 x 50 metres for sparse scrub (Rodwell 1995: 14). In a fascinating interdisciplinary study, the sociologist Claire Waterton (2003) has compared my use of dance phenomenology's four components of virtual force (Sheets-Johnstone 1979: 49-58, 112-28) and her use of the National Classification System (Rodwell 1995) to analyse plant species in the same 2 x 2 quadrant!

7. *Line* is 'the visual path that enables the eye to move within the piece'; *shape* is defined by the geometric or organic edges of areas within the painting, *colour* consists of the relative values and intensities of hues; *textures* consists of the illusion of tactility produced by the surface qualities of paint; *direction* is given by the vertical or horizontal pathways which the eye follows up and down and across the painting); *size* is created from the relative proportions and dimensions of different images and shapes within the painting; *perspective* is the expression of depth with its foreground, middle ground and background, and *space* consists of the particular combination of positive space (the space taken up by an object and negative space (the space between objects) (Dunstan 1979).

8. This is perfectly consistent with Husserl's phenomenology of internal time consciousness (Husserl 2002: 115). For Husserl, each moment contains not just a discrete impression but a *retention* of the previous moment *and* the succession between that moment and the moment before that. Furthermore, each moment contains a *protension* of a forthcoming moment and the succession between that and subsequent moments. Thus whilst photographs, in capturing single moments, normally epitomise the discrete impression - the 'severed' or sundered moment – the *Still Life* photographs had a retentive and protensive power by virtue of where and how they were exhibited.

9. Many of the spectators sensed this paradox. 'I really like [the] juxtapos[ition of the recordings] against our live experience', wrote one spectator. '[They] made me see the surroundings [...] in a different way. But, she added, 'they also spoke to me about how the manmade can never mimic the power of nature. [...] For the [recording] on bird flight a flock of oyster catchers rise from nowhere on the flats and circle twice over the finger of sky-colour water – perfectly timed to the length of the spoken text!'

Another spectator 'interpreted the empty photo frames as trying to frame nature and therefore denaturalise the natural. [...] The placing/framing is clever and makes me see particular things among the infinite possible things. [...] It made me think about the way we take in and acknowledge our surroundings (or not).

10. The term is Merleau-Ponty's, for whom analysis based on what we see does not 'conceive properly the natal bond between me who perceives and what I perceive' (Merleau-Ponty 1968:32); rather, '[t]he secret of the world we are seeing must necessarily be contained in my contact with it' (*ibid.*).

How did choreology influence the teaching process in artistic education of the French community of Belgium ?

Claudine Swann

As an inspector for dance education for more than twenty years in the Ministry of the French Community of Belgium, I have been watching people teaching dance in the context of artistic education and research. My missions in that system are amongst others:

- To control the application of the laws and study programmes, the quality and level of education;
- To represent the Ministry of the French Community of Belgium on several occasions, for example, as a member of the jury that awards the pedagogical certificate to the dance teachers and accompanists;
- To propose and supervise the content of professional development courses.

In that framework, I have participated in the complete revision of the artistic educational system that became law in 1998. The main and most important change was the introduction of the notions of competence, objective, content and study programme.

This has been a little revolution and has changed considerably the way of approaching the teaching of dance. Before, especially in classical dance, the objective of a class was essentially to teach the content and that content was the steps. Why should we learn the alphabet (of steps) if not to make words and then phrases to say something? Today those steps have become tools to teach something and that something has to be defined in the study programme in terms of educational objectives and content in order to allow the students to acquire competences in Autonomy, Creativity, Artistic Intelligence and Technical Mastery.

The new law allowed us also to ask ourselves those essential questions in education: WHY am I teaching WHAT, TO WHOM and HOW? Every teacher should be able to answer those questions and part of my work has been dedicated to helping them to do so. This was not an easy task ...

During my observation of classical dance classes I recognised immediately that what was missing the most was DANCE. Teachers were desperately concerned, by organising steps together, to be able to reach the unreachable

...virtuosity. Notice that the students, in the non- compulsory education system which is the most important part of it, are between 7 and 20 years old and come a maximum twice a week for an hour! So I had to confront them with the reality of that context and make them understand and accept that steps and virtuosity will not lead them to reach the objective of allowing students to acquire competences in 'A, C, AI, and TM'.

The hardest tasks for the teachers were Creativity and Artistic Intelligence because art and expression were absent in their teaching. Training is not synonymous with education, Technique does not imply Expression and it is also not the aim to put a smile on your pas de bourrée, Creativity is not, as I heard and saw many times, just improvisation. The majority of our students will not become professional dancers but are or will be the public of artistic performances so we have to give them tools and knowledge to appreciate and understand art. Making art needs also a sense of what you make and to know what and how you are making.

Before the law, in the frame of professional development, I invited 'Masters' of the Paris Opera Ballet and international well-known teachers to share their experience but the result was sixty teachers sitting in a studio and having arguments about vocabulary and the grammar of steps. Simply a disaster ...But while I was still working on the revision of the system, I met Rosemary Brandt in a conference demonstration and immediately, knowing the problems I was being confronted with, I recognised that her approach of choreology and its application in the teaching of dance could be a great help to us all.

It is now thirteen years that she has been coming for workshops in Belgium, and I can say that today we have some great teachers. What was impressive in the beginning was to see teachers of classical, contemporary and jazz dance working all together, speaking the same language, having a dialogue and sharing their experience. That was unusual. If dance has evolved, its transmission has not always followed. Most of the time people come to teaching after having been professional dancers and their methods come from the reproduction of their own experience, often archaic or, at worst, improvised day after day. With the study programme that had to be elaborated and the four basic competences this was no longer possible.

Choreology contains different models to analyse movement and those models have been tools that allowed teachers to change their methods and to speak about dance in terms of movement. I think that is clearer than using images that can be subject to different interpretations. Imagine explaining a movement to twenty children; it results in twenty different movements and that is not always what is required.

The models are the Structural Model, Choreutics, Principles of Movement, Strands of the Medium, Non-verbal Communication and a model for interpretation and evaluation. During the workshops we mainly investigated the first three and now the teachers have a completely different approach to dance. Actually they understand now, what Rosemary calls the raw material of dance movement. They know that dance is a result of transformation, manipulation of movement by choices you make deliberately on how to use its different components which will convey its specific aesthetic.

Even if every component of the movement is linked and has implications for one another I will take each aspect of the structural model separately, namely, Body, Space, Relationships, Dynamics and Action, in order to demonstrate what had to change and to give you some examples of how.

Before I examine the structure of the body, I have to be precise that the way we use the structural model is to NAME WHAT YOU CREATE TO BE SEEN AND WHAT YOU ACTUALLY DO. The Body used to be addressed as an instrument and too often one forgot the person that lives in there. You certainly have all heard the teacher in a dance class shouting 'your knee, your back, your foot'. Dancers were waiting for the right information to be given to fix the problem. It is better to speak to the person about her knee, her back and her foot. Let the students experiment and discover how to fix the problem, let them discover how they can bring attention to the different parts of their body via showing, hiding, leading with, looking at etc... Let them look and observe with a specific objective in mind, not just look at the chignon of their friend. In these activities you will progress towards autonomy, creativity, artistic intelligence and technical mastery. This process will be much more educative than mere shouting.

The structure of space

The vocabulary of classical dance includes positions; *attitude, arabesque*, positions of the arms and legs... In the teaching process, the tendency is often to organise the steps in several positions which result in a lack of movement and an addition of poses not linked together. Using choreutic units and their manner of materialisation, a theory of Valerie Preston Dunlop, we could observe that the result of that organisation was a series of body designs. This means that the shape in space is created by the body. One way to solve that problem was to introduce the notion of spatial progression, in other words to draw a shape in space with the movement. It was exactly what was missing.

As an example I take the teaching of the five positions of the arms in a *port de bras*. It is not necessary to stay in each position, once the child knows them theoretically you explain the exercise as passing through each of these positions; they know where the exercise starts and ends and you bring their attention to drawing in space, spatial progression. The result is much more interesting.

To be precise in space it is also necessary to learn about directions... where do I go? about orientation of the body in space... facing what? Where is up related to my body? ...when I stand, 'up' is above my head but if I lie down then 'up' is still above my head but not in the same direction in the general space. Teachers were fascinated because they had never thought about it before. It sounds so simple but those notions were very important revelations.

Did you ever think that when you do a *battement tendu* you don't only make a gesture with your leg which is already uncommon, but you can draw a straight line on the floor with your toes and for a child to draw, and especially with the foot, is much more interesting than to just stretch their leg in front of themselves.

The structure of dynamics

This has been the biggest key and particularly the notion of Rhythm of the movement.

Children are so tense in classical dance class so for them to learn how to use their energy in relation to gravity and to be subtle in accelerations and decelerations has been magical.

So when that child is drawing the straight line of the *battement tendu* with her foot and then can accelerate her movement with an impact or decelerate it in an impulse, then make it as a rebound or a swing, a *battement tendu* will never be the same again. To know you can maintain, increase or diminish the use of energy in order to create the rhythm and the quality that you want to give to your movement is quite essential in dance.

Another aspect that has been investigated is the relationship between music and dance. The rhythm of movement is not the same as the rhythm of music even if energy and gravity are common ingredients. The movement accents do not have to copy the music accents; surprise is more interesting than redundancy but in a dance class it is unfortunately not often the case. The accompanist wants to help the teacher or the children by hitting the keys so strongly on each accent to keep them in the measure that it becomes very hard to make a light or a soft movement. The student must be able to create and keep his movement accents, his own movement rhythm without being imposed upon by the music. But that is another debate and I will no longer speak about the relationship between music and dance even if I am passionate about it.

The structure of action

There are twelve basic actions: jump, transfer the weight, turn, travel, stillness, lean, scatter, gather, torsion, fall, gesture and unspecified. This sounds simple but in dance we combine those actions, simultaneously and sequentially. To make an action of course you use your energy so you create a rhythm but not every single action needs to have its own rhythm. To decide when a movement phrase begins and when it ends in one rhythmic structure was also an important key, because the trap that one can fall in, when you have just learned about rhythm as a teacher, is to give a rhythm to each action and you might put the children in a completely inorganic state. But being aware of it you can get much more flow in your exercises and the students will be no longer only concentrated on the actual combination of steps but on the energy they have to use to create the rhythm of that combination.

As a conclusion, I think that a dance teacher should not impose everything, but suggest, propose, inform, allow to experiment, to observe and to discover and it is that kind of methodology that gives the students a chance to construct, develop, understand and create their movement and their dance.

A teacher is not the master that has a body of knowledge that students should reproduce identically but a person able to give keys to the students to allow them to acquire competences and develop their skills, keeping the uniqueness of their individuality.

It is only then that they will demonstrate skills in artistic intelligence, autonomy, technical mastery and creativity.

Here are some of the answers that a few teachers agreed to allow me to quote on the question: *What did the choreology workshops bring and change in your teaching?*

The first thing I want to say is that choreology gave me incredible tools to use the knowledge that I had as a dancer when I started to teach. I would have loved to have known them when I was still dancing, no doubt I would have been a better dancer and would have had a better understanding of all the aspects of danced movement and will not have been only preoccupied to master my classical technique with a well trained body. I started that education when I started to teach...good for my students! It was a great relief to be able to give to the students, whatever their abilities were, knowledge not only about what the body has to do, but also about how you manage space, what does movement create in that space? How does energy function? How can we play with it to create different qualities of movement, ...this has been an extraordinary opportunity for me to reach my objectives. And for the student, he is engaged in a process of learning in which he will feel and be much more successful.

I work in a school where classical and contemporary dance are taught and even if I am classically trained today I can analyse and understand the work of my colleagues because I know how it works in relation to the different components of movement.

When I had been introduced to choreology, I understood very quickly that it would be a discovery that will become an inescapable tool in my teaching. It has allowed me to make choices about my objectives of education; it has helped me a lot in choreography, and to give information to external examiners about how to evaluate my students. I also think that the repetition of an exercise becomes less a routine when you can consider it using the different structures. My students are more often in a successful situation than before when I was mainly working on body and technique. To be honest I'm not sure I would still be teaching today with the same enthusiasm if had not had that wonderful tool.

I am sixty-three years old and have been a principal dancer, have danced more than 150 Aurors in *Sleeping Beauty*, 300 Kitris in *Don Quixote*, then I have been a ballet master in a company. During the rehearsal I could give the dancers many tricks and corrections about technical aspects but I could not speak about the subtleties, I could only show them. Now I am a teacher and I would have continued the same way if I had not met Rosemary Brandt and choreology and I would have been frustrated and my students too. Today I know how to speak about the nuance of a movement. I can say where in space I want my impulse to begin, I can ask for a soft impact. I also know that when my students have a low level of energy I have to work on dynamic and at the opposite, when they are hyper-kinetic, I work on space because it asks for more concentration. Because I speak with my students and do not keep anything secret my role has been demystified; it does not mean that they respect me less, it is the opposite.

Classical ballet pedagogy:
the dancer as active contributor

Cadence Whittier

Classical ballet classes consist of a traditional structure. Typically, beginning with barre and ending with grand allegro, the teacher presents a series of exercises and steps that the students reproduce and repeat from class to class. This structure influences the role of the teacher and the student during the class period. The teacher is usually viewed as the expert. S/he imparts the information, distributes the exercises, and serves as the 'eyes' for the students' technique. The students act as the receivers of the information. They embody the teacher's corrections and are expected to skillfully perform the artistic and technical parts of the exercises. In this traditional structure, information and knowledge often travel in one direction from teacher to student, and consequently, the dancers may come to depend on the teacher's corrections, praise, and directions in order to initiate technical and artistic changes. Dance scholar Doug Risner argues,

> traditional dance pedagogy teaches obedience and emphasises silent conformity in which dancers reproduce what they receive rather than critique, question, or create it.[1]

Clearly, it is important for teachers to design well-structured classes and provide critical and thoughtful feedback to their students, and clearly dancers must learn how to embody the choreographer's intent or the teacher's corrections. But, how do the dancers learn how to actualise that intent from their own expressive desires? And, how do they develop a sense of initiative in the ballet classroom?

The structure of the ballet class should challenge students to participate in the teacher's methodological tools. Students, too, can learn how to provide critical and thoughtful feedback to their peers, create movement phrases, assess their technique, and analyse the artistic and technical qualities that define the ballet aesthetic. As this happens, they learn to engage actively and creatively in the learning process.

This paper will present a methodological process that focuses on four components: developing body awareness, exercising choice, following through with intent, and providing peer feedback. Laban/Bartenieff Movement Analysis (LMA/BF) facilitates this methodological process.

A tool for communication and self-understanding, LMA sensitises students to their inner and outer experiences' which 'changes the way the dancers perceive and talk about their technique and their expressive capabilities as artists and individuals.[2]

Laban/Bartenieff Movement Analysis (LMA/BF)

The interplay of physical action and expressive desire are essential principles in LMA/BF, and they are also essential principles when studying ballet technique. According to dance scholar Elizabeth Dempster, 'dance can be thoughtful action, a movement of embodied mind.'[3] This sentiment parallels Rudolf Laban's and Irmgard Bartenieff's philosophy of movement. Their intent was to

> instill a personal mastery of the language of movement expression both in physical embodiment and conscious understanding.[4]

Whether we are analysing the movement of factory workers, improvising freely, or participating in a codified technique form, such as ballet. human expression and bodily movement are intelligent, dynamic, and expressive. LMA/BF provides a framework for deciphering the functional and expressive landscape of movement, and it provides

> a means to equip students with an understanding of movement such that they are in greater control of their own development and versatility.[5]

In my ballet classes, dancers use the LMA/BF theories of Body, Effort, Shape, and Space (BESS) in order to analyse body connectivity, movement phrasing, energy, form, and spatial intent.

When working from a LMA/BF perspective, there is a consistent focus on accessing three-dimensional space, a full range of motion in the body, and a large dynamic palette. For example, my students may use concepts from Bartenieff Fundamentals in order to analyse how particular movements are organised in the body or how those movements could be performed more efficiently. As another example, they might identify how different energy qualities from the Effort category change the expressive nature of the balletic phrases. There are, in fact, many ways that balletic steps can be performed and interpreted. Using LMA/BF as a navigational tool helps dancers nurture, strengthen, and experiment with the many possibilities. This process teaches them to interpret and 'color' the steps in personal ways, which in turn develops personal uniqueness and artistry.

Methodological process

How do ballet dancers:[6]
• relate to each other during class? Are there opportunities for them to interact with peers?
• develop personal uniqueness within the balletic form?
• actively contribute to the class experiences?
• develop body knowledge?
• come to understand the ballet aesthetic and the conversation that occurs between their personal movement style and the ballet aesthetic?
• learn to move from their inner impulses?
The following paragraphs present a four part methodological process that addresses the above questions: developing body awareness, exercising choice, following through with intent, and providing feedback to peers.

Developing body awareness

Students in my advanced ballet classes typically view their bodies as instruments. This simple metaphor has a profound effect on their self-perception and their approach to learning ballet technique. Instruments are objects and can therefore be fixed, manipulated, altered, broken down, and put back together. When this is the operative metaphor in the classroom, the dancers tend to approach their bodies with a 'fix-it' mentality. Instead of accepting that change is a process, they try to place their bodies in the 'right' and 'correct' postures and positions. In doing so, however, they fail to realise that change in one part of the body causes changes in other parts of the body. For example, when a dancer changes the placement of the pelvis, the placement of the entire spine, lower body joints, and feet are also affected. Furthermore, since each dancer's body is different, the 'right' position is not standardised. The process of change must be viewed as creative and ongoing, which requires that dancers learn to sense and perceive, rather than fix and imitate, the desired change being asked of them in technique classroom. Likewise, teachers need to carefully observe their students in order to provide them with individually tailored and appropriate feedback.

The following paragraphs and tables present various LMA/BF theories and concepts that develop movement literacy and body knowledge in the ballet classroom. These concepts and theories help my dancers develop a more mindful, sensitive, and holistic approach to their technique training.

Perceiving the body as a whole: As the movement shifts, the spatial integrity of the whole body shifts. Each position in ballet provides different spatial challenges. Table 1 investigates this concept. There are four LMA theories presented in Table 1: Spatial Intent and Countertensions (Space Category), Shape Qualities (Shape Category), and Free Flow (Effort Category).

Learning to move dynamically: Since ballet is position and step oriented, it is easy for dancers and teachers to become overly focused on the execution of correct shapes and positions. As a result, many of the ballet dancers I encounter are less skilled at analysing how the steps and positions can be performed in unique and dynamic ways. We therefore focus on the following questions during the class period: What is the pathway of movement between different steps? How do the positions move into space? How does experimentation with movement phrasing change the technical demands of the steps and positions? Even though form and accuracy are important in ballet, explorations in dynamics, phrasing, and movement pathways teach the form very well. Table 2 investigates this idea. Four LMA theories are presented: Traceforms (Space), Shape Qualities, Effort Elements, and Phrasing.

TABLE 1: PERCEIVING THE BODY AS A WHOLE
LMA/BF theories: brief definitions
Spatial Intent/Pull describe where in space a dancer intends the movement to go or where the movement is 'pulling' the dancer in space. For example, a changement has a strong upward pull, a chassé is initiated by a forward low pull in the lower body, a piqué arabesque typically rides a forward and upward pull.

Countertensions describe the oppositional lines of energy that stabilise the body. For example, upward and downward spatial pulls are engaged in equal proportion in order to stabilise a relevé sous-sus. Countertensions teach dancers to align their bodies along spatial through-lines, which in turn prevent misaligned positions.

There are six *Shape Qualities*: Rising, Sinking, Spreading, Enclosing, Advancing, and Retreating. Shape Qualities do not describe the static shape of the body (rounded, linear, twisted, etc), but instead describe the forming process of the body as it moves into space. For example, the body Rises and Spreads into piqué à la seconde and the lower body Sinks and Spreads into a 1st position grand plié. When performed with Breath Support, Shape Qualities teach dancers to initiate movement in the torso and pelvis, and to practice three-dimensional shape change in the body.

Free Flow is one of the eight Effort elements in the Effort category (see Table 2). In my experience, amateur ballet dancers perform ballet technique with a high degree of Bound (contained) Flow, which causes excess tension and holding in their shoulder and hip joints, and in the cervical and lumbar areas of the spine. Free Flow, or outpouring flow, in conjunction with Breath Support, lessens the excess bodily tension, which in turn, helps the dancers perform the movement with easefulness and adaptability.

Movement examples:
As you perform the following movement examples, imagine little balloons softly expanding in your shoulder and hip joints, rib cage, and in between each vertebrae of the spine. This image will reduce tension at these joints and will help you move your limbs into space with Free (outpouring) Flow. Exhale from your diaphragm as you reach the end of the movement. As you exhale, engage the Countertensional lines of energy and Shape Qualities more fully, by allowing the 'balloons' in the joints to expand. Remember, the supporting side of the body is as spatially active as the gesturing side.

1. *Developé à la seconde from fifth position.* As you develop the left leg to second, imagine that the balloons on the right side expand and widen to the right as your right arm and left leg Spread to second position. Don't just open the arm and leg to second position. Instead, the Widening of the torso at the midline of the body should initiate the Spreading of the arms into a Countertension from the left leg to the right arm, passing through an expanded and wide torso. As the left leg développés higher into space, simultaneously stabilise the right side of the body in a vertical Countertension from the foot to the head. Make sure the described Countertensional lines of energy engage the entire body, not just the arms and legs. In my experience dancers need to feel the oppositional lines of energy through the torso especially. They have a tendency to disconnect the movement of the thorax from the movement of the pelvis. The Countertensional lines of energy assist in connecting these two areas of the body. Additionally, allowing the form of the body to engage in Spreading, especially through the shoulder girdle and ribs, will help coordinate the torso with the arms and legs.

2. *Balançoire.* Begin in a battement degagé devant. Then, balançoire to battement degagé derrière. Notice how the top of pelvis, the ribs, and shoulder girdle Advanced slightly as the gesturing leg Retreated. If doing this at barre, notice how your barre arm also needed to slide forward along the barre in order to maintain the connection between the arm and scapula. At the end of the movement feel the Countertensional pull from Forward High (in the upper body) to Back Low (in the gesturing leg). The pelvis should be aligned along this

Countertensional Spatial Pull – subtle engagement of the abdominal muscles will help connect the base of the ribs that the top of the pelvis. Finally, move the leg from derrière to first position. As the pelvis returns to its vertical position, the ribcage and shoulder girdle Retreat slightly and the barre arm slides backward along the barre. In this one example, the dancers begin to feel how their upper bodies respond to their lower bodies in subtle ways. Furthermore, they learn to use the barre dynamically in the same way that they would use a partner's hand in a pas de deux. What they once thought was a static exercise for the upper body becomes a nuanced and subtle whole body exploration.[8]

Student responses: As college students, my dancers are expected to write bi-weekly responses that articulate their understanding of the class experiences. The following student responses refer to 'whole-body connectivity.'

Although I am working on breath support and spinal/pelvic alignment, I do so within the context of lines of energy and spatial intent. That is, I think of my spine and pelvis containing lines of energy that simultaneously ground and lift my body...When I développé, I think of my spine lengthening and my pelvis subtly shifting in order to accommodate my directional shifts from front to back, or side to front, or side to back, etc... Throughout the balletic sequence, I try to use my whole body, as well as my whole dancing space; I try to view my space and body as one. M.B., advanced ballet class, age 19.

There is something so light, yet so sharp about the movement of the arms... the back and arms work together to bring out movement from deep within... I used to just move my arms from point A to point B, but now my whole body is guided through space to accomplish what I had done before in a simple and boring gesture... I think the factor that intrigues me about the movement of the arms is that it comes from the core or the back. It is as though the arms must ask permission to move from the greater whole. N.G., advanced ballet class, age 18.

TABLE 2: LEARNING TO MOVE DYNAMICALLY
LMA/BF theories: basic definitions
Traceforms are created every time a dancer moves her/his body in space. The pathway of the movement may pierce the space (linear) or it may arc through the space (curvilinear) or it may spiral through the space (spiralinear). Regardless of the pathway, it is important for dancers to

realise that their movement leaves impressions in the space—they 'trace' and 'form' the space with their bodies.

In the below example, *Shape Qualities* (defined in Table 1) offer increased awareness about how the whole body grows and shrinks from one position to the next. Over time, dancers may learn to choose the Shape Quality they want to emphasise. For example, they may emphasise Rising out of a temps lié devant which would be a different feeling kinesthetically and visually than if they were to emphasise the quality of Advancing in this same movement.

Effort: There are four effort categories: Flow Effort (see Table 1), Space Effort, Time Effort, and Weight Effort. Space Effort refers to how a person attends to her/his environment – Is it Direct and pinpointed or is it Indirect and all-encompassing? Time Effort refers to a person's qualitative sense of time – does the person expand time, Sustaining from one moment to the next, or does the person condense time with Sudden, Quick impulses? Weight Effort refers to how a person uses her/his physical mass – does s/he engage her/his mass with a powerful and Strong energy, or a delicate and Light energy? Explorations in Effort teach dancers about dynamic variety.

Similarly to musical phrasing, *Movement Phrasing* involves making choices about accent, rhythm, syncopation, dynamic emphasis, stillness, and the length of the movement phrase. Changing the movement phrasing of a particular exercise will change the technical and artistic demands of the exercise. Take, for example, a typical movement phrase in ballet: piqué soutenu to tombé pas de bourrée en avant. A dancer may choose to perform this as one continuous long phrase or s/he may choose to perform the piqué soutenu as one phrase (stopping the movement at the end of the soutenu) and the tombé pas de bourée as another phrase. One choice plays with continuous linked movement and the other choice plays with 'stillness and stir' as Laban referred to it.[9]

Movement examples:
1. *Using Shape Qualities and Traceforms in a Port de bras exercise:* Create a port de bras exercise that moves through the many classical positions. Hold glow sticks or streamers while you perform the exercise. Notice the movement pathways your arms make in the space: Was it twisted, curved, or straight? Did the pathway change level? When does the movement Spread or Enclose into the next position? Rise or Sink? Advance or Retreat? Then, involve your torso more as you move through

the port de bras. How could your torso/spine grow and shrink in order to emphasise the movement of the arms in space? For example, does your spine need to twist and rotate more as your arms move from à la seconde to fourth arabesque port de bras? Does it need to lengthen and Rise as the arms move from à la seconde to fifth position? What if this same port de bras emphasised Spreading instead of Rising?

Once you become familiar with these concepts, try applying the same questions and explorations to movements of the lower body during a balancé or temps lié combination.

2. *Experiment with changes in movement energy in a barre combination.* Create a barre exercise of your choice and experiment with the energy quality of the exercise. Perform the exercise fluidly and then sharply, powerfully and then delicately, with quick or lingering accents, and so on. How did your exercise change as you played with the dynamic quality? What did you learn about artistic choice and movement expression?

3. *Experiment with Movement Phrasing in a center combination.* Create a simple center combination and experiment with the phrasing of the exercise.

a. First, play with the idea of *stillness and stir.* Find stillness in unexpected places (in the middle of a temps lié or fouetté, for example). Also link together movements that you normally do not link together. For example, if you always find stillness in fourth position at the end of a pirouette, try seamlessly connecting the landing in fourth to the next movement in your sequence.

b. Second, play with the idea of *long and short phrases.* How do you link together a long series of steps so that it becomes one large phrase? What if you split the series of step up into many short movement phrases? How does this change the technical challenges of the exercise?

c. Third, play with the idea of *dynamic rhythm.* Find a rhythm and flow between Quick and Sustained moments, Light and Strong moments, Free and Bound moments, Indirect and Direct moments.

Student responses:
How I use my energy when dancing....has helped me to discover that it is OK to dance at a different rhythm or style than your peers or how the teacher teaches or dances the movement...[this concept] allows each dancer to be individual and unique within the class... and to choreo-

graph and dance how they want based on their thoughts, interests, and what concepts they like. C.D., advanced ballet class, age 17.

Free flow and bound flow is like knowing when to let go of things in life, and when it is okay to hold on a little longer. I felt that deciding when to let go and when to hold on, I could more easily find a rhythm within the movement... B.E., advanced ballet class, age 20.

After taking this class I have a much greater understanding of how phrasing works in the counts, music, and especially in movement of the body... I feel and recognise which patterns work in my body at certain moments, thus allowing me to make the most of every movement in a combination. M.MC., advanced ballet class, age 22.

Parts 2 and 3: Exercising choice and following through with intent

When teachers and students approach ballet technique training with a curious and experimental attitude, they will likely avoid a 'fix-it' approach. This is in contrast to

> orthodox ballet training [which] tends to suppress precisely those qualities of independent judgment and self-definition considered essential to choreographical development and innovation.[10]

Teachers can ask dancers to make conscious decisions about their dancing throughout the class period:
- Experiment with dynamics and phrasing (as described in Table 2)
- Emphasise a technical or artistic movement quality in two or three places in a movement sequence
- Practise different ways to execute the Shape Qualities of movement phrases or steps (as described in Table 1)
- Create a movement sequence around a particular concept from class
- Employ different imagery or dynamic sounds for the same movements

Making choices and following through with those choices teaches dancers about their movement preferences and it deepens their understanding of the ballet aesthetic. Through this approach, students learn to perform repeated exercises differently from one class period to the next and they learn to interpret the movement exercises in personal ways. Ultimately, they learn to use the methods of experimentation and curiosity in order to initiate technical and artistic changes in their dancing.

Part 4: Interacting with peers
Many ballet students are used to taking class silently. Not surprisingly, inter-acting physically or verbally with their peers during the class period is usually a new experience for them. However, this process is critical to their development as active and intelligent dancers.

There are various ways that dancers in my classes interact with each other. Sometimes they embody how a peer is moving. This teaches them about the choices that other dancers are making, which may ultimately challenge them to move beyond their typical movement preferences. Some-times my students teach a peer how they worked with a particular movement theme, or they create balletic exercises together, or they perform barre exer-cises while facing each other. Even the simple act of facing each other at barre reminds them that they do not dance in isolation. Instead their danc-ing creates relationships, not only in space but also with other human beings. This gives them a tangible motivation for their movement.

Peer feedback teaches dancers about their own movement preferences and assumptions. As they witness and observe each other, they develop their observational skills and learn to articulate their differences and commonalities. Through this approach, the students also become the con-veyers of information and as a result the teacher is no longer the only expert in the technique class.

Translating dance experiences to life
Investigating creative possibilities... Taking risks... Learning to listen to sensory impulses... Understanding that change is a process... Discovering that movement is intrinsically meaningful...

Whether the dancers are beginning or advanced, young or old, it is impor-tant that they interact with each other, develop personal uniqueness, engage creatively in the class experiences, and learn to analyse the ballet aesthetic and their own dancing. LMA/BF has been useful in this process; it provides dancers with a framework for articulating their physical actions and expres-sive choices. As dancers develop bodily knowledge and movement literacy, they develop as artists and people:

> Through movement and expression, a dancer is able to come into con-tact with a more personal self. Movement creates different shapes, colors, smells or perhaps objects in a dancer's mind... through creativity and imagination. K.A., advanced ballet class, age 20.

> I have learned more about myself as a human being who moves: breath and alignment are fundamental to motion. Getting the air I need, as well as being in the place I need to be, are apt reminders that dancing is

not an activity disconnected from life; in fact, it is a fundamental expression of it. M.B., advanced ballet class, age 19.

Every day, each individual chooses to move to their own rhythm by choosing their style of life. Some like to 'take in the moment' and move slower through life. Some people like to always be on the go... each individual chooses how they want to live their life, this concept is no different than when we choose our own sequencing and timing in ballet. C.D., advanced ballet class, age 17.

As teachers, we must acknowledge the creative nature of learning and knowing; this will support the development of mindful, inventive, and artistic dancers. While it can be argued that the learning process is linear and certain, when viewing it from a larger perspective, it is also nonlinear, dynamic, and uncertain. Laban stated,

movement is man's magic mirror reflecting and creating the inner life in and by visible traceforms, and also reflecting and creating the visible traceforms in and by the inner life.[11]

Additionally, somatics educator Richard Strozzi Heckler notes,

How we actually are, in action, attitude, and the way we relate to others, is the basis for experiential learning. If we embody our ideas and opinions, we can participate more deeply in who we are and who we may become, and we will have at our disposal the primary ingredient for learning: ourself.[12]

Movement is the medium of discovery in a ballet technique class. The technique classroom can therefore become a place where students practice physically that which they want to become.

1. Risner, D. When Boys Dance: Cultural Resistance and Male Privilege in Dance Education. In: Shapiro, S.B. *Dance in a World of Change: Reflections on Globalisation and Cultural Differences.* Human Kinetics. 2008. p. 94.
2. Whittier, C. Laban Movement Analysis Approach to Classical Ballet Pedagogy. *Journal of Dance Education.* 6(4):132, 2006.
3. Dempster, E. Women Writing the Body: Let's Watch a Little How She Dances. In: Goellner, E.W and Murphy, J.S. *Bodies of the Text: Dance as Theory, Literature as Dance.* Rutgers University Press. 1995. p. 24.
4. Groff, E. Laban Movement Analysis: A Historical, Philosophical and Theoretical Perspective. Unpublished Masters Thesis. 1990. p. 61.
5. Groff, E. 1990. p. 61.

6. Whittier, C. Developing Artistry in Ballet through Personal Agency. 2008 National Dance Education Organisation Conference Proceedings. 2008.

7. Hackney, P. *Making Connections*. Amsterdam: Gordon and Breach Publishers. 1998. Breath Support is a concept important when practicing Breath Connectivity. Breath Connectivity is the first of six Total Patterns of Body Connectivity in the Bartenieff Fundamentals.

8. Whittier, C. National Dance Education Organisation Conference Proceedings. 2008.

9. Laban, R. and Ulmann, L. *A Vision of Dynamic Space*. Laban Archives in Association with The Falmer Press. 1984. pp. 68, 69.

10. Dempster, E. In: Goellner, E.W. and Murphy, J.S. 1995. p. 27.

11. Laban, R. Edited by Lisa Ullman. *Language of Movement: A Guidebook to Choreutics*. Boston: Plays, Inc.. 1966. pp. 48, 100.

12. Heckler, R.S. *Anatomy of Change: East/West Approaches to Body/Mind Therapy*. North Atlantic Books. 1993. p. 9.

Thoughts from Hong Kong:
conference closing address

Anita Donaldson

We've come to the end of three wonderful days – and it's fallen to me to do what is nigh impossible: the rather daunting task of drawing things together, and bringing the conference to some sort of conclusion.

So who's she: and why me? Partly because I was in the wrong place at the wrong time, and didn't heed Valerie's maxim 'beware of casual conversations in the corridor'. My conversation took place not in a corridor, but in the more salubrious Grosvenor Hotel in July, when I blithely said to VP-D 'I assume that you're having some kind of closing session, someone who's going to summarise the whole, and perhaps map out some future directions.' And so here I am!

But perhaps it's also because I stand as an example of the way the seeds of Laban's work (and Laban's work at Laban) have been sown and disseminated – spread far and wide. I first came to Laban 30 years ago to the month – in early October 1978 – and even then I knew that there was something in the man's work that was the key to understanding dance as an art form. And the title of my dissertation at the time spells that out – something to the effect that what was then called Movement Study (courtesy of VP-D, Walli Meier and Marion North), was the body of knowledge underpinning the performance, creation and understanding/appreciation of dance. I went back and forth between Laban and Australia for the next 26 or so years, during which time I experienced the transformation of Laban Movement Studies to its current Choreological Studies; sowed the antipodean seeds, watched them grow; did some cross pollination – and sadly also watched the early shoots die here and there along the way. But I've also been able to re-sow the seeds again in Hong Kong [at the Academy for Performing Arts] in a way that I've not been able to do before – in the form of Choreological Studies at both undergraduate and graduate level. But all of that has its roots here – in Laban, and Laban's work.

Now pulling together a three day conference in which there have been something in the order of 75 sessions on widely differing topics, has its challenges to put it mildly, so I can only skim the surface, and give some very broad brush strokes. And I'm going to do this in three ways:

• Offer some observations ... musings ... things that struck me for some reason or another ......
    • Pick out a few quotable quotes – but as food for thought ....
    • And then raise some issues/considerations for the future: no answers as such – but hopefully something to take away and think about ....

I was firstly struck by the amazing breadth and range of sessions – and who would not be? They reinforce – if indeed it needed reinforcing – the extra-ordinary mind that was Rudolf Laban's: the epitome of the visionary artist-researcher/artist-scholar who has left such a vast, enduring legacy. But interestingly, it's also a legacy that has not gone all that much beyond the dance community – and perhaps a relatively circumscribed dance community at that. And it begs the question as to why that should be the case .....

We had the pedagogical .... the historical ... the creative and the analytic ... We had actor training .... and fascinatingly – conductor training ... We had the sacred and the more profane... lectures ... lecture-demonstrations ... performances ... workshops and films ... green leaves and lettuces; mathematics and engineering. Wonderful breadth that, while it made it difficult to choose where to be when, at the same time underscored just how wide and extensive the Laban map.

Then there are the wonderful 'grand ladies' of Laban – the likes of Marion, VP-D, Walli Meier, Ann Hutchinson Guest, Geraldine Stephenson and others ... And the pioneering spirit that shines through still. Their tenacity, perseverance and drive; their refusal to take 'no' for an answer ... and what might be seen at times as bloody-mindedness – and in many cases, probably was! In many ways that is what has kept Laban alive: and that's what might still be needed to keep it alive and well into the future. The conference is, perhaps, as much an acknowledgement and celebration of their achievements, as of Laban's work.

The conjunction between theory and practice dominated the conference – so called 'academic' papers that were grounded firmly in practice, and performances that had a theoretical element to them: so Jean Jarrell's presentation on Sonia Rafferty's *Shoal* ... the *Green Clowns* Project ... Ana Sanchez-Colberg's *We*: implicated and complicated ... Johan Stjernholm's *Space Engineering No. 1*. The artist researcher/practitioner/ thinker at work. The practice-theory nexus is also there in the *Loss of Small Detail* project: mapping the creative process – implications that stretch wide: *Loss* is the first of what must inevitably be many such projects. To date dance has been poorly served in respect of its archives – and I'm not talking here of purely text-based archives, but archives of the creative process and product .... And Valerie made an important point yesterday: the need for young choreographers to start archiving their own processes and ways of working sooner rather than later .... The *Loss* mapping model is, I think, a breakthrough of rather momentous proportions in this respect.

I was also intrigued by two interesting connections: the fact that several people raised the notion of the 'space in-between', and the dynamic importance of this space. Johan Borghall referred to 'the spaces and places in-between' and the pivotal moment of change ... Charles Gambetta talked about what happens between the beats in music ... and Ana Sánchez-Colberg spoke of both the metaphoric and the real space between: no void or dead space, but something alive in the moment of becoming – whether in dance, in music, or in acting. And it is hopefully in the spaces in-between the 75 or so sessions that the organisers so wisely included in the conference, that memories were rekindled, old debates taken up, new ones begun ... where new connections were made, new ideas were shared, and new, exciting possibilities explored.

And I was also struck by two separate references to the freedom/release that contact with, and understanding of, Laban's work instigated: Rosemary Brandt spoke of being trapped in classical technique and not being able to move beyond it – until Laban gave her the tools to break through that impasse .... And for Charles Gambetta it was close encounters with Laban's effort factors that provided an escape from the tyranny of set beat patterns for a conductor – and the discovery of conducting the music, rather than conducting the beats or the metre: the 1... 2 ... . 3.. 4 – or as Laban would have said – the eins, zwei, drei – of music. For me this underlines the need for us to ensure that the freedom – both explicit and implicit – that comes from working with Laban's many different principles, stays one of our guiding principles. Not to set them in concrete, wrap them up in cotton wool, regulate and restrict them – but to let them breathe and develop how they need to.

So then what about those 'food-for-thought' quotable quotes? Just a few that had some resonance for me for one reason or another ...

Ana Catalina Román's reference to Bill Forsythe's 'always include some irregularity: it keeps the audience busy ...'

Rosemary Brandt's 'What I do creates something for you to see ...': the understanding by the performer of what they are doing, and why they are doing it: not just steps – but something that goes beyond.

Jean Jarrell's 'it does no harm to the mystery [of dance that is] to know a little about it'...

Ramsay Burt's 'the immanent potential of the dancing body' ...

Marion North's 'it's not right or wrong – it's different' ....

Anna Carlisle's 'it's impossible to stay with how one was taught': regardless of whether that was in the 1920s, 1940s, 1970s – or whenever.

VP-D's 'we swung about, whooshed around, all over the place ....': as one does!

And last but not least – Claudine Swann's probably unbeatable 'put a smile on your pas de bourée'.

.... And so, then, to some issues and considerations – some of which have their roots in that conversation in the Grosvenor:

•   Laban for the 21st century – what does that actually mean? That we keep on doing much the same thing as we've been doing since whenever, but just fast-forward the date? Or does it mean a rethink ... a reconsideration and reconceptualisation? ... Of pushing the envelope – of taking what we know further? And what are the hallmarks of the 21st century anyway? And how do we shape our Laban thinking and practice in response to them?

•   And following on from that – the relevance of Laban's work (and I take that rather over-generally I know) to the here and now. Not everything lends itself to Laban, and it may well be that we have to be prepared to discard some things, put others on ice – to reappear some time in the future in a different guise. And this goes back to my previous point about freedom ...

What is important, is that whatever it is that we do in respect of Laban keeps moving forward ... readily adapting to suit various widely differing contexts: little is carved in stone – and perhaps it's the 'why: what if?' principle that needs to become our major covenant...

•   But perhaps I'm wrong in talking about Laban's work in a single mouthful? Of course I am! Perhaps there are some areas that are strong and flourishing far and wide ... We'd all like to think so – but I'm not so sure ... Take Labanotation for instance – it's no secret that it's finding it tough going ... And I confess that in the School [at the Academy] in Hong Kong, we have de-emphasised it, and are now focusing more on the digital technologies as creative and documenting/archiving tools. But! as I said earlier, we now have Choreological Studies as a required core course in both the undergraduate and MFA programmes – so perhaps I can be forgiven for the Labanotation omission.
•   And I know there is some concern about quality control: how to protect the integrity – of the choreological itself ... Of what is being taught and how it's being taught... of the kammertanz works and their performances. None is under copyright, so are potentially open to misuse and abuse. Anyone for instance, can teach this thing called Choreological Studies – for better

or for worse. [And I think that many of us are aware of the damage that poor teaching and rigid interpretations of Laban's work back in the 1960s and 1970s especially, had on the acceptance and development of his work: the awful 'be like a tree waving in the wind' syndrome!] How do we weed out the bad, the indifferent, the outdated and the downright dangerous? Does it matter: isn't some better than none? And if the answer is 'no', then what can be done about it?

Well, one thing that can be done is about to be done: and hot off the press – an exciting move in the right direction has come with the recent securing of funding to negotiate for an intensive professional development unit in Laban Studies at Trinity Laban with the first course in 2009.

• Research is something else to think about. We've seen the start of this – the AHRC funding of the *Loss* project is a milestone by any reckoning: the ball has been set rolling: how to keep it going? There are masses of potential research projects just waiting to begin: so who, how, when and where?

• And the question of Laban the institution as the keeper of the Laban flame? It possibly goes without saying that it must be – but what does that actually mean? Is it a realistic expectation? What are the consequences? Has Choreological Studies for instance, finally found its space and time? And is it perhaps time to be thinking of an MA or similar in the choreological? For me – and as we've seen in several sessions this weekend – the choreological surely lies at the very heart of our embodied and conceptual/intellectual understanding of our art form: as such it lies at the very heart of dance education and training in the conservatoire context.

• And perhaps tied in with that – the handing of the flame to a new, younger generation (perhaps an apt metaphor in the year of the Beijing Olympics!) ... The likes of VP-D will not last forever – and even the next generation – the Rosemarys, Jeans, Anitas, Anna Carlisle's and Regina's etc., – are not 'spring chickens' any more. How do we ensure, then, that what we know can be, is? Time, then, for some succession planning, of looking ahead to the future.

And finally: the ultimate conference question: where to from here? How do we keep the momentum of this conference going – its spirit alive? There are no ready answers – and I don't intend to try: each of us will take it forward in our own particular way ... But these three days have surely stimulated our thinking about what that might mean, why it needs to be – and how it might be achieved. As Valerie said in her Keynote speech 'what we have now is not enough'.

Contributors

Linda Ashley MA
Linda Ashley is Senior Dance Lecturer and Research Leader at AUT University, School of Sport and Recreation, New Zealand. Linda has extensive academic, choreographic and educational experience in dance. She moved to New Zealand in 1997 and is currently pursuing doctorate studies at The University of Auckland.

Penelope Best PGCE, MCAT, ITLM, SrDMT
Penelope Best is a Senior Dance Movement Psychotherapy clinician, supervisor, facilitator, and researcher; Honorary Fellow ADMT UK; Honorary Research Fellow, Roehampton University; President European Network of Dance Movement Therapists; Co-ordinator DMP Programme, Warsaw; Core tutor DMP Programme, Rotterdam. She also undertakes private clinical supervision practice and is a mentor/consultant for creativity action research within education UK.

Sarah Burkhalter MA
Sarah Burkhalter is an art historian living and working in Geneva, Switzerland. She is interested in the interplay of dance and built spaces. Her current research focuses on kinaesthetic perception in turn-of-the 20th century performers.

Anna Carlisle MA, MBE
Anna Carlisle is President of the Laban Guild. She is a freelance practitioner, choreographer and Director of the Phoenix Project, a Professional Development Course in Laban Studies. Her research interests lie in Rudolf Laban's concepts of 'Living Architecture' – Choreutics and their relation to Sacred Geometry.

Jane Carr Ph.D.
Jane Carr spent many years developing access to dance in South London while also working on a number of mixed media collaborative arts projects. Her experiences prompted her to research aspects of the relationship between what is understood as embodied in dance and its appreciation for which she received her PhD from Roehampton University London in 2008. Jane currently lectures at Trinity Laban.

Melanie Clarke MA
Melanie Clarke is a graduate of Laban's BA and MA Dance Studies pro-

grammes. In 1998 she joined the Laban faculty teaching release-based Contemporary technique and Labanotation. Melanie is also a dancer and choreographer and is currently touring her solo work 'Half of One' and a Quartet 'Too...'

Anita Donaldson Ph.D. OAM
Anita Donaldson is currently Dean of the School of Dance at the Hong Kong Academy for Performing Arts, having come there via the Laban Centre, and the University of Adelaide in Australia. She has a long association with Trinity Laban, having first come to Laurie Grove in 1979 to undertake the Diploma in Education.

Dianne Dulicai Ph.D. ADTR
Dianne Dulicai is Senior Consultant, Hahnemann Creative Arts Therapies Department, Drexel University, Philadelphia, USA. She has 30 years of clinical practice and academic experience. Dianne founded the graduate programmes in dance/movement therapy at Hahnemann Medical College in Philadelphia and at the Laban Centre. She served as president of the American Dance Therapy Association, and has taught and published worldwide.

Catherine Foley Ph.D.
Catherine Foley designed and is course director of both the MA in Ethnochoreology and the MA in Irish Traditional Dance Performance at the Irish World Academy of Music and Dance, University of Limerick, Ireland; she also supervises doctorate research in dance at the Academy. She is founder and Chair of Dance Research Forum Ireland, and established and acted as Director of Tráth na gCos, the dance festival at the Irish World Academy, until recently. She choreographed The Sionna Set Dance (2005) and has published, lectured, and given dance workshops internationally.

Charles Gambetta Ph.D.
Conductor/composer Charles Gambetta is on the music faculties of Guilford College and Greensboro College USA. He began his conducting studies with Ansel Brusilow in 1974 at the University of North Texas where he was also Associate Conductor and Arranger for the One O'clock Lab Band. Known for his ground-breaking research in conductor training, Charles has developed a revolutionary movement-centered curriculum for conductors based on the principles of Laban Movement Analysis. In 2008 he accepted an appointment to the faculty of the prestigious International Institute for Conductors.

Julia Gleich MA, MFA
Julia Gleich teaches ballet at Trinity Laban and is Head of Choreography at London Studio Centre. She is Director of Gleich Dances New York/London, President of Norte Maar, NY, and a master teacher for Burklyn Ballet, Vermont. She has presented at CORPS de Ballet and is interested in ballet as a modern/ contemporary form.

Miriam Huberman MA
Miriam Huberman is based in Mexico and combines choreology, injury prevention, dance history and dance education in most of her work. Currently, she is involved in the creation of Tampico's first contemporary dance company, teaching injury prevention and choreology.

Michael Huxley MA
Michael Huxley is a researcher and Principal Lecturer in Dance at De Montfort University. At DMU he is Project Leader for the Centre for Excellence in Performance Arts and was Conference Chair for the CORD/CEPA Conference on Dance Pedagogy 2009. He is published in several books. He is Chair of the CORD Editorial Board for Dance Research Journal and Senior Academic Adviser Dance for PALATINE. He researches dance history and dance pedagogy.

Jean Jarrell MA
Jean Jarrell is a Senior Lecturer at Trinity Laban in charge of Notation Studies. She obtained an MA Dance Studies (Laban), a Licence ès Lettres (Grenoble, France) and is a Fellow of ICKL. She trained and performed in France before coming to the UK to teach. Currently semi retired, she retains some teaching including the Specialist Diploma in Dance Notating.

Maggie Killingbeck M.Phil
Maggie Killingbeck is a Principal Lecturer at the University of Bedfordshire where she leads the PGCE Dance course. She has been Chair of the Laban Guild for Movement and Dance since 2006. She is a member of Lisa Ullmann Travelling Scholarship Fund Management Committee.

Joukje Kolff M.Sc
Joukje Kolff received an MSc in Computational Linguistics (University of Amsterdam) and MFA in Dance (Ohio State University). She assisted Ann Hutchinson Guest in writing the Advanced Labanotation Textbook issues, has taught Labanotation at Laban and Roehampton University and is on the research committee of ICKL.

Monique Kroepfli MA
Monique Kroepfli completed her dance studies with an MA from the Laban Centre in 1995. She was a member of dance faculty at Basel University (Switzerland) from 1996 to 2007. Monique is a founder member of lost&found dance collective (Switzerland). Since 1997 she has been working as a freelance choreographer, dancer and pedagogue.

Milca Leon MA
Milca studied at the Laban Centre and went on to teach Choreological Studies there, Movement for Actors at Central School of Speech and Drama (London), and Choreography and Technique at the Dance Academy in Jerusalem. She now teaches dance and Laban Analysis for dance teachers, actors, and therapists in various institutions in Israel.

Loretta Livingston
Loretta Livingston is a downtown Los Angeles-based contemporary dance artist. A multi-award winning choreographer/performer and dance educator, Livingston mixes movement, vocal text, video art and live music. She works abroad, currently in Korea, Singapore and Turkey and is Associate Professor of Dance at the University of California, Irvine.

Isabel Marques Ph.D.
Isabel Marques achieved her MA in Dance Studies at the Laban Centre in 1989, and her PhD in Education from São Paulo University in 1996. She is director of Caleidos Dance Co. and Caleidos Institute and the author of Teaching Dance Today and Dancing at Schools. She was responsible for writing and introducing Dance in Brazilian Curriculum (1997) and UNESCO´s collaborator for Dance Education issues in Latin America (2002).

James McBride MA
James McBride is an MPA Practitioner, director of a management consultancy firm (www.coaction.dk) in Denmark, and the European coordinator for the Institute of Movement Pattern Analysis (www.iompa.com). He lectures regularly at the University of Copenhagen, Danish National School of Contemporary Dance and Danish Royal Academy of Music.

Marion North Ph.D. CBE
Marion North trained with Rudolf Laban, Sylvia Bodmer and Lisa Ullmann. She worked with Laban intensively for the last nine years of his life at the Youth Advisory Bureau (Y.A.B) where individuals came to work with him for personal, professional or therapeutic development. After Laban's death in

1958, Marion went on to develop this work and became the Principal and Chief Executive of the Laban Centre.

Gisela Peters-Rohse

Gisela Peters-Rohse undertook vocational training with Lola Rogge, Hamburg, and after working in the professional theatre she re-trained as a dance teacher. From 1970 onwards Gisela has been teaching in Cologne, directing the department of ballet for children at Rheinische Musikschule Köln and teaching at the Hochschule für Musik in Köln. Having developed her own method for childrens' dance, she writes, choreographs and teaches in Germany and abroad.

Valerie Preston-Dunlop Ph.D.

Valerie Preston-Dunlop studied and collaborated with Rudolf Laban for 12 years. She has researched Laban's life and work and has curated The Laban Collection of documentation and memorabilia. She is author of a number of books which focus on Rudolf Laban including the award winning 'Rudolf Laban, an extraordinary life' and co-author of 'Dance and the performative: A choreological perspective' with Ana Sanchez-Colberg (2002). Her recent DVDs include The American Invasion and Laban Dances 1923-28. Her current research projects are with William Forsythe's company and on the spiritual dimension of Rudolf Laban's work.

Dilys Price M.Ed., OBE

Dilys Price is Director of Touch Trust and Senior Lecturer in Movement & Dance, UWIC. Dilys was part of the team which built Wales Sports Centre for the Disabled, at UWIC, training elite able & disabled athletes together as equals.

Annabel Rutherford MA

Following a career in the performing arts as a dancer and an actor, Annabel Rutherford is studying for her PhD in English and Drama at York University, Toronto. She holds MAs in English, Russian Modernism, and Dance History and has published papers on ballet, drama and art history.

Lesley-Anne Sayers Ph.D

Lesley-Anne Sayers lectures in dance history at Trinity Laban, London and in art history for the Open University, Bristol. She studied at Laban after a first degree in drama, completing MPhil research in 1987 on the development of British Dance Criticism. Her doctoral research (Bristol 1999) explored the potential re-creation of a Diaghilev Ballets Russes work from the 1920s, accessing the ballet via its scenographic/musical relationships, later staged at

Princeton University in 2005. Her post-doctoral research continues to involve scenography, re-creation and interactions across the visual and performing arts.

Paula Salosaari Ph.D

Paula Salosaari is a dance teacher, lecturer and researcher based in Finland. After her MA in Dance Studies at the Laban Centre, her doctoral research proposed a new way to teach ballet, which acknowledges and gives space to the dancer's agency by introducing divergent teaching and structural images of the dance as tools to create with. Her post doctoral research continues to investigate ways of enhancing bodily knowledge in dance education.

Katia Savrami Ph.D.

Katia Savrami is a Choreographer, Dance Analyst and Theoretician and is a graduate of the Laban Centre's post-graduate and research programmes. Katia lectures at the University of Patras and at the State School of Dance, Athens as a choreologist. She is a member of the International Editorial Board in Research in Dance Education, UK and a tutor of the Imperial Society of Teachers of Dancing, London.

Nigel Stewart M.Litt

Nigel Stewart is Senior Lecturer in the Institute for Contemporary Arts at Lancaster University, and is the Artistic Director of Sap Dance. Nigel has danced with various UK and European companies, and as a solo artist. As a choreographer and director he has worked with Theatre Nova, TheatreáÁrks, Triangle and many other UK companies, and Odin Teatret in Denmark. He has published several articles and chapters, and is co-editor of the book Performing Nature: Explorations in Ecology and the Arts (Peter Lang 2005).

Claudine Swann

Claudine Swann has been Inspector for Dance Education at the Ministry of the French Community of Belgium since 1986. She has an extensive experience as a dance artist, choreographer, and teacher and has a special interest in ballet and choreology.

Cadence Whittier MFA

Cadence Whittier received her MFA from the University of Utah and her certification in Laban Movement Analysis/Bartenieff Fundamentals (LMA/BF) from Integrated Movement Studies. Currently, she is an Associate Professor in Dance at Hobart and William Smith Colleges in Geneva, New York where she teaches courses in LMA/BF, Kinesiology, and Advanced Ballet/Pointe.

Lightning Source UK Ltd.
Milton Keynes UK
01 May 2010

153599UK00001B/5/P

9 781852 731380